WARRIOR
ELITE

ROBERT MACKLIN

WARRIOR ELITE

AUSTRALIA'S SPECIAL FORCES
Z FORCE TO THE SAS
INTELLIGENCE OPERATIONS
TO CYBER WARFARE

hachette
AUSTRALIA

hachette
AUSTRALIA

First published in Australia and New Zealand in 2015
by Hachette Australia
(an imprint of Hachette Australia Pty Limited)
Level 17, 207 Kent Street, Sydney NSW 2000
www.hachette.com.au

This edition published in 2019

10 9 8 7 6 5 4 3 2 1

A catalogue record for this
book is available from the
National Library of Australia

ISBN 978 0 7336 4198 5 (paperback)

Cover design by Christabella Designs
Cover photographs courtesy of Australian War Memorial/076487 and AFP/Australian Defence Forc
Text design by Bookhouse, Sydney
Typeset in 13/16.3 pt Garamond Premier Pro by Bookhouse, Sydney
Printed and bound in Australia by McPherson's Printing Group

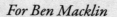

For Ben Macklin

CONTENTS

'The centurion in the infantry is chosen for his size, strength and dexterity in throwing his missile weapons and for his skill in the use of his sword and shield; in short for his expertness in all the exercises. He is to be vigilant, temperate, active and readier to execute the orders he receives than to talk.'

Vegetius, De Re Militari, II, 14

FOREWORD

BY PETER JENNINGS
DIRECTOR, AUSTRALIAN STRATEGIC POLICY INSTITUTE

My first encounter with Australia's Special Forces came when I was a young adviser to Alexander Downer, who in 1991 was shadow minister for defence. We visited the Campbell Barracks of the Special Air Service Regiment (SASR) in Perth to view the 'Killing House', where soldiers practise hunting terrorists and rescuing hostages. We were taken to a room where half a dozen shop dummies dressed in fatigues guarded live 'hostages' – SASR troopers. Our confident guide – a major, from memory – said to Downer and me, 'Don't move, and whatever you do stay behind that white line on the floor.' While he spoke he put his arms around the shoulders of two manikins as if they were about to pack down into a scrum.

The room suddenly went dark and in that instant two 'flash-bang' stun grenades exploded, disorienting us with intense light and noise. Our SASR rescuers pounded into the room shining torches in our faces before, in seconds, 'double-tapping' the dummies with two rounds to each forehead. With the hostages rescued, to everyone's surprise Downer seemed to break out in an impromptu foot-stomping dance. A white-hot flash-bang casing had rolled over the safety line and adhered to the rubber sole of Alexander's shoe. As his shoe got hotter, Downer danced harder until he dislodged the round, leaving a deep groove melted into the sole.

The early 1990s was a time with few opportunities for the SASR to use their training in combat, but in 1998 Prime Minister John Howard deployed a company of Special Forces soldiers to Kuwait as part of Operation Desert Fox. This was an international effort to pressure Saddam Hussein to open Iraq to inspections of weapons of mass destruction. Our troops were to act as a rescue force in the event that the Iraqis might shoot down an aircraft, leaving aircrew stranded in hostile territory. As chief of staff to Defence Minister Ian McLachlan, I faced the displeasure of surprised senior Defence officials who were alarmed by the government's forward-leaning decision to deploy Special Forces. 'Don't they understand just how dangerous this is? People could get killed!' one official railed. I had no doubt, though, that Howard and his Cabinet ministers had thoroughly considered the risks.

Our role in Operation Desert Fox was a defining moment for John Howard and the way he directed the Australian Defence Force (ADF). When he asked Defence what was available to commit to the operation, the sad reality was that few parts of the ADF were able to deploy. Aircraft and helicopters were not fitted with the electronic warfare protection needed to handle even the very limited Iraqi air defence network. Larger army units lacked necessary equipment. Defence thought the government would decide to send a ship, but Howard saw that option as too tokenistic, and was shocked by the lack of ready forces across Defence. Except, that is, for the Special Forces, which was ready to deploy, had the right training and most of the right equipment.

Australian governments of all political stripes are generally not very interested in strategic theory, but when a crisis develops they quickly want to know what the ADF can do. An important rule of thumb for Defence is that what gets used gets funded. The 1998 deployment of the SASR began a long period of growth for Australia's Special Forces, which in 2015 includes a Special Forces command headed by a two-star major general, the SASR in Perth and commandos in Sydney.

Sixteen years of continuous operational service, much of it involving high-intensity combat, has honed Special Forces' skills to the point that they are among the best small fighting units in the world. Taliban commanders in Afghanistan rightly feared the soldiers they called 'the bearded ones'. Our American allies saw Australia's willingness to close with the enemy on the battlefield as the key value of the alliance relationship. Successive prime ministers have repeatedly turned to the Special Forces when they have needed to put the ADF into harm's way to defend Australia's interests.

Warrior Elite is a lively study into the history and future of Australia's Special Forces, dating from the remarkable heroism of Sparrow Force in Timor in World War II and the eccentric innovations of the Nackeroos in northern Australia preparing for a Japanese invasion. Macklin's book is unique because he has tumbled to a reality that few people outside the official 'national security community' understand: the practical definition of what constitutes Australia's Special Forces has widened to include not only the SASR and the commandos but also Australia's intelligence agencies.

In a rare public speech in 2012, Nick Warner, the head of the Australian Secret Intelligence Service (ASIS), said it was 'difficult to see a situation in the future where the ADF would deploy without ASIS alongside'. Behind that statement sits the reality of a sophisticated military, police and intelligence machine, one that will dominate Australian defence thinking in coming decades, even at times against the instincts of the 'Big Army' – the conventional war fighters who are the recruitment base for the Special Forces.

It would be satisfying, but in my view ultimately wrong, to conclude that Australians have a special talent for the lateral, audacious type of thinking needed by Special Forces operators. Robert Macklin proves that the brave members of Sparrow Force in 1942 could easily fit into an SASR squadron today, but a lateral approach is often the forced result of lack of funds or inadequate pre-planning. For the most part, Australian strategic thinking is cautious and not very innovative.

As we enter a more competitive and risky strategic age it remains to be seen if that conventional approach is good enough to protect Australia's national interests. What is needed, in fact, is for our Warrior Elite to adopt a more consciously 'asymmetric' approach to national security. In Defence parlance, asymmetry simply means emphasising strengths that attack an opponent's weaknesses. As a country with a small but educated population and a small but high-technology-based defence, police and intelligence system, asymmetry is a natural fit for Australia. In a highly entertaining way, Robert Macklin's *Warrior Elite* charts what our military future will look like, based on some remarkable military and intelligence achievements of the past.

INTRODUCTION

Australia's defence strategy is at a tipping point – not for the first time nor the last, but the decisions facing our country today are as profound as any in the long history of warfare. We are not alone. Governments around the world are aware that the twenty-first-century battle space is almost unrecognisable from its predecessor. But in Australia's case there are special implications for the traditional 'Five Eyes' relationship that has both served and shackled the country's defence perceptions and priorities.

The alliance between Britain, the US, Canada, New Zealand and Australia emerged from an informal agreement for intelligence sharing between Britain and the US early in World War II. It was formalised as the BRUSA agreement in 1946 and later extended secretly to include the other three members of the Anglosphere. But while it remains focused on intelligence, it reflects a much broader relationship based upon 'shared values' that derive initially from the British colonial progenitor. Whether those values are sufficiently strong to warrant the continuance of an arrangement that has consequences for Australia is one of the issues successive governments will now be forced to confront.

Australia's geographical perspective and international priorities are very different from Britain's. This became glaringly obvious in World War II when both nations were fighting for survival. Prime Minister John Curtin's plea to America 'free of any pangs as to our traditional links or kinship with the United Kingdom' was a dramatic assertion of the notion that national self-interest trumps 'shared values' in defence of the realm. Nevertheless, it was to the US, another member of the Anglosphere, to which he turned for rescue.

A more pointed departure from tradition occurred in the post-war era when John McEwen, one of the more influential Australian political leaders of the century, negotiated the Japan–Australia Trade Agreement, which transferred Australia's mercantile allegiance from the UK at a time when Britain was itself preparing to enter a rival trading bloc in the European Common Market. However, as will be seen, McEwen and his successors actually increased the country's interdependence with the Five Eyes partners. And no one was more committed to encouraging the United States in its military adventurism in South-East Asia than McEwen and his conservative parliamentary colleagues.

America's subsequent, ill-judged military endeavours in Asia and the Middle East have provided the battlegrounds for Australia's forces over the last half-century, with the single exception of East Timor. And it is America's imperial pretensions that have created serious complications in Australia's relations with China and arguably affected the development of open-hearted, neighbourly relations with the Muslim nations of Indonesia and Malaysia.

This is not America's fault. Australia is a sovereign nation with an untrammelled right to an independent foreign and defence policy. It is also a proudly multicultural community. But the cosmopolitan nature of its population has yet to be reflected in the composition of its political establishment. The parliament, together with the judiciary, industry, bureaucracy and media, remain dominated by white Anglo-Australian men. And this establishment with its firm, if unconscious, attachment to an Anglophile past has dominated debate on Australia's defence posture.

It is a debate that has largely calcified to a choice between Indonesia and China as potential threats to the nation. Occasionally, there has been a verbal skirmish over 'forward' or 'continental' defence. But until very recently the issue has only been in which direction to point the naval flotillas, the air force squadrons and the seaborne transports of the serried army divisions – a military grouping characterised informally as 'Big Army'. The parameters of debate have been as restricted – and as racist – as the Anglo-Australian minds that formulated them.

In the last decade of the twentieth century, any perceived threat to the homeland became subsumed within the political need to march in step with America, initially into Kuwait and Iraq in the first Gulf War. Unfortunately, this lit the spark of Muslim fanaticism that resulted in Osama bin Laden's al-Qaeda tearing down New York's Twin Towers on 11 September 2001. And when America responded in Afghanistan, Pakistan and Iraq, the spark became a flame. Then, as America killed the firebrand and withdrew from the battle, a new spot fire of the Islamic State of Iraq and Syria (ISIS) – almost overnight, it seemed – became a blaze of insurrection in outbreaks across the globe.

ISIS is now perhaps the most potent insurrectionist force the world has known. And it uses a formidable mix of futurist electronic technology and atavistic brutality to spread its message. Its targets include the sectarian Shiite–Sunni divide within its own religious ranks, the detested Israeli enclave, the former colonial powers of the West and the Russian oppressors of Chechnya and its Muslim neighbours. Indonesia and China are themselves deeply vulnerable: Indonesia through its 95 per cent Muslim population and corrupt governance; China because of the substantial Muslim presence and its alienation due to its unyielding single-party government.

In this brave new world of the twenty-first century, Australia has found itself cruising in a seascape clouded by the fog of Anglo arrogance and wars past. While the New Zealanders maintain a matching course, the old marker buoys laid down in colonial days are no longer discernible, the way ahead wracked with hazard and uncertainty. The one saving grace has been Australasia's geographic location a hemisphere away from the barbarous outrages of Old World enmities.

We could feel sympathy for the British, who had to endure bus bombings and the savage public murder of a young soldier by half-deranged Muslim militants. We could mourn with the victims of the Boston Marathon bombings. We could empathise with the Canadians, whose parliament was invaded by a Muslim gunman. But though we had been shocked and enraged at the Bali bombings of 2002, we took Australian Security Intelligence Organisation (ASIO) chief David Irvine's recalibration of a terrorist threat on the homeland to 'high' on the eve of his retirement with the usual 'She'll be right'. It was almost unthinkable that we would suffer an outrage on Australian soil, that the anger we had sown in lock-step with America could reap the whirlwind of revenge.

That complacency ended when, on the morning of 15 December 2014, a Muslim neurotic, drawn to the ISIS fire, took 17 Australians hostage in a coffee shop in the heart of Sydney. And while the 50-year-old Iranian Shiite turned Sunni fanatic had few if any links to the ISIS caliphate, that only compounded the problem. As the Australian-born Muslim, lawyer, academic and media presenter Waleed Aly wrote at the time, 'Many deranged gunmen have gone before him. Only rarely do they associate themselves with the symbolic power of a global militant movement. At no point in the history of our species have such human satellites . . . had the power to become so much more than they are simply by attaching themselves to a symbol from another continent. And right now, there is no symbol more potent and available than that of Islamic terrorism.'[1]

Australian Strategic Policy Institute (ASPI) director Peter Jennings explained, 'For ISIS, lone wolves are useful cannon fodder, able to inflict damage in the homelands of their enemies, to garner further publicity and to inspire yet more recruits to the cause, yet ultimately cost the group nothing, even if their attacks fail. ISIS issued a fatwa in September [2014] calling on their supporters to "kill the disbeliever whether he is civilian or military" of any country that joined the coalition mounting air strikes in ISIS.

'Beyond the immediate to the siege though, difficult questions have to be asked about what further steps, if any, should be taken to reduce the possibility of further such crises.'

As the ISIS contagion spreads, alliances are in flux worldwide. But Australia remains locked in its Anglophile past. Uncomfortable as it may be, we have little choice but to ask whether this is a viable strategy for our long-term security. Is it wise to persist in seeking our symbol of nationhood in the imperial folly of Gallipoli, and in the shadow of a foreign monarch who is also the head of a Christian Church? Is it time, perhaps, to loosen the ties with the Anglosphere, to turn finally from our colonial past and embrace our cosmopolitan population, our secular, egalitarian values and our geographical good fortune in a new notion of defence and security?

This leads inevitably to a more focused debate about the recalibration of forces to meet the threat, now taking place among a high-level group of Australia's military planners in both official and informal meetings. And it goes to the heart of Australia's defence posture in the twenty-first century. The more perceptive among them embrace a future in which the front lines would be occupied by the expert cyber teams already assembled in Australia's ASIO headquarters in Canberra. But in physical combat the Big Army strategy of the twentieth century would be transformed in a measured pace to units of Special Forces – SAS and Commandos – equipped with an extraordinary capacity to determine the tide of battle. This highly trained cohort would incorporate the intelligence agencies, notably ASIO, ASIS, the Australian Signals Directorate (ASD), the Australian Geospatial-Intelligence Organisation (AGO) as well as the specific defence intelligence groupings.

Their operational brief would cover infiltration of enemy ranks, either as unseen observers or undercover participants; 'kill or capture' squads; platoon-level units with firepower easily surpassing a twentieth-century infantry battalion, but with speed and agility previously undreamt of.

They would be based in a greatly expanded SAS headquarters facility at Swanbourne, Western Australia, with regional HQs manned by a substantially enlarged commando force on the north and east coasts of the continent. Overwhelmingly their operations would be conducted on Australia's offshore perimeter and in domestic counterterrorism events. Only in the event of a major assault on the homeland would they deploy at battalion level, supplementing missile and air defences secretly located in unpopulated areas. In the order of battle, all communications and telemetry would be focused on the support of the Special Forces 'spearhead' and all air and sea assets designed to maximise their impact on the battlefield. The lines of separation between the individual services – army, navy and air force – would blur and eventually disappear.

The enormous savings in defence personnel, both civilian and military, will appeal strongly to the political leadership on both sides of the ideological divide. The sale of redundant facilities and assets will allow funding to be redirected to the Special Forces

Command and Control without further impost on the national budget.

However, if this transformation is to be achieved it will be in spite of the traditionalists within the Big Army and among the general public, whose views run deep. The diehards in the military establishment will fight a rearguard action worthy of Leonidas at Thermopylae. For what is a general without a division to command, or a brigadier *sans* brigade? But despite these obstacles the way ahead is inevitable: Special Forces units are the future of our defence preparedness. They are the new centurions, the Warrior Elite.

Their rise to the forefront of military priority is an extraordinary blend of happy chance, personal dedication and unanticipated technological leaps. And on the way they have carved a saga of courage, excitement, determination and ingenuity unparalleled in all other fields of human endeavour.

Robert Macklin, May 2015

1

EARLY DAYS

There is nothing new about the Big Army's hostility to Special Forces. It has been a feature of the relationship since the first 'irregulars' set foot on the battlefield either as enemies or allies. To the military establishment they have been upstarts with scant regard for the chain of command; insubordinate bounders who refuse to follow the rules of the game. In Ancient Rome, the greatest military force the world had known fell prey to the insurgent German tribes who declined to engage them in the set battles over which the centurions exercised such mastery.

In the modern era, the first appearance of the *guerrilla* was in Napoleon's Spanish campaign in 1808 where the people used hit-and-run tactics against the invader. They were highly effective and not only harassed the French soldiers but also recaptured towns and territory that had earlier fallen to Napoleon's armies. The British commanders of the Peninsular Wars were happy to accept their battlefield successes but looked askance at their methods, which were 'not the done thing'. They were even more aroused at the other end of the nineteenth century when a new irregular term entered the military lexicon with the appearance of the 'commando'. A Dutch derivative, it was used in the South African War of 1899–1902 to describe the small

1

Boer units – usually mounted on horseback – who harried their rival British colonialists.

Since that time they have reappeared in a myriad of nationalist, ideological and religious guises in conflicts around the globe. According to David Kilcullen, a highly respected Australian military theorist, 'Though military establishments persist in regarding it as "irregular" or "unconventional", guerrilla war has been the commonest of conflicts throughout history.'[1] Recent experience suggests that it will remain so.

Undoubtedly Winston Churchill's stint as a correspondent for the *Morning Post* in the Boer War sparked his enthusiasm for the first British commando operations in World War II. At his initiative, a force of 2,000 'special service' soldiers were assembled by June 1940 to carry out tactical raids on the German occupying forces in Europe.

They were trained at Lochailort on Scotland's rugged west coast by a talented band of instructors. They were led by a young Scottish aristocrat, Major Bill Stirling, his cousin Lord Lovat (also a major) and Captain Freddie Spencer Chapman, who before the war had been an Arctic explorer and mountaineer as well as a teacher at Gordonstoun School, the *alma mater* of Prince Philip and later Prince Charles. The training was intense, and when the units were let loose on the Continent they scored some minor successes. But when the main body of commandos under Captain Robert Laycock – known as Layforce – was sent to the Middle East for action in the eastern Mediterranean, the military establishment offered scant cooperation. The result was a series of costly failures, and by July 1941 Layforce was in tatters. It disintegrated during the Battle of Crete and many of its number became POWs. British High Command decided (with barely disguised satisfaction) to disband the unit.

Many of the men returned to their previous regiments, while others chose to remain in the Middle East. Among them was the devil-may-care Lieutenant David Stirling, the younger brother of Major Bill, who had abandoned plans to climb Mount Everest to join Layforce. He engaged the support of a family friend, the deputy commander Middle East, General Sir Neil Methuen Ritchie, for a smaller and more mobile unit that would operate behind enemy lines. Ritchie took the proposal to his commander-in-chief, Claude Auchinleck who, in deference to Churchill, signed off on it. Stirling immediately gathered a team of about 60 volunteers and after a short training regime set out to parachute into German-held North Africa and blow up enemy aircraft on the ground.

It was a disaster. In the face of an approaching storm, Stirling insisted on proceeding with the mission. When they jumped, the team were blown wildly off course. Many were dragged to their death on landing. Stirling himself seriously injured his back. Forty-two of his 61 officers and men were killed, wounded or captured. The survivors were rounded up by a New Zealand unit, the Long Range Desert Group, who were already operating behind the lines, but in more conventional mode. Stirling avoided censure by going to ground and then pulling strings to attach the remnant of his unit to a friendly command. Taking a leaf from the New Zealanders, he abandoned parachuting for vehicle insertion and in a series of raids on German-held ports rehabilitated his unit's reputation.

To disguise its real modus vivendi the force had initially been designated the Special Air Service Brigade. After some discussion with his men, Stirling decided to retain most of the nomenclature, which was soon abbreviated to the SAS. And though Stirling was captured by the Germans in January 1943, the unit would distinguish itself in his absence and subsequently set the tactical framework and the *esprit de corps* that would characterise Special

Forces units thereafter. From this unlikely beginning, the British 22 SAS Regiment became and remains a leader in the field.

The link to Australia's Special Forces occurred at their birth when in October 1940, five instructors, including Freddie Spencer Chapman in charge of field-craft, arrived to train Australian and New Zealand companies at a newly developed facility at Tidal River on Victoria's Wilsons Promontory. The Australians felt 'commando' was altogether too flashy and settled upon 'independent companies' to describe both their role and their relationship to the Big Army.

Unlike David Stirling, the man given charge of the first company raised, Major Alex Spence – a 35-year-old journalist from Bundaberg, Queensland – had no family ties to smooth the way. Nevertheless, he quickly earned the respect of his men and worked well with his immediate superiors. By August 1941, their training in the rugged mountains, dense bush, swamps and beaches of Wilsons Promontory was completed. The men were ready for action.

But it soon became clear that the High Command was divided on how best they could be used. Spencer Chapman saw their role as 'stay-behind' guerrillas, who in the event of a Japanese invasion of the mainland 'would be a thorn in the flesh of an occupying enemy, emerging in true guerrilla style to attack vital points and then disappear into the jungle'.[2] But informal instructions from the hierarchy alerted the officers and men of 2/2 Independent Company to prepare for shipment to the Middle East, where their compatriots in the 9th Division were besieged at Tobruk.

Fate had a very different theatre in store. By early September 1941, the Australian War Council had become deeply concerned about Japanese involvement in Portuguese Timor, where the colonial power was negotiating with Tokyo for a civil air service and the stationing of a Japanese consul in Dili. The following month, the newly installed Curtin Labor Government countered by appointing its own consul, David Ross, and declaring that, 'It is essential in the event of Japanese attack on this territory [that] Britain should declare war . . . Portuguese Timor is the entrance door to Australia.'[3]

While a British declaration was desirable, Curtin was well aware that Britain had its hands full defending its own turf and that Australia would have to take the military initiative. High Command chose the 2/40 Battalion and Spence's 2/2 Independent Company to defend Timor under the command of Lieutenant Colonel William Leggatt, a 47-year-old Melbourne lawyer. Together they would be codenamed Sparrow Force, a gently understated sobriquet for Australia's first entry to Special Forces combat. In fact, they were embarking on a classic guerrilla action to divert a vastly superior force from their drive towards the Australian mainland and with every intention of inflicting fierce casualties on the aggressors.

Five days after the 7 December attack on Pearl Harbor, Sparrow Force was ready to deploy. The plan was to land at Kupang on the Dutch side of the island, where they would link up with the Royal Netherlands East Indies contingent led by Lieutenant Colonel Nico Van Straaten, newly arrived from Java. By now the Japanese were carrying all before them in a headlong dash down the Malayan Peninsula. To counter their inevitable attack the Allies would reinforce the Dutch territory, while Spence's 2/2 Independent Company would occupy East Timor with the support of an additional 260 Netherlands East Indies troops.

By 13 December, they were established in Kupang and three days later they boarded the ancient Dutch training cruiser *Surabaya* for the overnight journey to Dili. With Royal Australian Air Force (RAAF) Hudson bombers in overwatch, the main force made their way stealthily along the coastline, with spotters alerted for Japanese submarines. Intelligence reported a substantial Portuguese force in the capital. Diplomatic negotiations with the colonial power had been inconclusive as Portugal asserted its neutrality and no one knew how the landing would be received. As the troopship approached its destination, Lieutenant Colonel Leggatt and his Dutch counterparts flew from Kupang to Dili and informed the governor, Manuel de Carvalho, that the Allied force intended to land.

The colonial administrator prevaricated. Leggatt joined Spence on board the *Surabaya* and gave the order to proceed. As the men of Sparrow Force climbed into the long boats for the journey to shore, visions of Anzac intruded. One soldier fingered his rifle and asked, 'Will I ram one up the spout?' Spence replied, 'No, but look as if you're prepared to meet a challenge.'[4]

When they reached the sandy beach, they were met only by the local bird life and the troops headed in combat formation for the airport about three kilometres from the capital. Once again there was no sign of resistance and they were soon digging defensive trenches around the airfield. Rumours spread that the Portuguese contingent under one Captain Da Costa was in the hills with a native force preparing to attack; but as time passed it became clear that Da Costa had abandoned the high ground (and the natives) for the creature comforts of Dili.

The Australians quickly realised why he had done so. They were poorly outfitted for the tropics and hordes of malarial mosquitoes attacked their bare arms and legs day and night. While the troops were ordered to dose themselves with quinine twice daily, the medicine came only in a powdered form that was thoroughly unpalatable. Many declined to take it and soon more than half of the 115-strong company were hospitalised with malaria.

Major Spence ordered a survey of the nearby hinterland, seeking a healthier campsite, and soon moved the field hospital to Three Spurs, well above the swampy lowlands. He also encouraged his men to make friends with the locals and, where possible, to learn the native Tetum language. It was becoming ever more likely that Spencer Chapman's vision of the independent company as a 'stay-behind' unit acting as a 'thorn in the flesh' of the invader would be realised, albeit in a different location from the North Queensland jungles he had expected.

Through Christmas, the tension rose and on 27 December Prime Minister John Curtin made his historic appeal to America for the defence of the homeland. Then, on 25 January, the Timorese defenders caught their first glimpse of the enemy when a Japanese reconnaissance plane flew over Kupang. The following day at 9 am seven Japanese fighters attacked the nearby Penfui airfield.

By now the Japanese Imperial Army was threatening Singapore and on 31 January the last Allied forces left Malaya and blew up the causeway to the island. Japanese infiltrators – often disguised as Singaporean civilians – crossed the Straits of Johor in their wake. Already their air force had sunk the British battleships *Repulse* and *Prince of Wales*. The 'impregnable fortress' would fall within 15 days.

The Australian command decided to reinforce the Timorese defenders and sent additional infantry and a light aircraft battery under Brigadier William Veale (a civil engineer in private life) to take command of the operation. The constant air attacks that followed blew the island's air defences away but troop casualties were light and morale remained relatively high. During one raid a soldier had the Australia badge shot off his epaulette, while a second round cut through his shirt under the armpit. His response: 'As well as khaki shorts and khaki shirt, I've now got khaki underpants!'[5]

However, the situation became deadly serious when on 19 February more than 240 Japanese aircraft from the same carriers used in the Pearl Harbor strike force bombed Darwin, with special attention to the harbour and the two airfields. The men on Timor knew nothing of this and at midnight a small fleet carrying 1,500 Japanese troops arrived at Dili. At first the ships were thought to be the expected Portuguese reinforcements from Mozambique. In fact, they had been intercepted by the Japanese and were now on their way to Goa, the tiny Portuguese colony in India. But once the Australians realised the invaders' identity they opened up with devastating crossfire, killing some 200 Japanese in five hours of battle. All the defenders then made an orderly withdrawal to the hills but for one unit – 7 Section – who drove into a Japanese roadblock. They surrendered and all but one were executed.

Later the same night the Japanese arrived in overwhelming force in Dutch Timor. A massive aerial bombardment spearheaded the landing of 4,000 men and five 'tankettes' on the south-west of the island and a paratroop attack on the Penfui airfield. Leggatt moved his Sparrow Force HQ to the east and at the same time engaged the 500 paratroopers. This culminated in a bayonet charge that killed all but 78 of the airborne invaders. However, the effort exhausted both the defenders and their ammunition and Lieutenant Colonel Leggatt had no choice but to surrender. Though he was not to know it then, he was sentencing his troops to a terrible fate as prisoners of war. Over the next two and a half years nearly 200 of them would perish through a combination of brutality and starvation.

The Japanese soon controlled most of Dutch Timor, while Spence and his commandos (who would eventually wear the name with pride) were consolidating their positions in the hills of East Timor. In the west, Brigadier Veale had withdrawn in haste after ordering 'Every man for himself'. The commandos were unimpressed. Veale escaped with 12 of his headquarters staff and struck out overland, eventually reaching Lebos, 80 kilometres south-west of Dili. In fact, they retreated so quickly that they left behind most of their small arms.

There was a further blow when on 9 March the Netherlands East Indies surrendered to the Japanese. This meant that the remaining 300 Australians on Timor were facing a force of 6,000 battle-hardened Japanese who would not only fight to the death but whose methods were unencumbered by any of the restraints codified in the Geneva convention.

Soon afterwards the invaders passed a message through Consul David Ross under house arrest that the 2/2 should follow Leggatt's lead and surrender. But when Spence put it to his men the response was immediate and unmistakably Australian: 'Surrender? Surrender be fucked!'[6]

Spence's counsel to make friends with the Timorese was literally bearing fruit. The Australians' informal demeanour and sense of humour struck a chord with the natives after their overbearing Portuguese colonial masters and they were happy to supply them with home-grown fruits and vegetables. The Australians paid with what little money they had and when that ran out they substituted a 'surat' system of IOUs that would be redeemed, they said, when they were able to make contact with their headquarters in Australia.

Having established their own modus operandi, the commandos didn't take kindly to Brigadier Veale's admonition to shave off their beards. The 2/2's Lieutenant David Dexter cracked, 'We lost our razors, not our rifles.' The brigadier's response is not recorded. The incident was one more illustration that an officer at general rank had become superfluous to requirements.

By the end of March, the commandos had consolidated their position. They were well established in the hills surrounding Dili. At platoon level they were setting ambushes along the rough roads and jungle tracks the Japanese travelled in their campaign to rid themselves of the Australian 'thorn in the flesh'. However, they were without any means to contact their compatriots in Darwin, since Veale's headquarters staff had been unable to salvage a radio during their wild retreat. This became their first priority and responsibility fell on 2/2 company's signaller, Max Loveless.

Wracked with malaria, Loveless led a small team of signallers in an attempt to cobble together a workable transmitter with parts from an American commercial medium-wave receiver, a damaged army 109 set, the power pack from a Dutch transmitter, aerial wire and a receiving set. Using the most primitive tools – pliers, a screwdriver and a tomahawk – Loveless worked around the clock but to no avail. Then word arrived from a Portuguese ally that there was a radio in the Qantas Airways office in Dili.

They mounted a raiding party and in the dead of night broke into the Qantas premises. The radio seemed perfectly intact and as a bonus there were half a dozen rifles with ammunition to match. Timorese bearers helped to carry their prize across the mountain spine to Veale's HQ in Mape. However, their joy was short-lived. The radio would not operate without powerful batteries, and those few they had were patently insufficient. Loveless was devastated and retired to his bunk. It took all the psychological subtlety of his section head, Captain George Parker, to revive his spirits; but when he returned to the workroom it was with a brilliant solution. He would hook up the powerful uncalibrated Qantas set to the weak set they had salvaged with a range of only 50 kilometres. The combination should do the trick. All they needed were four more batteries.

Parker organised a foraging party, which 'liberated' batteries from Dili plus enough petrol to run a charger. The extraordinary Heath Robinson contraption now occupied a room nearly three-metres square, with equipment on benches around the perimeter attached by various wires to a generator taken from an old car. A further attachment included a metre-diameter wheel with fixed handles to be turned by four native Timorese working in shifts.

On the night of 18 April, Loveless gave the order; the wheel began to turn and suddenly in Darwin the signallers heard a Morse code message from men they assumed had been either killed or captured by the Japanese. But before they could confirm their situation the batteries ran out. Loveless spent the next day refining his contraption, and that night Darwin was waiting. They were also highly suspicious of the contact as a Japanese ploy and when the first message arrived they demanded proof of identity.

'Do you know George Parker?'

'Yes, he is with us.'

'What is his rank? Answer immediately.'

'Captain.'

'Bring him to the transmitter. What is your wife's name, George?'

'Joan.'

'What is the street number of your house?'

'Ninety-four.'

It was enough. Darwin was satisfied. In Timor they were ecstatic. They christened their contraption 'Winnie the War Winner'. Then they tapped out the message that would send a bolt of pleasure through an Australian command under imminent threat of invasion: 'The Timor force is intact and still fighting. Badly needs boots, quinine, money and tommy-gun ammunition. Over . . .'

2

INDEPENDENT COMPANIES

That signal from Sparrow Force was the first positive news from the north since hostilities began. Until then, the Australian command had been rocked by one reversal after another. The fall of Singapore had been Australia's worst military disaster since Gallipoli, with the entire 8th Division – some 15,000 men – taken captive. In the Battle of the Java Sea on 27 February, a combined Allied strike force of American, British, Dutch and Australian ships (ABDA) under the Dutch Rear-Admiral Karel Doorman had suffered a shocking defeat at the hands of the Japanese Navy. The ABDA flotilla had intercepted the Eastern Invasion Force approaching the Indonesian archipelago through the Makassar Straits. But in a seven-hour battle every attempt to disable and destroy the Japanese troopships was repulsed by their powerful escorts. The battle expanded in a widening arc around the Sunda and Bali Straits over the next three days and a deadly combination of Allied confusion and superior Japanese firepower took a crushing toll. Ten Allied ships were sunk and more than 2,100 sailors – including Admiral Doorman – were killed in action.

The Japanese seemed irresistible. After landing in Java, the invaders fought a fierce war of attrition and the ABDA ground forces surrendered on 9 March. Eight days later, General Douglas

MacArthur and his family escaped the Japanese onslaught in the Philippines in a B-17 bomber, reaching the Australian coastline early next morning only to discover Darwin under Japanese attack. They diverted to Batchelor, 50 kilometres inland, and after refuelling flew on to Alice Springs, where the party transferred to a train headed for Adelaide. By 20 March, MacArthur had reached the small South Australian town of Terowie where he addressed an enthusiastic crowd of local farmers and their families at the station. There, for the first time (but by no means the last) he made his famous declaration: 'I came through and I shall return.'

Appointed supreme commander of the South-West Pacific area, MacArthur quickly discovered that Australia was almost bereft of military defences. There were fewer than 32,000 Allied troops in the whole country and less than 100 aircraft, many of them Gypsy Moths with fabric-covered wings and propellers that had to be spun by hand to start. 'God have mercy on us,' he said.[1]

The Pensacola Convoy of eight ships under the protection of the US Navy cruiser *Pensacola* and a single submarine chaser had been at sea heading for the Philippines, Guam and China when the Japanese attacked Pearl Harbor. The flotilla of troop transports and freighters carrying peacetime supplies as well as some boxed aircraft, bombs, guns and anti-aircraft ammunition steered a zigzag course across the Pacific and fetched up in Brisbane on 22 December. The Americans aboard the transports were designated Task Force South Pacific and given temporary quarters at Amberley airfield and two Brisbane racetracks. In the weeks to come, their naval compatriots would be put to work on resupply missions to the irregular forces holding out in the northern approaches. But their principal contribution to the war effort would be a measurable lift in local morale as symbols of America's commitment to Australia's defence. Prime Minister John Curtin quickly developed a strong working relationship with MacArthur, and Australia's highest ranked soldier, General Thomas Blamey, was appointed commander of the Allied land forces; though given MacArthur's one-man-band proclivities, Blamey's designation was somewhat overblown. And until the 7th Division could be returned from the Middle East and US infantry units arrived in force, his frontline resources were desperately few.

However, behind the scenes there was feverish activity among the Special Forces. As specialists arrived from Singapore and the UK, intelligence units such as Special Operations Australia (SOA), Secret Intelligence Australia (SIA) and the Far Eastern Liaison Office (FELO) would be controlled through the Australian Intelligence Bureau, which answered to both the Australian High Command and MacArthur's headquarters.

Colonel John Rogers, a highly decorated Australian intelligence officer, was recalled from the Middle East to take charge of revamping Australia's intelligence operations. In April, Blamey appointed him liaison officer with MacArthur's headquarters and three months later he became director of military intelligence (DMI), a role he would retain throughout the war. He worked closely with the director of naval intelligence, Commander Rupert Long, who had already developed a network of coast watchers around the vulnerable approaches to Papua New Guinea and the Australian mainland. Rogers' operation was a testing one given the traditional unwillingness of intelligence organisations to share information with each other. And it was not assisted by the military egos at the top, particularly in MacArthur's khaki court.

However, his relations with the American supremo would not be without its lighter moments. He arranged for MacArthur to call on Governor-General Lord Gowrie at Government House in Melbourne, and the American, who relished the ceremonial perquisites of his high rank, decked himself out in military splendour for the ride to the vice-regal mansion. As they approached the gates, Rogers reminded him that if he wished he could stop the car there and return the guard's salute before proceeding to the entrance. MacArthur was happy to oblige. But when the car slowed, the guard of the day casually strolled over, stuck his head through the window on the general's side and asked, 'Who are you?'[2] MacArthur's response is not recorded.

Rogers quickly learnt that in 1941 three additional independent companies had been turned out from the Wilsons Promontory training centre by Lieutenant Colonel J. C. Mawhood of the British Special Operations Executive (SOE). However, relations between Mawhood and the Australian military staff deteriorated and this led to SOE's control being terminated. In January 1942, the centre was upgraded and reopened as the Guerrilla Warfare School and after a six-week course specialising in reconnaissance and sabotage the 2/5th Independent Company was formed with 17 officers and 256 other ranks.

On 13 April, they shipped out of Townsville for Port Moresby, arriving during an air raid four days later. The following week, they were deployed to Wau in the mountains inland from Lae. There for the next 12 months in appalling conditions of soaking rain, insect attack, disease, food shortage and little medication, they would harass and demoralise the Japanese aggressors.

The company's most successful raid was on Salamaua on 30 June 1942, where they killed more than 120 Japanese for the loss of only three Australians wounded in action. When the Japanese were preparing a major attack on Wau, the 2/5th raided and ambushed enemy troops as they moved into position. But while they and Sparrow Force proved themselves potent thorns in the enemy's flesh, other independent companies were fighting losing battles against the Japanese in New Ireland, Bougainville and Manus Island.

Closer to home, a uniquely Australian special operation was being developed. In March, the deputy DMI, Lieutenant Colonel Bob Wake, toured northern Australia and reported, 'There is ample evidence . . . that the Northern Territory and adjacent areas have been a hotbed of Japanese espionage and that Darwin has been the centre of collation and communication of information. It would seem highly probable that enemy agents are being landed by parachutes from aircraft coming in over the Gulf of Carpentaria . . .'[3]

Wake and his small delegation followed this startling assertion with reports of 'evidence' of Japanese contact with 'the aboriginals and half-castes' of the area designed to spread terror among the whites. These same traitorous degenerates were primed 'to attack whites if and when landings are attempted by the enemy'. They recommended 'rounding up all uncontrolled aboriginals and half-castes and all low whites and "breeds"'. Moreover, they called for dummy air raids to flush out the traitors, who would then presumably be incarcerated (at the very least) until the end of the war.

It was an exercise in racist absurdity. But the report did contain one solid recommendation with immediate appeal to the Special Forces community: the raising of a North Australian Observer Unit (NAOU) to be trained as a guerrilla force to patrol the vast empty stretches of northern Australia and report on the expected Japanese invasion. If and when it came, they would not confront the invaders but, as suggested by Freddie Spencer Chapman and demonstrated by the men of Sparrow Force, would remain in place to harry and demoralise the occupying forces.

The idea had particular appeal to Army Minister Frank Forde, who had fiercely resisted earlier recommendations for a Brisbane Line approach to Australia's defence from the commander of home forces Lieutenant General Iven Mackay. He developed plans to consolidate the bulk of his forces between Brisbane and Melbourne to protect the nation's industrial base. The Curtin Government rejected the plan, much to Forde's satisfaction, since his electorate was situated well above it in central Queensland.

Forde was so enthusiastic that he chose one of his personal assistants, 37-year-old William Stanner, to follow the Observer Unit proposal through. Stanner had graduated in anthropology from Sydney University before joining the London School of Economics as a research assistant. After participating in an Oxford University expedition to Kenya, he returned to Australia and joined the staff of Percy Spender, the army minister in the Menzies Government, as a research officer. When Labor took power, he transferred to Forde's office in the same role.

Armed with his new brief, Stanner flew to Darwin for talks with the northern area commander, Major General Edmund Herring. By then he had roughed out a general idea of how the unit might operate. He said later, 'While working in Kenya in 1938–39 I had become quite knowledgeable about the commandos and their role in the Boer War, and about the Germans' remarkable performance in East Africa in World War I under von Lettow-Vorbeck, in country and circumstances not unlike those that might face us in North Australia. Both had a considerable effect on my mentality.'[4]

After a session with Herring and Brigadier Richard Sutherland, MacArthur's chief of staff, on a rare break from the khaki court, Stanner was told to flesh out his ideas on paper. 'I sat up all night doing so,' he says. He roughed out a plan that would provide 'a thin green line' of self-reliant soldiers across the 3,000 kilometres of northern Australia. He then concentrated on the logistics of supplying them with basic rations and the means to travel across their designated areas. 'Next day Sutherland put me through a grinder,' he says. 'He was a formidable, sceptical and very professional soldier . . . I have forgotten exactly what I said but it must have made a certain amount of sense because he took me to see the Major General again. After a little talk, I was staggered to hear Major General Herring say that I myself should raise and command the kind of special unit I had suggested.'[5]

Stanner's only military experience had been in a militia signals unit in the 1930s, but time was of the essence and good men in short supply. Two weeks later he found himself with the unexpected rank of major answering to Major General George Vasey, deputy chief of the general staff, and charged with recruiting 400 volunteers for one of the more unusual special operations of the war. It was a daunting task. Stanner had not the slightest idea how to begin. However, with Vasey's backing he sent circulars to all Australian Imperial Force (AIF) and Citizen Military Force (CMF) units seeking fit men with bush experience, horsemanship and initiative for 'adventurous duties requiring a high degree of endurance and ability to act independently'.

The response was overwhelming. 'It was like opening a flood-gate,' he says. 'I could have filled the unit twice over.'[6] The reason was not hard to divine. Stanner was offering his compatriots the chance to defend their country while avoiding the despised regimentation of army life. What's more, they would be joining the ranks of the legendary dashing bushmen from the pages of Henry Lawson and Banjo Paterson.

They arrived from across the continent at their temporary headquarters outside the village of Ingleburn, west of Sydney. Conditions were primitive, a foretaste of their mission in the lonely reaches of northern Australia. Their beds were straw mattresses on bare earth and they performed their ablutions with no hot water by hastily dug latrines. Their eight-week course consisted of daily route marches followed by lessons in map reading, guerrilla tactics, weapons handling and living off the land. The specialist signallers were then sent to the AWA Marconi School of Wireless in Sydney, where they learnt to transmit and receive in Morse code. The rough conditions helped to develop a group camaraderie and this was consolidated when one of the early recruits, Lieutenant Travers, provided the nickname that would replace the NAOU's awkward acronym: the 'Nackeroos'.

The unit's total complement would reach 550 and include farriers, saddlers and two anthropologists, no doubt to engage with any loyal 'aboriginals or half-castes' who might have escaped the clutches of the ubiquitous Japanese fifth columnists. They were equipped with telescopes, signalling flags, handcuffs and prisoner chains, axes, fishing lines, compasses and the all-important mosquito veils, nets and gloves. Their weapons were the standard .303 rifle plus light machine guns, tommy guns and .22 rifles, as well as 12-gauge shotguns for hunting game. For transport they were allocated 1,500 horses, 41 trucks, six motorbikes and 15 bicycles.

On 11 August, the first fully trained contingent of Nackeroos left Sydney for their forward base at Katherine in the Northern Territory. They had a brief leave in Brisbane, where they brawled with the dapper American servicemen whose luxury-stocked canteen in the city centre was a magnet for the local girls but off limits to the Australian soldiers. The clash was a forerunner of the Battle of Brisbane three months later, when an Australian soldier, Gunner Edward Webster, was shot dead by an American MP, Norbert J. Grant, and scores of combatants on both sides were injured.[7] The Nackeroos, however, escaped without serious harm, and 14 days after leaving Sydney finally reached their headquarters on the southern bank of the Katherine River.

Stanner was enthusiastic. 'It was a beautiful site,' he says, 'with fair cover from air observation, splendid water, and heavy grass, which we never burned but trampled underfoot to keep the dust from rising; a lesson many units were very slow to learn.'[8] For most of his men it was only a staging post and over the next two weeks he deployed three field companies to Normanton in the Gulf of Carpentaria all the way west to Wyndham in the Kimberleys.

Before they set out, Stanner addressed the men. 'I will not find it easy to forget this scene,' he says. 'Moon rose late . . . a calm, soft shiny night. I talked until late, a general air of tension and excitement in the atmosphere. I slept rather restlessly and lightly, continually waking up to look out on to brilliant moonlight and rustling grass. One of the men played a banjo till very late – old songs and new songs . . .'[9]

By 14 September, all three units were in place; then a remaining small contingent under Lieutenant Romney Cole was sent 1,000 kilometres north-east to Borroloola on the crocodile-infested coastal plain between the Barkly Tableland and the Gulf. On arrival, Romney Cole looked around the three buildings that made up the town – a pub, a dilapidated police station and a falling down store. 'Welcome,' he said, 'to the arsehole of the world.'[10]

Meanwhile, back on Timor, Major General Vasey was quietly repatriated. Spence took full command of Sparrow Force and was promoted to lieutenant colonel; Major Bernard Callinan became commanding officer (CO) of 2/2. They were digging a particularly painful thorn into the Japanese flesh. Time and again, they used their local knowledge of the terrain, ably guided by their Timorese helpers, to catch the invaders unawares and cut them down with rifle and light-machine-gun fire. And with the radio fully operational, Darwin was able to resupply them with airdrops and a monthly seaborne mission to an unguarded spot on the coastline. The commandos would then transport the supplies by pony to their mountain redoubts. In June, MacArthur told Blamey, 'The retention of these forces will greatly facilitate offensive action when the necessary means are at hand . . . they should remain and execute their present missions of harassment and sabotage.'

They were happy to oblige. They had even extended their operations to Dili. The previous month, an attacking force of 12 men moved stealthily at night through the side streets of the town heading for the Japanese headquarters near the sea. There they would burst in and kill as many as possible before withdrawing into the darkness. A small party armed with Bren guns was taking up a position on the foreshore overlooking the Japanese HQ to provide harassing fire during the attack and then cover the withdrawal of the main force. Platoon leader Captain Geoff 'Bull' Laidlaw, a former surfing champion, was moving ahead of his troops a short distance into the town when a Japanese sentry at a machine-gun post challenged the silhouetted Australian. Realising he'd been detected, Laidlaw opened fire with his .45 revolver from three metres. Commandos on both sides of him joined in and tossed grenades into two nearby shelters filled with Japanese guards.

The sentry was killed outright. The survivors in the shelters ran to machine-gun positions and began firing wildly. For the next ten minutes the Australians answered their fire, while the Bren-gun party near the beach raked the headquarters and its defences. The Japanese casualties piled up, while the Australians suffered no more than a few scratches. The main body of commandos then withdrew, and as their firing died away the Bren-gunners decamped.

Over the next three days, the Japanese carried out reprisals against the Timorese, whom they suspected of collaborating with the Australians. Throughout the following week all Japanese forces remained in the capital regrouping. Unbeknown to Spence and his men, when the Imperial Japanese Army's forward HQ in Singapore learnt of the raid they sent an unnamed enforcer known only as 'the Singapore Tiger' with orders to remove the Sparrow Force thorn forthwith.

On 22 May, an Australian raiding party led by Corporal Ray Aitkin was setting up an overwatch position on the main road from Dili about 40 metres above the thoroughfare. There was a noisy waterfall on their right flank and a bridge across the creek directly beneath. Aitkin says, 'It was a leisurely affair in that there was time to lay our spare clips on flat rocks and wipe away sweaty, fearful palms on the seat of swift-drying shorts. A monkey crossed the track below. A few minutes later a goshawk killed a rat in the same place. And then, or so it appeared to [my] half dozen [men], the whole bloody Japanese army burst around the spur in single file.

'The formation was four forward scouts, a gap of 20 yards, four more, another gap and then the main body led by a nuggetty lad with crossed straps and a sword. Naturally enough, when we opened fire these scouts and the boy with the sword copped most of the attention. Those uninjured in the vanguard flopped on the track, disconcerted by the noise of the waterfall and thinking the lead was coming from up the track rather than above.

'Five or six took shelter under a flame tree in a rock hole on the uphill side of the track. They would have been perfectly safe had not Norman Thornton been sitting above it and he proceeded to remove the leaves from the trees with systematic machine-gun fire. The main body did the only possible thing, which was to run like hell back down the track.'[11]

The 'nuggetty lad' with the sword was the Singapore Tiger. He had growled his last.

3

THE NACKEROOS

Once the Nackeroos were established in their far-flung forward bases, they began to patrol in ever-expanding arcs seeking evidence of Japanese infiltrators. At first they attacked the task with great enthusiasm. It was not long, however, before the immensity of the bush and the total absence of oriental intruders began to affect morale. 'I became aware of a constant battle with the psychology of the Australian soldier,' Stanner says. 'He wanted someone to fight!'[1]

Stanner was also aware of the difficulties of erecting a northern screen across an entire continent with only 550 men. 'One doesn't really appreciate the vast size of Australia from a map,' he says. 'But when you cross it on land that's a different matter.' This brought home to the unit the hit-and-miss nature of their task. And like their compatriots in Sparrow Force they had initial trouble staying in contact via radio. When their 300-watt transmitter – the '133' – arrived at Katherine, the American removalists mistook the pack for a refrigerator and dropped it off the truck. Every valve was smashed; the innards were damaged beyond repair. Months would pass before it could be replaced.

However, using a smaller set at night they were finally able to establish a network of 45 transmitter/receivers and develop a fraternity of the airwaves via coded Morse signals. The long hours on duty tested their mental stamina. One signaller near the coast, Doug Drinkwater, says, 'The midnight to daylight shift was the worst. It was scary sitting there alone with everyone else asleep. I had to have a light on when I was taking down messages and I often thought that if there were any Jap patrols about I would be the first one to get shot!'[2]

One big problem was keeping the radio batteries charged, as the tropic humidity played havoc with their armatures. They became adept at improvising with whatever was available, from replacement carbon rods from torch batteries to fencing wire as aerials. Another trial was finding suitable horses to negotiate the rough country of their patrols. They scoured the Top End for mounts and had to take a great many station discards and half-broken brumbies to make up the numbers. Donkeys and mules saw service as pack animals but they were not always easy to handle. Morrie Vane says, 'Mules are very spiteful animals and will kick you anywhere. I got flattened by a mule one day. Old Jimmy Gibbs, the manager of the station, said, "Forgot to tell you, but you can't put a halter on that bloke".[3] Arthur Winter recalls two particularly vicious mules: Centipede and Taxation. 'Centipede got his name because he could kick you with all four legs at once,' he says. 'And Taxation, well, that's a problem at all times.'

However, their most fearsome hazard was undoubtedly the several thousand saltwater crocodiles that frequented the rivers, creeks and waterholes near the Nackeroos' camps. They were a constant presence. Clem Muldoon says, 'One day we were beside the Ord River when a large bullock came down to the water to drink. A big croc grabbed it around the nose and pulled it straight in. There was hardly a bubble and we never saw that bullock again.' Alan Kearney tethered his horse Baldy at night by a creek that flowed into the Roper River. 'During the night it rained 16 inches [400 millimetres] and by daylight the water wasn't far from me,' he says. 'The creek had become a river and I went to find Baldy, but all I found was his hind leg and part of his shoulder.'

On one occasion, Sergeant Reg Oakley was riding across the flooded Gin Arm Creek in the Gulf country when he felt a thud and the water around him turned red. A crocodile had ripped open his horse's belly. Oakley says he swam 'Olympic strokes' to get to the other side. The horse and all his equipment disappeared beneath the torrent.

On another occasion, Corporal Tip Carty and a mate tried to cross a creek on a log. No sooner was his mate above the water when a three-metre crocodile reared out of the creek towards him. Tip says, 'I fired two shots from the hip but the croc kept coming. The fellow behind me was using high explosive ammunition from a crashed Spitfire and he managed to shoot the crocodile as I stepped back.'[4]

Soon afterwards, near a flooded part of the Adelaide River, the water rose and flooded their camp. A crocodile and a shark cruised by within a few metres. The Nackeroos raised their beds and posted a guard in a nearby tree. 'At 7 pm,' Tip says, 'the largest croc I have ever seen – over six metres – came out of the river at us. We fired at him but the bullets ricocheted off his skin. As he turned away I lobbed a hand grenade into the water ahead of him.' Two days later the croc returned. Once again they drove him off but Tip says the attack 'gave our driver, Jock Willis nightmares from which he never recovered. He used to wake at night screaming.'

Crocodiles aside, the Nackeroos enjoyed an unexpected bonus. The Aboriginal people of the north, rather than collaborating with the Japanese infiltrators of Colonel Bob Wake's perfervid imagination, became their indispensable guides and saviours. They taught the young soldiers how to live on the bush tucker of the north: the tasty turtles, ducks, yams, frogs, lizards and snakes that had been their staple diet, as well as the kangaroos and wallabies that filled the soldiers' meat safes when supplies from the south ran low. They showed them how to dig soaks in dry creek beds and to tap water from the bulbous swellings on the paperbark trees. They lent them their dugout canoes to patrol the tidal flats. And they shared with them the knowledge borne for thousands of years of how to navigate their way across the seemingly trackless territory of the far Outback.

The Nackeroos' radios, with their Japanese propaganda broadcasts from 'Tokyo Rose' and the 'Domei' news service, kept them on high alert. Usually the information in the broadcasts was well wide of the mark but occasionally a fact or two would strike home. For example, soon after Eric Wenban reached his observation post (OP) at East Point on the Cox Peninsula, he was startled to hear Tokyo Rose say, 'Now you boys out on East Point – have you dug in yet? Have you made yourselves comfortable?'[5]

The sense of impending invasion was intensified with every bombing raid on Darwin or the sighting of a Japanese reconnaissance aircraft. One morning, Sergeant-Farrier Tom Martin was tending a horse. 'There was this swishing noise above me and I looked up to see a twin engine Japanese plane gliding at tree-top level over our camp,' he says. 'It was so low that I could see two Japs inside it. Luckily they started their motors and flew away.'

Other groups on the coast spotted naval flotillas that turned out to be Allied hunting packs. Japanese submarines were frequently reported to be surfacing offshore – particularly at night, when it was thought they would be recharging their batteries and getting some fresh air. And on at least two occasions, Nackeroos mistakenly opened fire on Australian patrol boats. However, in December 1942 the exercise suddenly became critical with Australian intelligence reports that 12,000 Japanese combat troops had been massed on

Timor, with Japanese shipping concentrated in the islands to the north. This, they believed, could signal the invasion of northern Australia.

On Timor itself, Sparrow Force had been under siege almost from the time they disposed of the Singapore Tiger. The Japanese confined themselves to Dili for several weeks while their 48th Division, commanded by a lieutenant general, began arriving from the Philippines. Their plan was to outnumber Sparrow Force by 100 to one and to crush them without mercy. A big Japanese patrol moved out of the capital on 7 August. Two days later bombers raided the Australian strongholds of Mape and Bobonaro south of Balibo. Spence hastily moved his headquarters out of Mape and when a small party returned to collect their radios and other equipment they discovered the Timorese had looted them. This was the first troubling indication that their relationship with the local population was no longer entirely reliable.

It then became clear that the Japanese had decided to surround and remove the Australian thorn once and for all. Some 2,000 enemy troops were on the move in four columns converging from different directions. Bull Laidlaw was once again in the thick of the action. On the night of 10 August, a large force from Dili moved towards his patrol and they withdrew to the high ground. At dawn they watched as the Japanese surrounded the village they had passed through and machine-gunned it for half an hour before launching a charge on the mostly deserted huts. Reinforcements then joined the enemy and between 500 and 600 troops advanced on Laidlaw's well-prepared positions. A series of Australian ambushes hit the Japanese hard, and as they continued to advance over the next four days the Australians inflicted 100 enemy casualties for one commando killed in action.

Further east near Liltai, an Australian patrol led by Corporal Eddie Loud engaged a Japanese column and was almost taken by surprise when another approached from the opposite direction. Loud and his men melted into the bush, where they took special pleasure at the sound of a pitched battle between the two enemy units. In other areas across the colony, contact between the commandos and the invaders resulted in casualties on both sides. But it was soon clear that the Japanese show of force – together with their ruthless treatment of collaborators and their anti-white propaganda – was having its desired effect on the native Timorese. Moreover, some of the remaining Portuguese chose this time to raise a native force to put down an uprising against the colonial power at Maubisse in the geographical centre of the colony. According to the 2/2 War Diary, 'One of our patrols near Mape out hunting the Jap, encountered a Portuguese patrol out hunting some natives. They exchanged compliments and went their various ways. Company HQ witnessed the spectacle of about 3,000 natives all in war dress and armed to the teeth, also complete with drums and Portuguese flags, returning from the hunt with many of them nonchalantly swinging heads of the unfortunate in battle.'[6]

In September, the 2/2 was joined by an advance party of 12, including Major 'Mac' Walker of the 2/4 Independent Company, with plans to reinforce their compatriots. Lieutenant Colonel Spence welcomed them at his new HQ, and once arrangements had been concluded Walker returned to prepare his troops for their new deployment. On 21 September, the 450-strong 2/4 – known as Lancer Force – embarked on the destroyer HMAS *Voyager* in Darwin for the hazardous journey across the Timor Sea.

They arrived at Betano Bay on the south coast in the late afternoon of 23 September, but as the troops disembarked the destroyer drifted into the shallows where it stuck fast. Increasingly desperate attempts to refloat her were in vain and at 1.30 pm the next day the regular Japanese reconnaissance plane spotted the stranded warship. *Voyager* was doomed.

Though the destroyer's gunners brought down the reconnaissance plane, the crew had already radioed her plight. Shortly afterwards, a squadron of bombers pounded the Australian ship with high explosives.

In Darwin, two corvettes, the *Warrnambool* and the *Kalgoorlie*, were dispatched to recover the crew, which they accomplished without further loss. However, the incident encouraged the Japanese aggressors, and despite the reinforcements Sparrow Force were soon under siege by a far superior force. The Japanese had abandoned all civilised restraints. They now tortured anyone they believed might have information about the Australians' whereabouts, and in a particularly vicious interrogation they tormented and murdered two Portuguese priests.

Another small contingent of Dutch troops linked up with the defenders and were assigned to assist Lieutenant Colin Doig with his H Detachment, maintaining a reconnaissance over the eastern end of the island. A party from the newly raised Australian Z Special Force had arrived in the east and were arming and training native Timorese to resist the Japanese. Z Force had been raised in June as a commando strike force of the Allied Military Intelligence group. Lieutenant Doig was impressed with the support they received from HQ in Darwin. '[They] could get things done that we found nigh impossible,' he says. 'As a small unit they were superbly equipped and had just about everything.'[7]

The Timorese were becoming a lost cause. They realised that the Australians might well be driven out and the Japanese would exact a high price among known collaborators. Australian currency lost its value, its possession a telltale sign to the Japanese of cooperation with the enemy. The result was that fresh food became harder for the Australians to acquire and their condition suffered accordingly. In some areas, the Japanese had even recruited Timorese as frontline troops; and though in battle they were little more than cannon fodder, the native tide had clearly turned against the commandos.

The remaining Portuguese were also fiercely pressured to take the Japanese side and the Allied High Command offered them weaponry to resist. Most preferred flight, and eventually the Allies evacuated more than 300 women and children. Spence himself was a marked man, and on 11 November he was ordered to evacuate. Major Callinan took over as Allied commander.

At the end of the month, the Australian Navy mounted a daring exercise to land fresh Dutch troops and evacuate Portuguese civilians and exhausted Dutch fighters at Betano, the site of the *Voyager* disaster. The patrol boat HMAS *Kuru*, which would ferry the soldiers from ship to shore, departed Darwin early on 29 November; the faster corvettes HMAS *Armidale* and *Castlemaine* followed at midday carrying the reinforcements. The following day at 9 am, the two larger warships were spotted by a Japanese reconnaissance plane and took evasive action, but in the afternoon they were twice attacked by Japanese bombers. With assistance from RAAF Beaufighters they escaped undamaged, but the delays meant that when they reached Betano on the afternoon of 1 December the *Kuru* had departed with the civilians. *Castlemaine* caught her up next morning and took the passengers aboard. *Kuru* and *Armidale*, which was carrying the fresh troops, made for Betano by separate routes. Then followed one of the most heroic naval engagements of the war.

The *Armidale* was attacked by five Japanese dive-bombers at 1.30 pm. She fought them off and seriously damaged two of the attackers. Half an hour later, five Zero fighters distracted the corvette's guns while nine torpedo bombers attacked her flanks. Two struck her port side in quick succession, one smashing into the engine room, the other destroying the mess deck. As soldiers and sailors abandoned ship, the Zeros began strafing the men in the water. Ordinary Sailor Edward 'Teddy' Sheean, who had been wounded in the initial attack, strapped himself into one of the *Armidale*'s 20-mm Oerlikon guns and opened fire on the planes. He hit one Zero, which then crashed into the sea, and he damaged at least two others. He was still firing as the *Armidale* sank beneath the waves. Despite a round-the-clock search, there were few survivors.

The failed operation was a further blow to the men on Timor and by the end of December a top-level meeting of the Australian chiefs of staff concluded that at least three Allied divisions would be required to defeat the invaders. And by now the natives were increasingly hostile. The chiefs decided to order a tactical withdrawal.

As the New Year dawned, Timor was gradually emptied of its Australian Special Forces, the final Australian–British Z Force unit departing on the American submarine USS *Gudgeon* on 10 February 1943. They did so in the knowledge that in a critical phase of the war, when Japan was crushing all resistance before it, a small band of tough, independent and endlessly innovative Australians had checked its advance and given their Allies time to consolidate their forces in preparation for the all-important counterattack.

In the Northern Territory, the Nackeroos were unsure where they figured in the overall war effort. After the massive bombing raid on Darwin in February, there had been more than 60 additional bombings of the Territory and the north of Western Australia. But despite their best efforts the Nackeroos had found no evidence of enemy landings and had captured no infiltrators or fifth columnists. In Roper Bar, Rod Dunwoodie was getting restless. 'I felt we were wasting our time,' he says. 'We wanted to get into a fighting unit in New Guinea where we could pull our weight.'[8] A few of his mates decided they were fed up. 'It doesn't look like we'll ever go into action,' one said. 'Why don't we go down to Brisbane and join up with General MacArthur?'

Albeit with the best intentions, 12 Nackeroo non-commissioned officers (NCOs) and troopers went AWOL at precisely the time the *Armidale* was engaged in her final operation in the Timor Sea. Travelling in a three-ton Chevrolet 'blitz buggy', they made it the 3,400 kilometres to Brisbane where they reported to the military police HQ in the naive belief that they could sort out the AWOL situation and transfer to a fighting unit. Fortunately the provost commander, Lieutenant Colonel Joe Courtney, was sympathetic. He gave them tea and scones, and listened to their story; then he sent them back to their Katherine HQ where they arrived on 6 January to cries of, 'The prodigals have returned!' However, the court martial that followed was no laughing matter. The corporals received sentences of 180 days in detention, while the men got 150. Eric Wenban says, 'We thought we were lucky to get off with such a light sentence . . . they could have shot us for desertion.'

It was now becoming clear that the crisis of imminent Japanese invasion was fading fast. The Battle of the Coral Sea in May 1942 and the decisive action at Milne Bay in September of that year, where Australian and American forces stopped the Japanese advance, had rebalanced strategic superiority. The Nackeroos were becoming redundant. General Blamey wrote, 'The present organisation was set up at the time when an enemy combined land, sea and air attack on the shores of Australia seemed probable. It seems reasonable to rule out this contingency at the present time.' Therefore, the unit would be disbanded. William Stanner says, 'With a bit more luck we could have gone on to other roles . . . but it was not to be; it was probably a good decision although at the time I took it badly.'[9]

However, the experience gained by his men living off the land and cooperating with the Aboriginal people would have far-reaching consequences in the evolution of Australia's Special Forces. And some who cut their commando teeth as Nackeroos would put their skills to work in Z Force and other units that did vital work behind enemy lines throughout the war.

4

SINGAPORE ATTACK

By 1943, MacArthur had moved his headquarters to Lennons Hotel, Brisbane, and most of the Allied intelligence services had moved with him to the Queensland capital. Colonel John Rogers, as Australia's DMI, established his base at the recently completed Forgan Smith Building of the University of Queensland's suburban campus at St Lucia. (The university would remain at its city campus until war's end.) Rogers made regular trips to Port Moresby to assess Australian intelligence gathering in the field and monthly visits to the Naval Intelligence and SOA headquarters in Melbourne.

While MacArthur and his khaki court had overall command of the intelligence flow, the Melbourne group – known collectively as the Inter-Allied Services Department (ISD) – was particularly attuned to British interests and this was reflected in their separate Special Forces priorities. MacArthur was the quintessential Big Army commander to whom intelligence gathering was a vital tool in the military planning process. The British, backed by the traditionalists of the Royal Australian Navy (RAN), saw covert operations as the means to reassert their credentials for a return to their lost colonies after the war. Rogers frequently found himself caught between the two, and it required all his diplomatic skills to navigate a course that would satisfy both sides. He was not always successful.

Fortunately, MacArthur had committed himself to a triumphant return to the Philippines, and his island-hopping strategy was directed to that end. Moreover, his chief of staff, Richard Sutherland, despised the risky adventurism of special operations. This allowed the ISD to develop Z Force for missions behind Japanese lines in Singapore and Malaya without bothering the imperious American and his khaki court. The ISD established training schools in Broken Bay north of Sydney, Fraser Commando School on Queensland's Fraser Island, Z Experimental Station outside Cairns and the Special Boat Section on Garden Island in Western Australia. The training standards were very high – on one occasion a team rowed canoes the hundreds of kilometres from Fraser Island to Cairns – and the planning was both detailed and meticulous.

Its operators were mainly Australians but also included Dutchmen, New Zealanders, Indonesians and Timorese. They would mount more than 80 commando missions throughout the war, many of them conceived and commanded by experienced and well-connected British officers. Some would be costly failures and there were times when British colonial enthusiasm overrode more worthy aims such as the liberation of Australian prisoners of war. But others were spectacularly successful, none more so than Operation Jaywick, designed to sink Japanese ships at their moorings in Singapore Harbour, Japan's 'Light of the South'.

Jaywick was the brainchild of 28-year-old Captain Ivan Lyon, who shared a family descent with Queen Elizabeth, formerly Elizabeth Bowes-Lyon. He had escaped the Japanese advance on Singapore by sailing a native *prahu* to India. There he met a 61-year-old Australian, Bill Reynolds, who had made the same journey carrying British refugees in a converted Japanese fishing boat, the *Kofuku Maru*. When the British SOE transferred its headquarters to Ceylon (Sri Lanka), Lyon went with it and in planning sessions with Reynolds developed his ideas for a raid on Japan's southern base.

He navigated his plan, which he named Jaywick (after a deodoriser that banished noxious smells from Singapore homes), up the British chain of command and arrived in Melbourne on 6 July 1942 with the enthusiastic backing of the English establishment. He stayed at Government House as guest of a family friend, the Victorian governor, Sir Winston Duggan, from whom he enlisted the support of Governor-General Lord Gowrie. The viceroy arranged a meeting with the director of naval intelligence, Commander Rupert Long, who in turn brought the Naval Board chairman, Admiral Guy Royle, aboard. Finally Blamey himself signed off on the operation.

Lyon then arranged for the *Kofuku Maru* to be transported to Australia, where he renamed it MV *Krait* after a small but deadly Asian snake. Working with Lieutenant Colonel G. Egerton Mott, the chief of the Services Reconnaissance Department (SRD), Lyon recruited a team of 11 Australians and four British operators and began training in March 1943. Chief among the recruits were Lieutenant Don Davidson of the Royal Naval Reserve and Australian Army lieutenant Bob Page, the nephew of the former deputy prime minister Sir Earle Page. Davidson had escaped from Singapore at the same time as Lyon but had taken a circuitous route to Australia through Borneo and the islands. Page's father, a hero of World War I, had been the deputy Australian administrator in Rabaul when the Japanese invaded. His fate was unknown.

In January, Lieutenant Sam Carey of the Z Experimental Station in Cairns had proposed a raid on Rabaul to blow up Japanese ships with limpet mines and to rescue their civilian captives. Page volunteered for the mission, codenamed Operation

Scorpion, but first Carey had to demonstrate that his plan was feasible. Unfortunately, he succeeded too well. He and his team mounted a secret night attack from Folbots (folding kayaks), attaching dummy mines to Allied ships in Townsville harbour. To the navy's intense embarrassment, he theoretically blew half the fleet out of the water. Carey was arrested and Mott was only able to secure his release on condition that he left Z Special Unit. Scorpion was shelved indefinitely. However, the exercise proved to Lyon that his plan was workable and he was delighted when Page, who had played a leading role in the Townsville caper, volunteered for Jaywick.

After an intense training regime on the east coast, Lyon and his men sailed the *Krait* to Western Australia for a final check and resupply before heading out of the US naval base at Exmouth Gulf on 2 September 1943. Dressed in sarongs as Malay fishermen and with dyed hair and skin, they negotiated the Lombok Strait in a big swell without attracting the attention of intense Japanese activity on shore. Once in the Java Sea they made for Pompong Island, reaching their planned forward base on 16 September. However, they were surrounded by so much maritime traffic that Lyon decided to press on to Panjang Island in the Riau Archipelago, about 60 kilometres from Singapore, on 18 September. Now they were poised to strike.

Two days later, the six-man sabotage team in three Folbots commanded by Lyon, Davidson and Page began the long paddle to Singapore Harbour. Each man wore a black two-piece suit of waterproof silk, two pairs of black cotton socks and black sandshoes with reinforced soles, and all were armed with a .38 revolver and 100 rounds of ammunition. On their belts they carried a knife, a compass and a first-aid kit. Lyon also gave every man a cyanide capsule in case of capture. Each Folbot carried 300 kilograms of equipment – mostly the magnetic limpet mines – and food and water for a week. The canoes sat low in the water.

At their first staging post, tiny Bulat Island, the men left their canoes on the beach and went to sleep. They were awakened by the approach of a motorised sampan but it remained offshore for an hour while the crew breakfasted and then sailed away. Further stops were made at Bulan, Boyan and Dongas Islands from which they could see the lights of Singapore only 12 kilometres away. Lyon observed the harbour traffic through a powerful telescope and by late afternoon on the 24th he calculated that about 65,000 tons of shipping had assembled in the Roads area. It was time to go.

At 2000 hours that night, they pushed off and set a direct course for the harbour. The journey was uneventful until suddenly a searchlight from the top of a building illuminated the canoes in its beam. They froze, pointing the canoes to the shore to present the smallest target possible. After 30 seconds, the light moved on. They listened for an alarm, but all was silent except for the lapping of the water around their flimsy craft. They pressed on, but as they approached the island they were suddenly caught in a swirling current and could make no headway whatever. Lyon called off the attempt and they returned to Dongas.

Strong tides and bad weather frustrated their attack for the next 24 hours until finally, on 26 September, with the planned 1 October rendezvous with the *Krait* on Pompong Island looming, they had no options left. This time they split their forces, each canoe taking a separate wharf and at 2200 hours they reached their targets. Page, Davidson and their compatriots set their mines without incident. Lyon and his crewman, Able Seaman Andrew Huston, were spotted. Lyon says, 'Halfway through the work Huston drew my attention to a man who was watching us intently from a porthole ten feet above. He continued to gaze until just before we left the ship when he withdrew his head and lighted his bedside lamp.'[1]

Unaccountably, the seaman didn't raise the alarm. The two commandos set further mines and then headed for Dongas. All three canoes were well away when the first mine exploded. Davidson and his partner, Able Seaman 'Poppa' Falls, were about 20 kilometres from the island when at least seven explosions echoed across the water. Fifteen minutes later, ships' sirens began to blare and Singapore's lights were blacked out; some ships raised anchor and cruised aimlessly about. 'Our speed increased phenomenally', Davidson says.[2] As the strongest canoeists they headed directly for Pompong to hold the *Krait* until the others arrived. Lyon and Huston paddled to Dongas, reaching their redoubt at 0500 the next morning, while Page and Able Seaman Alf Jones had already arrived half an hour earlier. At daybreak they could see a black pall of smoke from burning oil over Singapore and at least one ship sunk by the stern with its bow protruding from the water. Later intelligence would confirm that at least four ships totalling more than 39,000 tons and possibly seven enemy vessels had been sunk or incapacitated.

Davidson and Falls covered the 100 kilometres to Pompong in brisk time, reaching the island at dusk on 1 October; the *Krait* arrived shortly after midnight and took them aboard. Lyon and Page reached the island at 3 am, all four canoeists totally exhausted. They fell asleep on the beach and awoke to find the *Krait* about a kilometre offshore heading for Temiang Strait. They were on the wrong beach! Unable to attract the boat's attention, the four men prepared for a long wait. Lyon made plans to commandeer a *prahu* from the Malay settlement on the island and repeat his earlier journey to India.

Meanwhile, there was drama at sea, as Davidson insisted the *Krait* return, and there are reports – later fiercely denied – that the officer commanding (OC) threatened sailing master Lieutenant Ted Carse before he altered course. They returned to Pompong on 3 October and picked up four greatly relieved commandos. Soon they were heading for the Lombok Strait where a Japanese destroyer came alongside for a closer look. After a tense ten minutes, it turned away and the *Krait* pressed on to Exmouth Gulf, arriving at dawn on 19 October, having covered more than 8,000 kilometres in one of the more daring Special Forces exploits of the war.

Lyon and Page were flown to Melbourne for debriefing at SRD headquarters. Prime Minister Curtin nominated Lyon for the Victoria Cross but once again the niggling relationship between Special Forces and the Big Army intervened and all three officers were eventually awarded the Distinguished Service Order (DSO). Only when the operation had ended successfully was General MacArthur fully informed. He then met with Lyon and promised full support for his subsequent missions – a promise that Lyon took with the proverbial grain of salt. He was wise to do so.

Back in Singapore, the Japanese gave little thought to the possibility of a Special Forces attack. Instead they rounded up local Chinese community leaders and executed scores of suspects in yet another atrocity perpetrated on their Asian progenitors.

However, Jaywick's success was powerful encouragement to the British Empire loyalists in the SRD, and when Lyon proposed an even more ambitious mission – Operation Hornbill – they backed him to the hilt. Lord Louis Mountbatten, a royal family intimate with an appetite for grandiosity that rivalled even MacArthur's, had been appointed the supreme allied commander South-East Asia Command in August 1943. No one was more determined than he to make a big splash in pursuit of Britain's colonial ambitions. Hornbill was certainly that.

Lyon's plan centred on the Natuna Islands between Borneo and the South-East Asian mainland. Allied forces, including native Malays but with Americans deliberately excluded, would secretly occupy the small archipelago 1,000 kilometres behind enemy lines. Operating a fleet of three motorised junks custom made in Melbourne and dubbed 'Country Craft', they would raid Japanese naval assets in French Indochina, Malaya and Singapore. The colonial nature of the exercise was underlined by the presence of 12 Free French commandos in the early plans.

It was a massive undertaking. Literally hundreds of intelligence flights would be mounted in the planning stage. Spies in Saigon and Singapore, escaped Allied prisoners and Japanese POWs would be milked for the latest information. An advance party landed by submarine would establish the base at Great Natuna in July 1944. They would be followed in September by 35 Z Force operators, while the Country Craft, under Davidson's command and carrying ten tons of stores each, would set out from Exmouth Gulf to join them. Lyon would run the show from the Natuna base but Davidson would have charge of the commando fleet. Bob Page would command the top-secret attack craft: one-man submersible mild steel and aluminium canoes four metres long and dubbed 'Sleeping Beauties' (SBs). Driven by a silent electric motor powered by four car batteries, they could travel 50 kilometres to a target area at a top speed of four and a half knots, then submerge for a limpet-mine attack at three and a half knots. The pilots, clad in rubber diving suits with breathing apparatus, stretched prone in the cockpit and controlled the canoe with a joystick. Developed and tested in Britain, the SBs performed well in trials at Portsmouth where Lyon himself took the controls and emerged well pleased.

They would be carried to the target area by the disguised Country Craft junks, which would wait offshore to spirit them away after the attack. The first target would be the Japanese naval base in Singapore, followed by massive attacks on the wharves and ships at anchor. Next would come a joint SB and Folbot assault on Port Saigon, after which, Lyon believed, the Japanese would be thrown into total confusion.

Sixty officers and men were selected for training at Exmouth Gulf and at Careening Bay on Garden Island south of Perth, where in three months they mastered the intricacies of the SBs delivered by the submarine HMS *Porpoise*. The RAAF provided radio equipment for the Country Craft being built in Melbourne and the project was proceeding on schedule until waterside and dockyard workers there went on strike for better pay and conditions.

Government secrecy about Japanese raids on the north – as well as the presence of thousands of American servicemen – had lulled the workers into the belief that the war was virtually won. Lyon and his compatriots were outraged but there was little they could do. Further complications arose when MacArthur reneged on his promise to provide a submarine for the advance party, and at a London meeting Curtin refused to permit British troops to operate from Australian soil in case it created conflict with the Americans. Lyon was forced to revise his plans radically.

On 17 July, Lyon emerged from his Perth headquarters with a new proposal. The SBs would still play a vital role. But the Country Craft would be discarded, as would the Free French and the Malay contingents. With his flair for the dramatic, Lyon had renamed the operation 'Rimau', the Malay word for Tiger, and as it happened he carried a likeness of the Asian beast of prey tattooed on his chest. In place of the American sub, they settled for HMS *Porpoise*. Instead of the Country Craft, they would capture a junk, load the SBs aboard and sail to their target: their earlier scene of triumph, Singapore Harbour. And once they had extinguished Japan's Southern Light they would rendezvous with the *Porpoise* on Merapas Island, the furthest easterly speck of the Riau Archipelago.

Lyon and his 21 hand-picked compatriots – a mix of British and Australian commandos – enjoyed a farewell party on Garden Island with the crew of the *Porpoise* on 10 September. It was a convivial evening, the one jarring note being the absence of the captain, Lieutenant Commander Hubert Marsham, who was suffering from nervous exhaustion and remained on the mainland. It was an unhappy portent of things to come.

Nevertheless, Marsham was well enough to take command the following day as the heavily laden *Porpoise* headed out carrying the 22 men of Rimau, their SBs, enough stores to sustain them for several weeks and sufficient explosives to destroy every ship in Singapore Harbour. The men carried Bren guns, 9-mm Sten guns fitted with silencers, hand grenades and an anti-tank gun to respond to any attack on the junk they intended to appropriate. Lyon struck a sobering note soon after departure, when he distributed cyanide pills to the team and to the two conducting officers, Major Walter Chapman and Naval Lieutenant Walter Carey.

The journey was uneventful until they reached Lombok Strait, where the *Porpoise* surfaced under cover of darkness and powered full speed into the Java Sea. It then travelled under water along the same route that the *Krait* had taken the previous year. Lyon's principal concern was for the health of Commander Marsham, who seemed on the brink of a complete nervous breakdown. However, they reached Merapas on 23 September and were about to unload the stores on the uninhabited islet when they spotted a group of Malays sitting by a canoe on the beach. This meant a slight change of plans, as they would have to leave a guard on the stores they intended to bury there. They selected one of the two conducting officers, Lieutenant Walter Carey, who would have the added task of coordinating the rendezvous when both the commandos and the *Porpoise* returned as scheduled on 10 October.

Once the unloading was complete, *Porpoise* set off to find a suitable vessel to deliver the Rimaus and their SBs to the target. And on 28 September they spotted an 18-metre, 40-ton Indonesian junk, about 50 kilometres off Pontianak, Borneo. The *Porpoise* surfaced beside it and ordered the *Mustika* to heave-to. The nine Malay crew members offered no resistance. Lyon took possession of the boat and the boarding party herded the Malays into the submarine as prisoners to be taken back to Fremantle. There they were released into the community and repatriated to Malaya after the war.

On 30 September, the *Porpoise* and the *Mustika* parted company, the submarine heading back to Perth, the junk making due west for Singapore with Ivan Lyon at the helm like some pirate king of the Caribbean.

5

Z FORCE

Lyon had second thoughts about leaving Carey alone on Merapas and returned to the island, where he assigned three of his commandos to join the naval lieutenant. He briefed them that after the attack on Singapore he and the offensive force would rendezvous with the *Porpoise* back at Merapas on the night of 7/8 November. If the sub failed to make contact, it would return every night until 8 December. Those on the island were to keep the captain informed via their powerful walkie-talkie radio.

Lyon then charted a course for Laban Island 20 kilometres from Singapore, arriving on 8 October, two days before the planned attack. They anchored the *Mustika* offshore and used the time to rehearse the operation in detail. Then, as they travelled slowly towards their jumping-off point on the afternoon of 10 October, they attracted the attention of a Malay police contingent on the tiny island of Kasu. The Malays set out in a launch to investigate, but before they reached the junk one of the commandos panicked and opened fire, killing three of the five men in the boat. The other two swam back to shore and raised the alarm.

Lyon, Davidson and Page caucused. The top-secret SBs could not be allowed to fall into enemy hands, so they had no choice but to scuttle the *Mustika* with the SBs aboard. But all was not lost; they would unload the stores and Folbots into a big rubber craft carried on deck. Lyon, Davidson and three others would paddle the craft to Subar, where they had dropped off Huston and a companion to observe shipping movements into the harbour. That would become their forward attack base. Lyon and Davidson would lead three Folbots into the harbour for a Jaywick-style attack, then reassemble on Pangkil Island in the Riau group for a second strike, this time on the Japanese fleet anchorage on the south of Bintan Island. Meanwhile, the 12 other commandos under Bob Page would make for distant Merapas.

Lyon and Davidson led the tiny flotilla into the teeth of the enemy HQ, and it seems likely that the Singapore attack sank three Japanese ships. But even before the strike the Japanese had assigned a company of 100 men under a Major Fujita from Singapore Garrison to hunt down the commandos. In the wake of the attack, they tracked Lyon, Davidson and at least eight others to Soreh Island, where the commandos were trapped. Over several days and against overwhelming odds, the commandos fought to the death.

Unaware of their fate, Page and his team were island hopping the 100 kilometres to Merapas in Folbots through tropical rainstorms and swollen seas, finally reaching their base on 4 November. Now they needed only to survive three days before the *Porpoise* surfaced offshore and gathered them in. Unfortunately, the *Porpoise* was no longer part of the operation. On its return to Fremantle, the stricken Commander Marsham had asked to be relieved from duty. The vital rendezvous with the Rimau party was passed to HMS *Tantalus*, captained by the Royal Navy's Lieutenant Commander Hugh Mackenzie.

Known as 'Rufus', Mackenzie was the quintessential establishment figure, and had little time for the 'hijinks' of the 'cloak and dagger boys' in Special Forces.[1] A gruff, headstrong figure, he had been on patrol in the Malacca Straits since April 1944. Pickings had been decidedly slim, and he was now fiercely impatient to score some 'kills' on enemy shipping. Also on board was the conducting officer, Walter Chapman of the Royal Engineers, who had been instrumental in the development of the SBs but was a rather diffident and retiring character. It was his task to ensure that the *Tantalus* made the rendezvous and to coordinate with the Rimau team on Merapas.

Meanwhile, Major Fujita followed the tracks of Bob Page and his men through the islands and closed in on them on the night of 4 November. Page split his team in two, and after a firefight he and several others escaped by Folbot under cover of darkness to the much larger Mapor Island nearby. The second party stole two Malay sailing boats and headed south towards Australia. Page was determined to make contact with the submarine, and from 7 to 8 November made his way each night back to Merapas.

He waited in vain; the *Tantalus* was well out of radio range, and despite Chapman's pleas Mackenzie chose to continue his hunt for targets. He later justified his decision on the grounds that 'the orders for the party were that they might expect to be picked up any time up to a month after the official date, 8 November'. He then wrote in bold hand, 'Major Chapman was naturally consulted and concurred.'[2]

When they did sight Merapas on 21 November and Chapman went ashore, he found no sign of the survivors. Indeed, the Australian commando who accompanied him, Corporal Croton, was forced to draw his pistol and order the nervous Chapman to remain on the island overnight. When they returned to the ship in the morning, they reported that there were no immediate signs of the Rimau party. This was enough for Mackenzie; he sailed away without a backward glance.

Page kept returning until the first week of December, but then he gave up and joined with his compatriots in attempting a return to Australia. None made it. Some drowned; others were killed in shootouts or beaten to death by their Japanese captors. Page and nine others were returned to Singapore, where they were imprisoned, interrogated and tortured for months in Outram jail. Then, after a farcical trial, they were taken from their cells on 7 July 1945 to the rough execution ground near a reform school. There they were beheaded, less than six weeks before the Japanese surrender on 15 August.

Mackenzie later became an admiral of the British Fleet. In May 1964, a remorseful Walter Chapman finally swallowed the cyanide pill given to him by Ivan Lyon when they set out on the *Porpoise* 20 years before. The *Krait* is today proudly displayed at anchor by the Australian National Maritime Museum in Sydney Harbour.

•

Through 1944 and 1945, Z Special Unit conducted surveillance, harassing attacks and sabotage behind Japanese lines in Borneo, as well as the training of locals to fight the invaders. However, the Allies continued to be divided on the best way to employ their Special Forces. MacArthur remained fixated on his glorious return to the Philippines and the ultimate conquest in Tokyo. Mountbatten and the British were equally tunnel-visioned about asserting their right of colonial return in the face of a strong undercurrent of American opposition. One tragic side effect was the low priority given to assisting the release of thousands of Australian POWs held in atrocious conditions by the Japanese. This is nowhere better illustrated than in the fate of the over 1,000 prisoners who perished on the Sandakan death marches.

They had been captured in the Battle of Singapore and shipped to North Borneo (now Sabah) to build a military airstrip and POW camps. Over the next year, they worked at gunpoint and were slowly starved. Medical supplies were practically non-existent. In August 1943, they were further demoralised by the Japanese moving their officers to Kuching, now the capital of neighbouring Sarawak.

From October 1943, two British Army officers, Major Gort Chester, a former rubber-plantation manager in Borneo, and Captain Doug Broadhurst, former commissioner of police in Malaya, led Operation Python in the area from Tarakan to Sandakan. Their first landing was at Labian Point about 200 kilometres from Sandakan, and using native and Chinese contacts they were able to radio back to Australia details of the prisoners and the airfield they were building.

A second group from Z Special Force arrived in January 1944 under Major Bill Jinkins. They too were principally concerned with organising the natives for guerrilla warfare. However, one of the party, Sergeant W. Brandis, was captured and interrogated. This led to a full-scale Japanese search for the other Australians, and two were captured before the rest escaped to the coast and were picked up by submarine, arriving back in Australia in June 1944 with the latest intelligence.

In January 1945, the Allies bombed and destroyed the airfield. The Japanese camp commandant decided to move the surviving 1,900 prisoners 260 kilometres west through marshland and dense jungle to Ranau. The first group of 470 set out with rations for four days, carrying baggage and supplies for a Japanese battalion relocating to the west coast. In one of the more horrific Japanese atrocities in World War II, those who fell out were shot, bayoneted or left to starve. When they reached Ranau, they were ordered to build a new 'temporary' camp. By June, only five Australians and one British soldier were still alive.

The second march, of about 540 prisoners, began on 29 May. The horror was repeated; only 183 survived to reach Ranau on

24 June. Of the 250 remaining at Sandakan, only 75 were fit enough to begin the final walk. None survived; those remaining all perished by starvation or illness before the Japanese surrender.

The POWs were not entirely forgotten. In November, Colonel Rogers put forward a proposal, codenamed Kingfisher, for 'reconnaissance prior to forming a plan for rescue of AIF Prisoners of War', and this was signed off by Lieutenant General Richard Sutherland on 7 December 1944. After the war, (Sir) Thomas Blamey said that paratroops had been ready to drop into Sandakan to rescue the prisoners but that 'Higher Command' required the necessary planes and ships for 'another purpose', the inference being that MacArthur and his khaki court had vetoed the plan. Indeed, the 1st Australian Parachute Battalion of 800 men was in training on the Atherton Tableland for this and other possible rescue operations.[3]

The British-dominated SRD was also active in the area, but they were less concerned with the prisoners than with establishing and maintaining links with locals for a subsequent return to the colony. Despite the obvious plight of the POWs, Gort Chester had made barely a mention of them when drawing up plans for subsequent action in Project Agas. When it was submitted to Colonel Roberts, he reordered its priorities. First remained establishing a military intelligence network in the area; but second (of four) was 'Ascertaining location and conditions of POW in the area with a view to assistance in escape or rescue later'.

Chester remained the guiding hand in Borneo, and SRD's instructions to him in January 1945 gave overwhelming priority to guerrilla actions. Their ninth and final objective was, 'To establish a party in the area of Sandakan . . . for the purpose of obtaining and relaying to Australia the detailed intelligence essential for the planning of a combined airborne naval operation on the POW camps in this area, aimed at effecting the rescue and withdrawal by sea of the prisoners therein, and such other information as is laid down under the project known as Kingfisher.' Alas, by then the first of the fatal marches was underway. Kingfisher never progressed beyond the planning stage.

Special Forces remained active in Borneo and the islands until the end of the war. On 25 March 1945, Tom Harrisson was parachuted with seven Z Force operatives from a Consolidated Liberator onto a high plateau occupied by the Kelabit people. Their efforts to rescue stranded American airmen shot down over Borneo were the highlights of their operations. Other units were highly effective in laying the groundwork for the subsequent recapture of Borneo.

Operation Copper was one of the last Z special operations in New Guinea. On the night of 11 April 1945, eight operatives were landed near Muschu Island by patrol boat to report on Japanese defences, particularly two 140-mm long-range naval guns believed to be back in service. They could prove particularly dangerous during the forthcoming invasion of Wewak, as they had sufficient range to reach the proposed landing areas.

Strong currents pushed their Folbots well south of their landing area and a powerful surf swamped them as they reached the shore. At daybreak the commandos began their reconnaissance, but the Japanese had discovered some equipment from the wrecked Folbots and soon 1,000 enemy soldiers were hunting them. Since their radio was among the equipment lost in the surf, they were unable to call for help or to be picked up. Of the eight men in the patrol only one survived: Sapper Mick Dennis fought his way through Japanese patrols, swam the channel to Wewak and struggled through enemy territory for nine days until he eventually met an Australian patrol on 20 April. His information was vital in putting the Japanese guns out of action during the Wewak landings a month later.

From 1943 onwards, the independent companies had been increasingly used in screening and intelligence gathering for the Big Army. Though they had received commando training, the companies were not well suited to operations that involved small groups using boats, submarines, aircraft and parachute drops. However, they did play an important part in some significant operations, none more so than the Australian-initiated coup in New Caledonia early in the war.

The brainchild of then air minister John McEwen, it was designed to prevent the island falling into enemy hands and becoming a staging base for Japanese air attacks on Australia. Working through Churchill and de Gaulle, McEwen gained permission for an operation to rout the local government, load them onto a Norwegian freighter and dump them on a beach in French Indochina.

The 2/3 Independent Company was deployed to Noumea on 23 December 1941 to assist a hastily assembled Free French administration to maintain order until US forces flooded into New Caledonia in 1942. The company then trained for service in New Guinea and carried out almost continuous operations against the Japanese in dense jungle and mountain country between Wau and Salamaua. Their most outstanding operation was the defence of Wau in 1943 and the capture of Bobdubi Ridge in May of that year. They took heavy casualties and were posted to the Atherton Tableland, where replacements were integrated into the unit. On 1 July 1945, they took part in one of Australia's biggest amphibious landings with the invasion of Balikpapan in Borneo.

After its withdrawal from Timor, the 2/4 Independent Company also re-formed and retrained at the Atherton Tableland and Canungra before sailing from Cairns to Milne Bay for a four-month tour of duty until January 1944. Tragedy struck during their amphibious landing to recapture Lae when a Japanese bomb hit their landing craft and 40 members of the unit were killed outright. Many others were seriously wounded. They re-formed as 2/4 Commando Squadron and were still fighting fiercely in Borneo when the Japanese surrendered.

On the morning of 12 September 1945, Colonel John Rogers was Australia's senior representative at the surrender ceremony in Singapore's Municipal Building, which faced a harbour now filled with Allied ships ranging from battleships and aircraft carriers to small amphibious landing craft. Lord Louis Mountbatten, resplendent in his white uniform, inspected the guard of Royal Navy, Royal Air Force and Indian Army men together with 120 members of the 1st Australian Parachute Battalion. The Australians had been personally chosen by Rogers, since they had trained and been ready to rescue prisoners from both Sandakan and Singapore. At the conclusion of the ceremony, Mountbatten called for 'Three cheers for the King!'. As Rogers drove through the streets, he noticed that the Chinese shopkeepers, who had ignored the colonial panoply, were already open for business with goods that must have been hidden through the entire duration.

Australia's independent companies had fought with distinction in the islands, and throughout the war retained their long-range patrolling capability and their Special Forces ethos. However, while in the UK the commandos were retained and rebadged as Royal Marines, Australia's Special Forces were deemed superfluous to postwar requirements and were disbanded. There was some resistance from among the officer corps, but the men who had risked life and limb in the hellish conditions of tropical warfare in the jungles of Borneo and the islands were more than happy to return to the comfort and security of civilian life. Once again, the Big Army ruled.

6

COLD WAR BEGINNINGS

No sooner had the hot war ended than the Cold War began. In the European theatre, the fascist dictatorship of Adolf Hitler was replaced by the communist tyranny of Joseph Stalin. In South-East Asia, Britain's return to her colonies would be challenged by nationalist movements powered by communist ideology. Once again Australia's defence forces were called to alert. And the techniques of Special Forces – notably surveillance and intelligence gathering – would play an increasingly important role.

John Rogers had retired from the army at the end of the war and returned to his peacetime occupation as an executive of the Vacuum Oil Company. However, as Soviet aggression became ever more apparent in Europe, communist activity in Australia, particularly in the trade unions, was on the rise. Rogers and others in the intelligence community were also aware of serious leakages of top-secret information to the Soviets via the Tokyo ring formed by the Main Intelligence Directorate (GRU) spy Richard Sorge. So alarmed was he by the postwar turn of events that, according to his daughter Judith, he joined some of his former military colleagues in a covert organisation with the deceptively bland title The Association.

'Its members were not aligned to a political party,' she says, 'but swore allegiance to the British Crown and the Australian Commonwealth and to uphold the Constitution. The Victorian section was headed by his former colleague and chief of signals Major General Colin Simpson, while General Blamey was ready to take the helm if required. Small groups were formed, ready to mobilise if a communist takeover seemed imminent. Members would be sworn in as special constables in the event of a paralysing strike or a violent coup.'[1]

It had happened before. In the wake of World War I, former officers of the AIF formed themselves into a paramilitary group – later known as the Old Guard – to fight Bolshevik activity in the Seamen's Union. One of the organisers, Lieutenant Colonel Eric Campbell, broke away in 1931 and founded the New Guard, dedicated to 'the throne and British Empire', and rumours spread that he and his group planned to kidnap the New South Wales Labor premier Jack Lang. In the event, the antics of his associate Captain Francis de Groot at the opening of the Sydney Harbour Bridge were a laughable anticlimax, and the New Guard's influence declined. But 15 years later, there was a sense that Australia was threatened and the country's security apparatus was in an unusually excitable and unstable state.

During the war, Australia's military intelligence had coexisted uneasily with the civilian security authorities directed through the Commonwealth Security Service (CSS), a branch of the Attorney-General's Department and headed by Eric Longfield Lloyd. In 1947, Lloyd was appointed director-general of security and later that year director of the Commonwealth Investigation Service (CIS). A softly spoken, deferential and modest character, Lloyd was regarded as a 'dependable' public servant. But as communist trade union leaders fomented strikes on the Queensland railways and industrial unrest in New South Wales coalmines, he was temperamentally unfitted for the times.

The Labor Government of Ben Chifley took up the cudgels against the Communist Party of Australia (CPA) and some trade union leaders were jailed. But Labor was indelibly associated with trade unionism and press coverage of industrial 'sabotage' took on hysterical overtones. Within the Australian Labor Party (ALP) there was growing division between members of the Socialist Left, who adhered to the party creed of the nationalisation of the means of production, distribution and exchange, and the Catholic Right, who saw 'Godless communism' as the principal enemy.

In the United States, fear of the 'red menace' was even more pervasive. According to a diplomatic note from the Australian Embassy in Washington, 'The whole country is in the grip of an extremely dangerous and mounting Russophobia, not unlike in its nature the Red hysteria of the early 1920s. It manifests itself both in the present Administration's policy of containing Russia from further expansion, and at home by the loyalty check of civil servants which is being carried out by the FBI . . .'[2]

The American ambassador in Canberra, Myron C. Cohen, and his most influential staffer, the naval attaché Commander Stephen Jurika Jr, believed the Chifley Government was tarred with the CPA brush. Jurika reported, '. . . Australia, its life and industry, are dominated by the Communist controlled unions and a Commonwealth Government which condones the actions of these unions . . . I would consider any information given to the Commonwealth Government to be almost immediately available to the USSR.'[3]

On 22 June 1947, the Australian ambassador in Washington, Norman Makin, a former minister in the Chifley Cabinet, received formal notification that some classified information normally released to Australia would now be restricted. Behind the scenes, further restrictions were progressively applied. The issue came to a head in February 1948, when Sir Percy Sillitoe, director-general of Britain's MI5, accompanied by Roger Hollis, his chief spycatcher, flew to Australia. According to Rob Foot, a highly placed intelligence historian, they were caught on the horns of a dilemma not uncommon in the world of espionage. The Americans had learnt of a series of leaks to the Soviets emanating from Australia by cracking a Soviet code in a Washington-based operation known as Venona. They demanded action to repair the leak, but the British officials were forbidden from giving the slightest hint of the source of their knowledge. 'An elaborate cover story was concocted,' Foot says. 'The Australians were to be informed that the information had come from a Soviet defector who had sighted [a leaked] document in a Soviet intelligence facility in Europe, and had been told it came from Australia.'[4] It was a tall order. 'They were rather churlishly received by Chifley and Evatt,' Foot says, 'and because of the limitations placed on them by the cover story they had great difficulty persuading them that the leaks were serious or, indeed, that any had actually occurred.'

Part of the reason for Sillitoe's concern was the decision by the British Government to develop its own atomic bomb – to be tested at the Montebello Islands off the Western Australian coast – and a missile delivery system at Woomera rocket range in South Australia. The sharing of American atom bomb technology already achieved at Los Alamos, New Mexico, and delivery systems at the Nevada missile proving grounds, were at the top of the British agenda. Australia's suspect security was frustrating it.

The American suspicions were well founded. When Sillitoe met with the secretary of defence, Sir Frederick Shedden, at Chifley's request, he found him more accommodating. Shedden ordered an immediate investigation into the access within Australia to a UK planning paper that had found its way to the Soviet Union.

Foot says, 'Within a few days Brigadier Frederick Chilton, the Controller of Joint Intelligence, was able to report that, other than very senior officials within Defence, the paper had been passed only to a certain Ian Milner of External Affairs who twice had it in his possession.'[5]

A Soviet spy-ring had indeed been operating undetected in Canberra virtually since the Soviet Embassy was established in 1943, and Milner was an important cog in the wheel.

The spymaster was a leading CPA official, Walter Seddon Clayton. Born in New Zealand in 1906 and educated at Christ College in Christchurch, Clayton left school at 16 and worked in several of the city's sports stores. In 1930, he had a fateful meeting with a visiting opera singer, Hilda Mary Lane, the niece of the socialist William Lane, who had led a group of Australians seeking 'utopia' in Paraguay, where Hilda was born. Clayton was in the audience and sought her out afterwards. He was enthralled by her; followed her to Australia and pressed his suit until they married in Melbourne the next year.

In 1933, Clayton joined the CPA, and by 1935 he was a full-time functionary. He organised and spoke at public meetings, wrote articles that followed the Moscow party line, and distributed pamphlets around the suburbs and at the University of Melbourne. In 1939, he moved to Sydney and became the driving force of the New South Wales branch.

In 1940, after the fall of France, the CPA was declared an 'illegal organisation' by Prime Minister Menzies. Clayton, a thin, shadowy figure habitually dressed in a grubby gabardine topcoat, seemed to relish the clandestine activities imposed on the party. He organised secret hideouts, underground propaganda operations and all the panoply of tradecraft – aliases, cut-out addresses, dead drops, codenames and contact arrangements – that he would soon employ in his espionage activities.

The CPA was partially rehabilitated in 1941 when Hitler attacked the Russian homeland, but by then Clayton was not only alienated from Australian democracy but was also being run by a Soviet controller in the Sydney office of the Tass news agency. He possessed all the resources required to run a successful spy-ring, including the spies themselves. Chief among them were two men and one woman with access to information valuable to his Soviet controllers in the KGB's Moscow Centre. The men – dedicated communists Ian Milner and Jim Hill – were both officers of the Department of External Affairs in Canberra. The woman, Frances Bernie, was a secretarial assistant in the office of the minister, the mercurial H. V. 'Doc' Evatt.

Clayton probably met Milner, a fellow New Zealander, and Hill, a native Victorian, at Melbourne CPA meetings. Milner had been a Rhodes Scholar who joined Melbourne University's Political Science Department in 1940. He was recruited to External Affairs in 1944 by the journalist-turned-diplomat Paul Hasluck (to his later intense embarrassment). At the time Hasluck was director of the Post-Hostilities Division and offered Milner the chance to work with him on international peace agreements and the creation of the United Nations Organisation. He accepted with alacrity. Hill was also at the University of Melbourne in the 1940s and on 25 June 1945, on Milner's recommendation, he too joined the Post-Hostilities Division.

By then Clayton was visiting Canberra regularly, where he met with Frances Bernie and fellow traveller Doris Beeby, whose flat was a frequent rendezvous. Other members of his group included a third External Affairs officer, Ric Throssell, son of the flagrantly communist author Katharine Susannah Prichard, and Dorothy Jordan, who would become Mrs Throssell in 1947.

However, while Sillitoe and Hollis were in no doubt that a spy-ring was operating, they were still unable to tell the prime minister or other Australian authorities the source of their information. (Ironically, unbeknown to the British spycatchers, their own Kim Philby had been initiated into Venona's secrets and was using his knowledge to protect his own Cambridge spy-ring of Maclean, Burgess and Blunt.)

When Sillitoe returned to Britain, Hollis remained in Australia and pressed the need for a security service along MI5 lines. He was frustrated by the attitudes of Evatt and particularly the minister's idiosyncratic departmental head, John Burton, who maintained that such organisations 'do more harm than good'.[6] But then in May 1948 the US authorities decided to institute a complete embargo on the transfer of all classified information to Australia. Suddenly and without any reason given, Canberra was informed of the US action on 3 July.[7]

This came as a shock to the Chifley Government. Soon afterwards, the prime minister visited London and, to dramatise the issue, his British counterpart, Clement Attlee, arranged for him to travel to Germany where the Berlin airlift to run the Soviet blockade was in full swing. After removing references to Venona, the British intelligence chiefs showed him a damning report on the leaks from External Affairs. It was decisive; Chifley immediately agreed that Hollis and another MI5 operative, Robert Hemblys-Scales, should go to Australia to investigate the leaks. Unstated but implied was Chifley's agreement that this was the first step in establishing what would eventually become ASIO – one of the pillars of Australia's Special Forces regime.

The formal decision to create an MI5-style security organisation was taken on 20 September 1948 in a meeting between Chifley and three of his senior Cabinet colleagues. In early 1949, a South Australian judge, Justice Geoffrey Reed, was approached by the Commonwealth solicitor-general Professor Ken Bailey to head the new service. Reed had been involved on the periphery of intelligence during the war when he conducted an inquiry into the lack of cooperation between the CSS and Military Intelligence. This resulted in the demotion of the Queensland head of the CSS, Robert Wake, who had previously authored the extraordinary report on Japanese fifth columnists and potentially traitorous 'aboriginals and half-castes' in the Northern Territory that led to the raising of the Nackeroos. Ironically, Reed had later investigated complaints against Wake, and not only cleared him but also developed a relationship that resulted in Reed appointing him ASIO's first director of operations.

Reed took up his duties on 16 March 1949. His organisation's first and most pressing task was to crack the Clayton spy-ring in an operation that became known as 'the case' and would engage ASIO's full attention for the first half-decade of its existence. In the event, none of the principals would be charged, since to do so would expose not only Venona but also the hearsay nature of the evidence. In the event, Milner defected and took up an academic post in Prague, while Hill and Clayton were neutralised and cut loose by Moscow in the face of ASIO's obvious attention.

Following the election of the vigorously anti-communist Menzies Government in December 1949, Justice Reed was replaced by the deputy DMI, Colonel Charles Spry, and Robert Wake resigned soon after. Spry continued to pursue 'the case' and partly as a consequence ASIO enhanced its credentials with the defection of the Russian spymaster Vladimir Petrov and his wife Evdokia in 1954. While the political left would remain suspicious of the organisation's modus operandi, in time it would be recognised as a vital element in Australia's counterespionage and counterterrorism armoury.

Another of the pillars of Special Forces – the Australian Secret Intelligence Service (ASIS) – also came into being during the early 1950s, though its existence would not become publicly known for two decades, and then only through a foolish slip of the tongue by an Australian prime minister. William McMahon, the last of Menzies' successors in the 23-year rule of the conservative coalition, embarrassed his government and the agency in 1972 by referring to it in a television interview. However, by 2012 its director-general Nick Warner felt sufficiently comfortable with its operational profile to deliver a wide-ranging public address setting out 'the unique contribution ASIS makes to our foreign policy and security'.

Its first director, Alfred Deakin Brookes, was the grandson of Australia's second prime minister, the broad-minded Alfred Deakin, who in 1908 wrote a personal letter of introduction for a young journalist friend about to leave Melbourne for London to pursue her writing career: one Katharine Susannah Prichard. Grandson Alfred, while personally charming, was cut from a different ideological cloth. He was drawn to the world of intelligence even before completing his Commerce Degree at the University of Melbourne, and soon found himself answering to General MacArthur as the chief of the Australian Army's FELO. His section was responsible for anti-Japanese propaganda and deception of the enemy.

In 1945, he transferred to the Department of External Affairs and was posted to Indonesia as assistant to Professor Macmahon Ball, Australia's political representative for the South-East Asia Command. Coincidentally, Macmahon Ball had been head of Melbourne University's Political Science Department, which employed both Ian Milner and Jim Hill prior to their recruitment to External Affairs. Indeed, Brookes was seconded for a time to Evatt's personal staff. However, Brookes's political instincts and ambitions led him in the opposite direction and in 1947 he joined the Liberal Party's Federal Secretariat at the instigation of party president Richard Casey.

An Anglophile of enduring enthusiasm, Casey had a long-standing fascination with the secret world. He had been an intelligence officer in World War I and was elected to federal parliament in 1931. He interrupted his political career to become Australia's first minister to Washington in 1939. After war broke out, he transferred to London where he served in the British ministry for two years as minister of state for the Middle East. He was appointed governor of Bengal in 1944 and relinquished the post in 1946 to resume his political career in Australia. He would be re-elected to parliament in Menzies' triumphal return to power in 1949.

Brookes was a family friend and they enjoyed an increasingly close working relationship. They exchanged many private letters and gifts, the latter usually from Brookes to Casey. Even when the politician became minister for external affairs he addressed the public servant Brookes as 'My Dear Alfred'.[8] Together they formed a vigorous duo with a mission to create an intelligence service in response to 'communist victories in China; the rise of nationalism in Asia; [and] the gradual but perceptible resurgence of Japan'.[9]

Casey was greatly assisted by an Australian-born MI6 officer, Charles 'Dick' Ellis, with whom he had worked when he was British minister for state based for a time in Cairo. Ellis made a number of visits from London, and in May 1950 Casey arranged a Cabinet-level meeting for him with Menzies and other senior ministers. Brookes also attended. Ellis pressed the case for an Australian secret service along MI6 lines and offered to take six suitable young men into the British service for three years' training.

The Cabinet committee was impressed. On 24 May 1950, they took the formal decision to establish a secret intelligence service with a capacity for both intelligence gathering and undercover operations, euphemistically termed 'Special Political Action'. However, it would be some time before the formal decision could be translated into political and bureaucratic reality.

ESTABLISHING INTELLIGENCE SERVICES

The first step in establishing a secret intelligence service was to send Brookes and his newly recruited colleague Bill Robertson to London for the intensive training promised by Ellis. Robertson had been recommended by Colonel Spry, who had met him in 1942 aboard ship returning from Tobruk and Greece, where he had won the Military Cross. He then fought in New Guinea and in 1944 was posted to the British Army, becoming one of the few Australians to land at Normandy on D-Day. He married Jean Spark-King in London in 1946 and by then he had added the OBE and the French Legion of Honour to his decorations. He had been schooled at Geelong Grammar and attended Wadham College, Oxford, where he read chemistry but devoted himself mainly to rowing for the university. When the war ended, he returned to Australia and worked for the Lysaght steel company but retained his links with Charles Spry, who had become a close friend. He could hardly have been better qualified for the Anglo-Australian operation.

The tyro spies carried with them a copy of the handwritten message Menzies had sent to Prime Minister Attlee that he had decided 'to establish a Secret Intelligence Service which, when organised, will operate on South-East Asia and in Pacific areas adjacent to Australia. Recent developments in Asia and our "near north", he wrote, 'make this a prudent and urgent measure . . . I trust that an Australian Service may in some small measure reduce the onerous worldwide commitments of the United Kingdom.'[1]

In this formative period, the agency operated within the Defence Department, where they answered to Deputy Secretary Frederick Chilton, who had resigned from the army and was now the driving force in the Joint Intelligence Bureau. Chilton was opposed to ASIS having a CIA-style 'dirty tricks' capability, and believed that any such actions should be conducted by the military. To underline his attitude he dispatched an army officer, Lieutenant Colonel Roblin Hearder, to join Brookes and Robertson in London. Brookes responded with a blizzard of letters to Menzies, Chilton and Defence Secretary Sir Frederick Shedden protesting that the British Secret Intelligence Service (SIS) remit included both secret intelligence collection 'and Special Operations'.[2]

He then wrote to Chilton asking if he and Bill Robertson could attend the SIS course on special operations because, 'It's most desirable that both activities should be closely linked together and can best work in closest association with your department.' He was boyishly delighted when Chilton consented. 'Bill and I are both looking forward to doing the course,' he wrote. '. . . I can get a grip on the theoretical side . . . my wartime SO [special operations] background will be extremely useful to build on.'[3]

Brookes pressed home his advantage when Menzies visited London in January 1951 with a private dinner for the prime minister attended by the head of SIS, Sir Stewart Menzies, as well as Shedden, Hearder, Robertson and himself. It did the trick. By April, it had been agreed that 'a Secret Service combining the responsibilities for secret intelligence and special operations activities is essential to the defence and security of Australia and the British Commonwealth in the Pacific'.[4]

However, there were still more bureaucratic fences to leap – particularly the use of diplomatic cover for Australia's overseas spies, a concession hard won from the public service mandarins running the Department of External Affairs. It would not be until 13 May 1952 that the governor-general in council signed the formal minutes that created ASIS and appointed Alfred Brookes its foundation director for five years.

Alas, the boyish enthusiasm that invigorated his and Casey's quest to establish the service would not sit well with the entrenched powers that be in the Australian politico-bureaucracy of the day. As we shall see, he barely made it through his term of office and his actions threatened the dissolution of the entire agency.

It was during this period that the third – and the least appreciated – pillar of Australia's Special Forces came into being. It arose from a military decision taken in September 1954 to raise commando companies in New South Wales and Victoria within the CMF. Once again, the move was justified by British precedence. The Military Board press release for the army minister Sir Jos Francis called on the World War II 'tradition of commando units in Britain and the Dominions' and declared, 'Australia does not intend to let it die out.'

Each unit would number about 250 soldiers – double the strength of a normal infantry company – and would be commanded by a major. 'These men,' it asserted, 'must have volunteered for overseas service in the war and represent the highest possible physical standards. Their training will follow the silent, highly mobile, hard-hitting tactics that had such a demoralising effect on Axis troops in all theatres of World War II.

'The new units, it is felt, should be trained to fit themselves for any type of terrain where their flexible, lethal type of close operations can be used to best effect.'[5]

The New South Wales and Victorian troops would be designated 1 and 2 Commando Company respectively. They would be headquartered in the leafy suburbs of Sydney's Mosman and Melbourne's Sandringham, in each case 'handy to facilities for training and watermanship'. In addition to the major as OC, the officer corps would comprise five captains with six sergeant NCOs. They would be armed with 87 Owen guns, five Bren guns, and a .303 rifle for each soldier.

At the time, all Australian 18-year-old males were required to undergo ten weeks' full-time training under the National Service Scheme followed by three years part-time in the CMF. And the army was flush with trainers from the war qualified for transfer to the units. The two OCs, Majors William 'Mac' Grant in Sydney and Peter Seddon in Melbourne, were appointed by the end of 1954.

Seddon was a Duntroon graduate, an artilleryman who had completed a parachute training course at Williamtown. When given the news that he had been appointed OC 2 Company, he replied, 'I've never heard of them. Where are they based?'

His CO responded, 'They don't exist yet. You are it.'

Mac Grant had served in the British Commonwealth Occupation Force in Japan and later in battle with the infantry during the Korean War.

They quickly developed their own distinctive headgear, uniform accoutrements and a motto: 'Strike Swiftly'. And from the beginning there was a healthy intra-service rivalry. They were deeply conscious even then of the symbiotic nature of their operations with the intelligence community. Mac Grant says, 'The post-war intelligence bodies had a large input into the creation and organisation of the new Special Forces.

'Their role [would be] conducting clandestine operations similar to those mounted by special operations and also those of the independent companies/commando squadrons during the war.

'It was envisaged that by raising units capable of performing such a dual role, a pool of trained manpower would be available to be "farmed off" as necessary to a special operations unit while the remainder would be used in more conventional commando operations.'[6]

Grant was just the man for the job. In the first six months of 1955, operating from a single office in Sydney's Victoria Barracks, he assembled the core of his unit, and was able to hold his first parade with 100 recruits. They enlisted for two years, but it was a catch-as-catch-can operation with minimal assistance from the Big Army. They were only able to scrounge a Reader's Digest condensed version of the Bible upon which to swear the oath of allegiance. On that first parade, Grant told his men, 'Our nearest counterparts in the British service today are the Royal Marine Commandos and the SAS Regiment at present operating in Malaya . . . Irrespective of your reasons for belonging to this unit, you are here to train for war, or to put it more bluntly, to learn to "kill some bastard" . . . In a unit of this nature I don't expect to be worried with petty offences. As in the war, I consider the greatest punishment I can inflict is to dismiss you from the unit.'[7]

In Victoria, the first members of Peter Seddon's 2 Commando Company paraded at Albert Park on 7 July 1955. Seddon was appointed for only 12 months, and during this time his permanent successor Major Jack Anderson would travel to the UK with Mac Grant for instruction with the Royal Marines. Anderson was also a Duntroon graduate and had served in Papua New Guinea and with 1 Royal Australian Regiment (RAR) on the front lines in Korea.

However, during their Royal Marine training, tragedy struck. Grant says, 'I had a sore ankle, and it was courtesy in those days that if the man behind you caught up you would allow him to pass. I was in front and when Anderson came up behind me I allowed him to overtake. On reaching the river crossing there were normally two ropes – one high, one low – and the top rope was gone . . . Jack Anderson took the single rope but lost his grip in the now swirling torrent. He was gone, swept away in a flash. I was the last person to see Jack Anderson alive.'[8]

Peter Seddon's appointment was extended through 1956, when he would be replaced by Major John Hutcheson.

The connection to the British commando unit was strengthened with the posting of two Royal Marine sergeants, Len Holmes and Mac MacDermott, to Australia in October 1955. Both had distinguished themselves in training as winners of the King's Badge and were highly qualified for their task. Holmes was appointed to 1 Commando in Mosman and MacDermott remained with the Victorians. They also conducted combined operations, and in January 1956 on Sydney Harbour they taught both units the special skills of small-scale amphibious raids using World War II Folbots similar to the ones Ivan Lyon had employed on the Jaywick and Rimau raids.

Also instructing on the course was Major John Slim, son of the then governor-general Sir William Slim. John was a member of Britain's 22 SAS Regiment, and both he and his father would have a hand in the subsequent development of the fourth pillar of Australia's Special Forces, the SAS.

At this stage, Melbourne provided a congenial and collegiate home to Australia's military and intelligence establishment. The Defence Department had not yet moved to Canberra; similarly, ASIO and the code breakers of the Defence Signals Bureau – a new organisation created in 1947 but with expertise gained in the war – were located in St Kilda Road not far from the CBD. The bureau was renamed the Defence Signals Branch in 1949, a title it retained until January 1964, when it became the Defence Signals Division (DSD). Moreover, the Liberal Party powerbrokers from Menzies and Casey down were dedicated Melburnians. So it was natural for Alfred Brookes to establish his ASIS headquarters within the gracious environs of his home town.

In 1952, his small team occupied a wartime pre-fab building in Albert Park, but soon shifted to Melbourne's Victoria Barracks. Despite Menzies' assertion that they would concentrate their activities independently on South-East Asia and the Pacific, in reality they were little more than a branch office of MI6 (then still known as SIS). And when the 'mother' agency was revealed to have been penetrated by Soviet spies Donald Maclean and Guy Burgess – and Kim Philby was suspended from the service – the fledgling Australian operation caught some of the odium in the fallout. It arrived at a particularly sensitive time, since Menzies and his External Affairs minister Casey had just negotiated the ANZUS Treaty, which envisaged a tripartite sharing of covert intelligence.

The Americans had begun to open the intelligence doors soon after Menzies replaced Chifley in the Lodge. But the Cambridge spy-ring revelations slowed the process markedly. It would take until 1954 before the two-way traffic between Washington and Canberra was allowed to flow unimpeded by Pentagon and CIA restrictions. Nevertheless, in the interim they were prepared to 'duchess' Brookes personally with a lengthy briefing at the CIA headquarters at 2430 E Street Washington. (It would move to its permanent site at Langley, Virginia, in the 1960s.)

Brookes was thrilled by the experience, as indeed was Casey, to whom he now answered, particularly as America's worldwide commitments were fast supplanting Britain's. Indeed, by 1953 the

CIA dwarfed SIS in manpower and resources with more than 14,000 operators – including more than 400 undercover agents in South-East Asia alone.

However, ASIS remained closely linked to its British parent. That year, the two services agreed that Australian field operatives in South-East Asia would be 'blooded' by their British counterparts on station. Australia also agreed to Britain opening a combined ASIS/SIS radio station at Kowandi near Darwin, and to a Joint Clandestine Organisation that would operate against insurgents in the British colonies.

The following year, ASIS took over some covert intelligence gathering from SIS in the region, finally fulfilling Menzies' promise to Attlee that the Australian organisation would 'reduce the onerous worldwide commitments of the United Kingdom'. Moreover, the British stations continued to supply Australia with a steady flow of intelligence reports from around the world. At the same time, Australia became the centre of international attention among intelligence services with the Petrov defections. Not surprisingly, this coincided with the arrival on 30 April 1954 of the first declared CIA officer, Colonel Sam Sanders, in Melbourne under diplomatic cover as assistant naval and air attaché.

Brookes set about building his intelligence empire within the bureaucracy, and immediately encountered resistance from his nominal head in the Defence Department, Sir Frederick Shedden. He appealed directly to Menzies, seeking either transfer to the External Affairs Department or 'the creation of a unit with no association with the Secretary of a Department but responsible directly to a Minister'. The External Affairs secretary, Arthur Tange, wanted no part of the agency, but he was forced to accept it when Menzies issued a new charter in December 1954. However, he was able to avoid responsibility for its covert actions since under the new arrangements Brookes reported directly to a Cabinet subcommittee comprising the prime minister and the minister for external affairs (Casey). And as Menzies was usually preoccupied with whole-of-government issues, the effect was the re-establishment of the initial ASIS duopoly.

However, Brookes's official status in the charter had brought a significant shift in the balance of power between himself and Casey, and the ASIS chief was not immune to the hubris of command. He became what the entrenched public service chiefs regarded as a 'loose cannon', bypassing them to deal directly with their ministers. That was unconscionable. But his cardinal sin, it would seem, was his predilection for engaging Allied intelligence and political leaders in policy discussions without reference to the Australian bureaucratic chain of command.

It is difficult to avoid the impression that he felt he was acting with Casey's tacit approval. The minister maintained his very close relationship with Brookes and included him in top-level talks with Britain's SIS chief of the Far East, James Fulton, with a visiting Dick Ellis (now under suspicion as a double agent in Britain), with CIA chief Allen Dulles and in meetings with Dulles's new Australian representative Lieutenant Colonel Collas G. Harris. Indeed, according to his diary, Casey, 'discussed [with Brookes] the possibility of a SEATO [Southeast Asia Treaty Organization] operation to cope with Chin Peng [the Malayan communist rebel leader] in Southern Thailand'.[9]

However, it would seem that Brookes overstepped the mark when, on a visit to Washington, he engaged in discussions with Dulles and his brother John Foster Dulles, then the US secretary of state, that touched upon the Americans using Australia as another possible launching pad for their nuclear deterrent strategy against the Soviets. When that news filtered back to Canberra, the reaction was immediate. Suddenly Casey found himself besieged on all sides with demands that Brookes be sacked and ASIS disbanded entirely.

Political expediency trumped personal friendship. On 14 May 1956, Casey resolved to cast his protégé adrift. He arranged a meeting between the acting prime minister, Arthur Fadden, the defence minister, Phillip McBride, and the department heads of External Affairs, Defence, Prime Minister and Treasury. Brookes and his vice-head, Roblin Hearder, were also present to hear Casey recommend that the agency be dissolved.

The meeting accepted the recommendation. While Brookes's reaction is not recorded, he would undoubtedly have been personally devastated. However, all was not quite lost. Some of the top bureaucrats, particularly Sir Allen Brown, the head of the Prime Minister's Department, were not convinced that Australia should be totally bereft of an overseas-intelligence-gathering agency, particularly as its most populous neighbour, Indonesia, was being ruled by an increasingly erratic President Sukarno. And while Brookes himself was put into suspended animation, his founding colleague Bill Robertson, who had been posted to Singapore, recommended vigorously that at least the agency's Indonesian operations be retained. He was supported by the ASIO chief, Brigadier Spry, whose friendship remained constant.

When Casey brought CIA resident Harris into the discussion a fortnight later, the return message from E Street HQ was one of 'dismay'.[10] The British Government was sufficiently disturbed to immediately dispatch the vice-chief of SIS, Sir James Easton, to Canberra. There followed a new round of talks in the intelligence community while Brookes remained in bureaucratic limbo and his erstwhile political partner sharpened the axe.

On execution day, 2 August, Casey first lunched at the Melbourne Club with his departmental secretary Arthur Tange and his choice for Brookes's replacement, Ralph Harry, at the time Australia's ambassador to Singapore. Casey then turned his attention to the chopping block. 'I saw A.B. and told him my decision about his immediate termination of his appointment,' he told his diary. 'Then also saw Colonel Hearder and told him the same thing and the reasons for it. Not very agreeable interviews but it had to be done.'[11] Hearder's departure would signal the end – at least for the moment – of the special operations element of ASIS.

While both men received a golden handshake – £120,000 between them – there was little professional consolation. Hearder found work as a security officer for the payroll trucking company Mayne Nickless, while Brookes became a habitué of the Melbourne Club as a consultant on international affairs.

8

THE SAS EMERGES

It was no coincidence that the loss of special operations from the ASIS arsenal would coincide with the raising of the next pillar of Australia's Special Forces establishment, an organisation devoted specifically to special operations: the SAS.

The unit's official historian David Horner, professor of Australian defence history at the ANU's Strategic and Defence Studies Centre, freely admits that he has been unable to untangle the official strands that combined to create the SAS. 'It is difficult to determine who was the main advocate for an SAS capability among the higher echelons of Australian defence,' he says.[1] He then parades a number of senior army figures, each of whom is equivocal about his role in its formation.

Horner's problem is understandable, since he worked almost exclusively from military sources. He touches upon a British journalist, Stewart Harris, who migrated to Australia in 1951, as the unlikely catalyst. He says Harris, who had been a member of Britain's 21 SAS and became an editorial writer on the Brisbane *Courier-Mail*, saw the need for an Australian equivalent and made the case in a meeting with the head of the British Army staff in Australia, Major General Jim Cassels. Cassels passed him on to the Australian chief of the general staff, Lieutenant General Sir Sydney

Rowell, who in a classic buck-passing exercise told him to write to the army minister, Sir Jos Francis. The politician responded with some soothing words that 'training along the lines you describe is receiving attention . . . [and] in this regard Australia is in constant touch with the United Kingdom'.[2] But he was almost certainly referring to the possibility of raising Commando Companies 1 and 2 in Sydney and Melbourne.

It is now clear that Harris continued to agitate, and on his transfer to Canberra as a correspondent for *The Times* of London he had personal access to the political and bureaucratic powerbrokers. Chief among them from 1953 was Governor-General Sir William Slim, who had fought with the Anzacs at Gallipoli, led the 'forgotten army' against the Japanese in Burma, and whose son John was a captain in Britain's 22 SAS. After serving with his unit in Malaya, John Slim was posted in 1954 to Melbourne to join the UK Services Liaison staff. As we have seen, he involved himself in training operations with the commando companies.

Apart from the officer cadre, the commandos were only part-time reserve units. The younger Slim became a strong supporter of an Australian counterpart to his Special Forces squadron. His distinguished parent gave him access to Australia's top brass and to the unashamedly Anglophile Prime Minister Menzies. Moreover, senior Australian military commanders observed 22 SAS actions in Malaya and returned moderately impressed.

The raising of the commando units in 1954–55 would have fully satisfied the appetite of the defence establishment for an irregular force within its ranks, but the imbroglio within ASIS demanded a professional military response. For, while the commando units would prove to be a fertile field for recruitment into Australia's security community, as a reserve force they were only marginally suited to the cloak-and-dagger operations that were intrinsic to an overseas espionage agency. Moreover, the British Special Forces establishment continued to press for an Australian SAS to assist their Malayan campaign.

The various meetings among intelligence officers, departmental heads and the subsequent Cabinet subcommittees to officially sanction the creation of the SAS remain classified, or so obfuscated within the archives as to defy a clear narrative pathway. That they occurred is not in doubt, and it is clear that the two most influential ministers in the Cabinet – Casey and the Country Party's deputy leader John McEwen – strongly supported it. Both were greatly attracted to the dark arts of undercover operations – Casey from the beginning and McEwen at least from his triumph in New Caledonia. Together they were a formidable team, no better demonstrated than in 1967, when, as governor-general, Casey appointed McEwen prime minister on the death of Harold Holt despite objections from senior Liberals.[3]

In this case, their success was real but publicly understated. On 4 April 1957, Menzies duly announced the results of a wide-ranging review of defence policy. Three days later his new army minister John Cramer said Australia's defence effort would henceforth be concentrated on South-East Asia and would include an SAS company, which an army spokesman described as 'a form of commando group'.[4]

A lively internal debate ensued as to its strength, equipment, role and location. For it was immediately clear that no one in the Big Army wanted to be responsible for it, and the more distant its location the happier everyone would be. It was not even officially acknowledged for the next five months, and then, according to Horner, 'The only mention of the SAS was in [a] staff table which showed that the company was to have an authorised strength of sixteen officers and 144 other ranks and the equipment of a standard rifle company less one platoon. Since [it] was to be substantially larger than an infantry company it is difficult to see why it was given a reduced equipment table.'

The reason, of course, was the traditional suspicion of the Big Army towards the irregulars. The attitude was nicely encapsulated by retired SAS major Jim Truscott. 'The term "special" in a unit's name is an enigma in Australia's defence force, often demanding exceptional results and causing military bureaucracy to query SAS cost-effectiveness,' he says. 'There are many who see the SAS as no more than super infantry soon to be done away with . . .'[5]

At first the company was to be located in New South Wales, but after objections were raised in Eastern Command (among others), it could not even find a home on the Australian mainland. It was slated for Rottnest Island in the Indian Ocean 18 kilometres off the Western Australian coast. However, eventually a compromise was reached and it found a home base at Swanbourne, a Perth suburb with a coastal frontage, while its principal training area remained among the quokkas on Rottnest.

Its first commander was Major Len Eyles, at the time only second-in-command of the army's parachute training wing at Williamtown. Moreover, High Command decided he could not be released until the following year, and until then the unit would have to make do with a 40-year-old infantryman, Major Wally Gook, who was training National Servicemen at Swanbourne.

No doubt Major Gook was both surprised and flattered by his new appointment. But when he officially took up his post in old timber buildings at Swanbourne's Campbell Barracks, with one captain, three lieutenants and a handful of hastily recruited soldiers, he had no stores, no equipment, no weapons and no training directives. His soldiers were a decidedly mixed bunch. Some had completed the parachute course, but selection was based purely on service records, and 'some soldiers were allocated to the

SAS simply on compassionate grounds to enable them to return to their home state'.[6]

Nevertheless, Gook applied himself admirably to the task and when he handed over command to Major Eyles on 1 February 1958 he had assembled a core group of fine soldiers with experience in World War II, Korea and the Long Range Desert Group that had rescued David Stirling and his nascent SAS team from their disastrous initial operation in North Africa. They also harboured one of Australia's legendary NCOs, Ray Simpson, who in subsequent actions would gain the supreme battlefield distinction of the Victoria Cross.

At this stage the other combat arm of Australia's Special Forces, the commando companies, were also undergoing important developments. Ironically, Mac Grant's 1 Commando provided the new SAS unit with their first instructors in canoeing, climbing and roping in Sydney, and aspects of infantry tactics at Gan Gan near Nelson Bay on the New South Wales Central Coast. By then 1 Commando had been redesignated 1 Infantry Battalion Royal New South Wales Regiment (Commando), (City of Sydney's Own Regiment). The change was basically cosmetic but it did provide the unit with a prestige that no doubt assisted its recruitment in periods of a high turnover among the reservists. It also lent a sense of occasion to Mac Grant's 1959 departure for higher duties . . . and with much more of a bang than he expected.

The night before, the company conducted an exercise on Sydney Harbour – with the navy's permission – to mine a couple of warships à la Jaywick. But to add an air of verisimilitude for the CO's benefit, Lance Corporal Ian McGuire employed his amateur chemistry skills in creating a harmless explosive device to make the appropriate sound of a mine detonating.

In the dead of night, he sighted one of the departing canoes and tossed his device into the water; he was almost deafened by the explosion. 'The noise was unbelievable,' he says. 'It reflected back and forth across the harbour three times. In Taronga Park Zoo, not only did the lions roar, but every damn animal which had the power to yell, shriek, scream, squawk, trumpet, bark or make any sound added their voice to the cacophony.' Mac Grant was not best pleased. Ian McGuire lost his single stripe but according to company historian Peter Collins, 'Far from being castigated by the press, the unit enjoyed some positive publicity, a four-page photo feature in the popular *PIX* magazine.'[7]

Grant's replacement was Major Jack Skipper, who shepherded the unit fairly uneventfully into the 1960s. It now comprised Alpha and Bravo Companies, Transition Company, Support Company (including the Signal Platoon), Assault Pioneer Platoon, Weapons Platoon and Transport Section. At full strength it numbered 264 soldiers.

It was a time of increased defence awareness. President Sukarno was becoming ever more bellicose as his country's economy stalled and the local Communist Party gained strength among the people and influence in high councils. Similarly, the anti-colonial war in Vietnam was moving into a new phase as the communist leadership in the north attempted to reunify the country by force and in defiance of international agreements. This resulted in an influx of new recruits and a substantial waiting list.

The situation in Victoria was similar. Its commando company had flourished after the early setback of losing its commander and by 1960 it had established an enviable reputation as a reserve unit. Its CO, Major Phillip Bennett, had graduated from Duntroon, fought in Korea, where he was mentioned in dispatches, and on his return to Australia was appointed tactics instructor at the School of Infantry. Just prior to his posting to 2 Commando he had served with the Royal Marines in Cyprus.

But on the night of 17 February 1960, his unit suffered another tragedy. Bennett used his training with Britain's Special Boat Squadron to plan a waterborne exercise through The Rip – the three-kilometre opening to Port Phillip Bay between Point Lonsdale and Point Nepean. A force of 74 commandos set out from Point Lonsdale in canoes and Zodiacs with two lumbering army DUKWs ('Ducks') in support. Almost immediately they were in trouble from the giant swells rolling in from Bass Strait against an eight-knot current heading seaward. According to Collins, 'The commando force was swept helplessly into the dark, boiling Bass Strait and seven to eight metre high waves. Neither frantic paddling on the Zodiac nor the twin truck engines on the DUKWs made any difference. In the terrifying darkness, the commandos were sucked out into the sea as if the entire Bay were emptying down a plughole.'[8]

A passing passenger ship, the *Toscana*, and the pilot boat MV *Akuna* came to the rescue, but two men went down with their upturned DUKW and a third was swept away from a rope ladder as he attempted to climb aboard the *Toscana*. Bennett was grief-stricken and would maintain an emotional attachment to the unit throughout a military career that saw him rise to become the first chief of the Australian Defence Force (ADF) in 1984.

Later that year, 2 Commando bonded even closer with the Royal Marines when the Royal Marines commandant, General Sir Ian Riches, visited them and sealed the alliance with the presentation to the CO of a distinctive upturned-blade commando fighting knife. Bennett was succeeded in 1961 by Major James Stewart, a Korean and Malayan veteran who did much to enhance the unit's *esprit de corps* through the development of a Mountain Leader's Course in the Snowy Mountains, a forerunner of a more exacting training regime designed for the SAS.

The following year, the company parachuted into the Laverton RAAF base area for the biggest joint air and land exercise in Victoria since the war. And in 1963 the association with the SAS was strengthened with the arrival of a new CO, Major Geoffrey Cohen, direct from command of the premier Special Forces unit. Cohen trained the unit to conduct small-scale raids in South-East Asia and reported in 1964 that, if required, the entire company could be deployed in a combat role in 16 weeks. However, while military activity in the north was raising interest among potential recruits, the company was progressively losing instructors for duty in Vietnam. The commando reservists were reduced to the role of home-based support, while the SAS was fully operational.

Since Major Len Eyles had taken charge, the SAS had played an increasingly important role in training exercises in Western Australia and joint operations on the east coast. By mid-1960, the unit had acquired its full establishment of 12 officers and 182 other ranks. Already it was becoming noted for the outspoken individualism that would become its hallmark. In 1959, for example, a visiting lieutenant general, Sir Ragnar Garrett, expressed himself 'dismayed' at the colourful language used by Sergeant Ray Simpson and complained to his superior, Major General Tom Daly, that the company appeared to be 'lacking in discipline and perhaps should be disbanded'.[9]

Daly sought a second opinion from the commandant of the Canungra Jungle Training Centre in Queensland, Colonel Arthur MacDonald, who then spent several weeks with the unit. His highly favourable report ensured that the SAS would remain the cornerstone of the army's Special Forces cohort.

In September 1960, a new CO, Major Lawrie Clarke, a 1947 Duntroon graduate who won the Military Cross in Korea, took up his appointment. Clarke broke with the earlier pattern of British patronage, having spent time at the Canadian Staff College and completed ranger and parachute courses in the United States. He personified the gradual redefining of Australia's military alignment from one major imperial ally to another. However, his first priority was to organise his company to meet the latest demands of the ADF. A High Command conference in Canberra in August 1961 decided that its primary role was medium- and long-range reconnaissance, with a secondary task of small-scale raids and, where necessary, assistance in internal security operations.

After a series of major training exercises in the north of Western Australia, the company left Australia's shores for the first time for the SEATO exercise Air Cobra in Thailand, where 3 Platoon was attached to a US Marine unit. Their role was medium-range reconnaissance and an operational tactic that would assume ever-increasing importance in the years ahead: calling in air strikes to take out attacking enemy forces. It also marked the beginning of a close association between the SAS and their Thai counterparts.

It was during this exercise that the Australian defence minister Athol Townley took the first step in an ill-fated partnership with the Americans in Vietnam with the announcement that Australia would provide a team of 30 army instructors to assist the South Vietnamese Army in jungle warfare, village defence and signals. Two SAS officers, Major Lawrie Clark and Lieutenant Ian Gollings, would be joined by four NCOs – Sergeants Joe Flannery, Des Kennedy, Ray Simpson and Roy Weir, secretly under the control of the CIA. The choice of some senior men for overseas service was gratifying, but according to Horner, 'It was clear that many high ranking officers in the remainder of the army had no idea how the SAS could be employed . . . there seemed little possibility of the SAS being deployed as a company or even as a platoon.'[10]

Britain's continuing quest to reclaim a role in its colonial outposts would ensure that the intense jungle training the company had undertaken at Canungra would be put to good use. In fact, the company's operations in Malaysia would begin its combat tradition.

The conflict was essentially between the ambitions of President Sukarno to project Indonesia's influence in the region and Britain's active role in asserting its somewhat anachronistic colonial influence. In May 1961, the British and Malayan governments had proposed a federation of Malaysia comprising Singapore, Malaya, Sarawak, Sabah and Brunei. At first Indonesia found the arrangement unobjectionable, but after Sukarno scored a diplomatic triumph in 1962 by forcing the Netherlands to accept Indonesia's claim to West Irian, his taste was whetted for a bigger say on the international stage. So when voices against the new Malaysian arrangement were raised in Brunei, Sukarno authorised his army to train a small volunteer force across the border in Indonesian Kalimantan to assist the dissidents.

In December 1962, they staged an insurrection. British forces in Singapore mobilised and, while the rebellion was quickly neutralised, sporadic fighting continued until May 1963. On 20 January of that year, the Indonesian foreign minister, Dr Subandrio, had announced that his country would henceforth pursue a policy of confrontation with the proposed federation. Three months later, Indonesian forces attacked a police station in Sarawak to which some of the Brunei insurrectionists had fled. There followed an undeclared war in the jungles of Borneo on the border between Indonesia and East Malaysia. Both sides employed light infantry operations, air and sea insertions and classic jungle-warfare tactics.

Despite Australia's military dalliance with the United States in its hour of need, the colonial offspring still retained strong links with its progenitor. The conservative government of Robert Menzies was unabashed in its affection for the mother country and maintained a residual European suspicion of all things Asian. So when the 14th Earl of Home, who had renounced his peerage to become Prime Minister Sir Alec Douglas-Home, asked his Australian counterpart to join the fight, Menzies and his Cabinet readily complied. His military hierarchy was not at all enthusiastic about committing regular forces to the campaign. However, they felt it was a perfectly appropriate battle space in which to blood the SAS.

9

AN INTELLIGENCE NETWORK

By 1963, the intelligence agencies had outgrown their inevitable birth pangs. But it had been a lengthy and tortuous process, not least for ASIO. The Petrov Affair led to the closure of the Soviet Embassy from 1954 to 1959 and this allowed Brigadier Spry to redirect his resources to other areas while maintaining a network of undercover sources within the CPA and a watching brief on known sympathisers. Through the 1950s his officers vetted military personnel with access to classified information and even those charged with 'educational duties' among the National Service trainees. He also extended the agency's international footprint at a time of record immigration intake by appointing ASIO officers overseas to liaise with local security services in no fewer than 16 countries in Europe, the Middle East, South America, the United States and South Africa.

Prior to the Soviet Embassy's reopening, Spry flew to Britain for advice from MI5 on how best to bug it. The British spycatcher Peter Wright, who would later retire to Tasmania and accuse his former boss, Roger Hollis, of being a Soviet mole, suggested a listening device be installed in a window frame. Spry took the advice and the bug worked perfectly. It transmitted every footstep in the office and every rustle of paper but alas not one spoken word. Clearly, the brigadier's plot had been detected and foiled.[1]

However, soon afterwards he tasted sweet revenge when his people discovered that the first secretary (and KGB officer) Ivan Fedorovich Skripov was engaged in espionage activities. Indeed, his informant, Kay Marshall, an attractive brunette in her 30s, was able to provide chapter and verse of the spymaster's modus operandi. A British national, she had come to Australia from New Zealand where she had worked for the UK High Commission in Wellington. When the Soviet third secretary there attempted to recruit her, she reported the contact to her superiors; they alerted the NZ Secret Intelligence Service, who encouraged her to continue the contact.

In December 1960, she came to Australia where, with ASIO's encouragement, she liaised with Skripov who gave her lessons in espionage tradecraft and tasks that would prove her loyalty to the Soviet cause. In December 1962, Skripov gave her a package – a communications device the size of a small flowerpot – to deliver to a Soviet 'illegal' in Adelaide. ASIO then mounted a major surveillance operation in the hope of identifying the mole, but while Marshall took the reassembled package to the rendezvous as requested, to the agency's immediate consternation Skripov's spy did not arrive.

Spry briefed Casey's successor as minister for external affairs, Sir Garfield Barwick, and on 3 February 1963 Barwick announced that the KGB man was now *persona non grata* and required his removal. He released photographs of the spying equipment and the several rendezvous with ASIO's Kay Marshall to seal the case against him. Skripov returned to Moscow and a familiar fate for failed Russian spies. He disappeared. But ASIO was left deeply concerned that the failure of their surveillance operation meant they had been penetrated by the Soviets. It is a question that remains unanswered.

The agency moved into new purpose-built premises at 469 St Kilda Road, Melbourne, that year, just as the Vietnam War was beginning to engage Australia's political establishment. The timing was fortuitous. In the years ahead, as increasing numbers of young Australians were conscripted and joined the casualty lists, opposition would grow exponentially. By the late 1960s, these anti-war groups had coalesced into a moratorium movement that was fast becoming mainstream. ASIO and the state police special branches were almost overwhelmed monitoring their marches and demonstrations with still photographs and moving picture footage. They would record almost half a million names of these 'extremists', including many members of the Labor Party's left-wing hierarchy. A hard core within the anti-war movement responded by attempting to identify and publicise the names of ASIO staff, and even to harass their families.

Since the ALP officially opposed the war the agency became a lightning rod for political controversy in the Commonwealth parliament. Indeed, there was a widespread view that should Labor win the 1972 election one of its first acts would be to dismantle ASIO. This added to the turmoil as the agency fought to secure its continued role in the system by engaging with selected journalists and feeding them information it had uncovered on communist and 'new left' activities. The first Hope Royal Commission into Australia's security services in 1974 discovered no fewer than 67 briefing papers directed to journalists in the decade from 1962. There were even plans to create a monthly journal titled *Analysis* that would use ASIO material to discredit political radicals. The idea came to naught, but it was within this fevered atmosphere that Sir Charles Spry retired in 1970, passing the reins to Peter Barbour, a 19-year veteran of the organisation.

Barbour was unsuited for the political cut and thrust of an incoming Labor Government. And the agency was vulnerable to the charge that it paid undue attention to extremists of the left while ignoring the excesses at the other end of the political spectrum. Like other Allied nations after the war, ASIO had a chequered record in dealing with former Nazis, particularly those with special knowledge of Soviet tradecraft. Australia proved particularly vulnerable to the Ustashi, a right-wing Croatian revolutionary movement that had collaborated with the Nazis in opposition to Yugoslavia's communist partisans.

Barbour's political master, Attorney-General Lionel Murphy, believed ASIO was withholding Ustashi files from him and conducted a much publicised 'raid' on ASIO's offices in Canberra and Melbourne. According to Harvey Barnett, later director-general of ASIO, the agency 'knew it was on thin ice' when Gough Whitlam appointed Murphy as its minister. '[Murphy] had a subsidiary interest in the raid – to inquire if ASIO held a file in his name,' he says. 'He was disappointed on both counts.'[2]

In his autobiography, *Tale of the Scorpion*, Barnett says the raid 'sent shockwaves round Australia and the Western world'. And in somewhat overblown terms he claims that, 'For a Cabinet minister to intrude in such an undisciplined and peremptory way into the sensitive centre of a nation's security organisation – even though he was the minister responsible – caused grave concern at home and abroad. Many thought the Westminster system was at risk and wondered if they were witnessing the emergence of a new draconian political order of the left in Australia. Some Australians of central European background were drawn to make parallels with Gestapo chief Himmler.'

In any case, the effect on morale was disastrous. Added to this were suggestions, later echoed by Royal Commissioner Justice Hope, that the agency had been 'penetrated by a hostile intelligence service'.[3]

Barbour's extended insulation from the real world gave the ASIO boss a somewhat distorted self-perception at a time when Sean Connery's James Bond bestrode the world's movie houses and glamorised the spy business. When Barbour was removed by the Whitlam Government in 1973 (with the secret approval of Opposition Leader Malcolm Fraser), it was for taking his 'beautiful Eurasian secretary' with him on a lengthy overseas trip to other security agencies and producing no report or 'anything else of benefit to ASIO'.[4] Barbour was appointed to the sinecure of consul-general in New York and would later occupy relatively minor diplomatic posts. By then the agency was in such a parlous state that in 1974 Justice Hope recommended that its sister agency ASIS establish a second level of electronic security at its Melbourne headquarters without ASIO's knowledge.

ASIS in the meantime had prospered under the leadership of Ralph Harry, whose grandfather had been a good friend of Alfred Brookes's grandfather Alfred Deakin's. Harry operated under a reworked 1958 government directive charging him with 'promoting Australian security by obtaining clandestine intelligence relating to other countries; by planning for clandestine operations in war; and by carrying out . . . special political action in other countries . . .' It also required ASIS to collect clandestine intelligence in Australia 'from travellers to and from other countries'.[5]

He was ordered to report his agency's activities to the External Affairs minister every six months. The minister would then forward the report to his colleague in Defence and the prime minister himself. And though it was not specifically authorised, during the 1960s the deputy prime minister, John McEwen, was also regularly briefed, not least because he was frequently acting prime minister in the absence of Menzies, Holt and Gorton.[6]

Harry's stewardship ran for three years until April 1960. By then he had established a strong working relationship with MI6 (still called SIS) and the CIA, particularly in South-East Asia. He had created or maintained three overseas stations under exclusive ASIS control – Jakarta, Tokyo and Dili – while several Australian staffers operated from the Crown Colonies of Hong Kong and Singapore. In 1964, the government declared the existence of the ASIS operation to the newly independent Singapore Government and shortly afterwards an ASIS officer was appointed to liaise with the Singapore Special Branch. Six years later the Singaporeans created their own Security Intelligence Division in the Ministry of Defence and Australia negotiated a formal agreement for liaison between the two agencies.

Harry had also overseen the establishment and expansion of 'special ops' training areas on Swan Island, off Queenscliff in Port Phillip Bay, at Middle Head, in Sydney Harbour, and in two North Queensland facilities. They would be used increasingly to equip not only the hardcore ASIS officers but also selected ASIO officers, commandos, SAS operatives and occasional police Special Branch officers for hazardous assignment.

When he departed from the Secret Service, Harry expunged it entirely from the public record of his career, and even from his published memoir, *The Diplomat Who Laughed*. He was replaced by 64-year-old Major General Walter Joseph 'Bill' Cawthorn, a career soldier and diplomat born in Melbourne and trained initially as a teacher. He fought at Gallipoli and with the British Army on the North-West Frontier and the Khyber Pass. In London on 10 March 1927, he married a widow, Mary Wyman Varley, and the following year their only son, Michael, was born.

In 1939, he was given charge of the Middle East Intelligence Centre in Cairo and rose through the ranks to become Lord Mountbatten's deputy director of intelligence in the South-East Area command HQ in Kandy. It was there in 1945 that he met Colonel Spry whose recommendation would be helpful to his ASIS appointment. From 1948 to 1951 he was deputy chief of staff of the army of newly independent Pakistan. He was responsible for the creation of Pakistan's Inter-Service Intelligence directorate (ISI) whose later activities would bedevil Australia's Special Forces in Afghanistan. His son, Michael, was killed fighting in Korea in 1951.

His experience on the subcontinent endeared him to Casey, the former governor of Bengal, and in 1952 he helped to secure him the task of director of Australia's Joint Intelligence Bureau. As minister for external affairs in 1954, Casey appointed him high commissioner to Pakistan, where he backed that country's claims over India's in the Kashmir dispute. Pakistan had joined the anti-communist SEATO bloc in 1954 but, by the time Cawthorn departed as Sir Walter, having been created a Knight Bachelor in 1958, the Pakistanis had spurned SEATO in favour of friendship agreement with China. Nevertheless, Cawthorn took up his new post as high commissioner in Ottawa with the full backing of Menzies, Casey and their senior ministerial colleagues. Indeed, he was also a chum of Governor-General Sir William Slim's.

Casey's selection of the ageing rhododendron breeder, bibliophile and Anglophile to head Australia's Secret Service was one of his final decisions in government. It was quietly applauded around the luncheon tables of the Melbourne Club, where both were members. Even the doughty opposition leader Arthur Calwell, whose preference was for the North Melbourne Football Club, gave the appointment his blessing.

The agency's vigorous, experienced Bill Robertson as second-in-command accepted the appointment without rancour and is believed to have continued to run the 'special ops' as he had under Brookes and Harry. He would do so unmolested throughout Cawthorn's eight-year tenure – a period of intense activity in South-East Asia, with competing demands in the Malaysian confrontation with Indonesia's Sukarno and the American-led war against Ho Chi Minh's forces in Vietnam.

There were deep divisions of priorities between Australia's two great Secret Service progenitors, the SIS and the CIA. The SIS head in Singapore, Sir Maurice Oldfield, who would later head the service, exerted a very strong influence over Australia's spymasters in Singapore such as a young Harvey Barnett. Oldfield's priority was Sukarno's *konfrontasi* with Malaysia. But since the late 1950s, the CIA had been keenly interested in thwarting communist political influence in Indonesia; so the potential for confusion and conflict was manifest.

In February 1958, dissident military commanders in central Sumatra and North Sulawesi declared the Revolutionary Government of the Republic of Indonesia – Permesta Movement – aimed at overthrowing the Sukarno regime. They were joined by a number of civilian politicians who were opposed to the growing influence of the Communist Party. The CIA backed the rebels with training and weaponry, while Sukarno appointed his army commander, General Nasution, to put down the rebellion.

On 18 May, much to the CIA's embarrassment, a B-26 was shot down during a bombing and strafing mission on government-held Ambon, and its American pilot captured. The CIA aborted the mission. Nasution's forces then launched airborne and seaborne invasions of the rebel strongholds and by the end of 1958, the rebels were defeated. A contrite President Kennedy later invited Sukarno to Washington, and eventually provided Indonesia with billions of dollars in civilian and military aid.

However, the CIA continued to suspect Sukarno of anti-American activities, particularly as the Indonesian Communist Party (PKI) gained increasing influence over his foreign policy. By 1964, they detected 'early stirrings' of an anti-communist movement in Indonesia.[7] At government level it was cloaked in the guise of *pancasila*, the five moral principles[8] that they further designated 'Sukarnoism' to gain his approval.

Indonesia's army leaders quietly supported the Sukarnoists, while the PKI labelled them victims of 'anti-communist phobia'. The situation became more confused when the Sukarnoists urged that *konfrontasi* be recalibrated from a military to an economic struggle. The CIA threw its weight behind them, while the president himself became increasingly aligned with the PKI, which the Americans now portrayed as 'an instrument of Chinese neo-imperialism'. Indeed, in its black propaganda the CIA characterised the PKI as leading the country 'in a march to the Chinese camp'. At the same time Sukarno's health was rapidly deteriorating, allegedly from syphilis in its tertiary stage.

A July 1965 CIA report, recently declassified, opined, 'should Sukarno die or become incapacitated, he would be likely to be replaced by a non-communist coalition . . . Friction with Malaysia will intensify, but is unlikely to break up the Malayan federation. Malaysia is both totally dependent on the UK and the Commonwealth, has a foreign policy allied with them, but also is adequately defended by forces committed by the UK, Australia and New Zealand. Malaysia will still seek US defence commitment.' But *konfrontasi* was clearly a secondary issue for the Americans; by 1965 they were waging an all-out war against the unlikely combination of Soviet and Chinese communism throughout South-East Asia.

However, that year would see Indonesia provide the only gain for the American cause when on the evening of 30 September six generals were killed by a group calling themselves the 30 September Movement, widely believed to be an instrument of the PKI. General Suharto escaped and took control of the army. President Sukarno refused to commit himself to either side but soon afterwards the military began a propaganda campaign that resulted in the slaughter of at least 500,000 Indonesians, many of them ethnic Chinese with no political affiliations, and others victims of longstanding family feuds.[9]

Acting on excellent reportage from his expanded Jakarta office, Cawthorn applied all available resources in support of the army and the subsequent moves to depose Sukarno. On 11 March 1966, a decree transferred much of Sukarno's power over the army and the parliament to Suharto; one year later Sukarno was stripped of his remaining power by Indonesia's provisional parliament and Suharto was named acting president.

By now, ASIS was stretched to its limits, since it had also been instructing the Australian Army Training Team for clandestine operations in Vietnam for three years and it had redoubled its efforts as the SAS deployed in Borneo and then in Phuoc Tuy Province, Australia's area of responsibility in the Vietnam conflict. At the same time the agency was incorporating a fifth pillar into Australia's Special Forces establishment: the DSD. This division was providing signals interception (Sigint) material from its listening posts in ever-increasing volumes, and it would assume increasing importance in the years ahead.

In 1964 DSD was charged with 'exploiting foreign communications' as well as 'responsibility for communications security in the armed forces and government departments'. It operated initially under the UKUSA ('Five Eyes') agreement signed by Britain (UK), America (USA) and Canada, Australia and New Zealand, providing cooperation on a global scale. To avoid duplication the signatories took responsibility for particular geographic sectors.[10]

Its principal sources of 'foreign communications' were radio listening posts at Coonawarra in the Northern Territory, HMAS *Harmon* in Canberra, Pearce Air Force Base outside Perth, Cabarlah near Toowoomba and a signals relay station at Watsonia in Melbourne. It had an arrangement with Britain's Government

Communications Headquarters (GCHQ) to share signals interception gathered from its Hong Kong facility since 1949 and it installed listening devices in its overseas embassies to intercept traffic within and between its host nations and their friends and allies. The Singapore and Darwin stations were used in *konfrontasi* operations in Borneo and were regarded by the SAS fighting forces as 'tremendously helpful'.[11] And in 1966 the Australian and US governments signed the Pine Gap Treaty for the construction and operation of a signals interception facility in Central Australia. The isolated site was chosen because it was too remote for opposition spy ships to pick up its signals. It began operations in 1970 when about 400 American families moved in to monitor the intercepts with two large antennas. It would later grow exponentially.

DSD operations were, and remain, the most secret weapon in Australia's Special Forces armoury. In the 1960s and up to 1975, even ministers for the army were not briefed on DSD and its American links, even though they bore ministerial responsibility for some of their operations. When awkward questions were asked by ministerial staffers, or the minister himself, responsible officers were instructed to evade any confirmation of the existence or role of the division.[12]

As the balance of Western power in the region moved inexorably from the UK to the USA, ASIS found itself drawn ever more deeply into the CIA net. Britain's decision to decline any meaningful involvement in the Vietnam War – following strong recommendations by Oldfield and other influential colleagues in SIS – sharpened the division between Australia's two great and powerful friends. And while ASIS would also express strong reservations about Australia's participation, the political pressure to put its servicemen in harm's way was overwhelming.

First Menzies then Holt and McEwen were determined to engage America as a shield between the homeland and the threat of the 'Yellow Hordes'. All three men were products of a country with a racist colonial past; but equally, all were witness to the attempt by Japan to invade Australia and overwhelm its sovereignty. All had vivid memories of General MacArthur and the thousands of American servicemen who joined the 2nd AIF in turning the tide. So, despite the total absence of any evidence of Chinese expansionism, they went to great lengths to encourage the Americans to 'stay the course' in Vietnam. And if that meant the sacrifice of Australian lives on the battlefield and the deployment of every available Special Forces unit, it was a price they were more than willing to pay. It was an entirely self-protective policy, though McEwen as minister for trade did take the opportunity to negotiate an agreement that the American forces in Vietnam would use Australian sugar exclusively in their coffee.[13]

Sir Walter Cawthorn was spared much of the backlash from the Vietnam misadventure. He retired from ASIS in July 1968. He then lived at 'Kallista' in the Dandenong Ranges, but in early 1970 he was admitted to hospital following a vicious attack by an unknown assailant near the Melbourne Club. He died on 4 December that year and was survived by his wife, herself a former special agent. By then the nation's premier Special Forces unit – the SAS – which his agency had helped to train in the 'black arts' of soldiery, had developed into a formidable fighting force in the jungles of Borneo and the paddy fields of Vietnam.

FIRST ACTION IN BORNEO

In 1962, the SAS, still at company strength, tested its newly acquired battle skills in jungle warfare against two companies of Papua New Guinea's Pacific Island Regiment (PIR) in a rerun of the Japanese advance along the Kokoda Track. The SAS played the defenders, and all concerned were no doubt gratified when once again the 'Japanese' were stopped in their tracks.

The exercise coincided with the arrival of a new CO, 31-year-old Major Alf Garland, a Duntroon graduate with a longstanding interest in Special Forces and a strong training background with American units. While he had completed the parachute course, he believed the SAS should be principally a reconnaissance and intelligence-gathering operation. This accorded with the view of Lieutenant Colonel John Woodhouse, the CO of Britain's 22 SAS Regiment, who visited Swanbourne in July 1963. Woodhouse indicated he would welcome the Australians' participation in the response to Sukarno's *konfrontasi* in Borneo and Garland was eager to comply. However, when Prime Minister Menzies received the formal request from his British counterpart, Sir Alec Douglas-Home, he equivocated on grounds that it might lessen Australia's influence in Indonesia. For the Anglophile Menzies this represented a significant break with tradition. However, he didn't close the door entirely and early in 1964 Garland was summoned to High Command in Canberra and advised to prepare his men for action if the situation in Borneo didn't improve.

Garland used a forthcoming SEATO exercise to test a new arrangement of his forces, turning platoons into troops of 21 men commanded by a lieutenant and containing three patrols of six men each, with two admin/intelligence personnel making up the number. The exercise, LITGAS, was carried out in the Philippines with US and Royal Marines against an assaulting force of 20,000 men in 75 ships with 300 aircraft in support. It was the biggest Allied operation since Korea. The Australians parachuted into their area of operations (AO) and their actions on the ground validated Garland's reorganisation.

However, if the SAS were to be deployed in combat, the exercise revealed the need for a second squadron for reinforcement and secondary operations. So on 20 August 1964, Canberra HQ ordered the creation of the Special Air Service Regiment (SASR), with 15 officers and 209 other ranks. It would be divided into two SAS squadrons to be deployed on the organisational template devised by Garland but with the addition of a headquarters staff of three officers and 37 other ranks.

While Major Garland would remain OC of 1 Squadron and his former adjutant captain Reg Beesley would command 2 Squadron, Major G. R. S. 'Bill' Brathwaite would be brought in as OC headquarters and the formal CO of the regiment. Brathwaite was 44 at the time, a World War II veteran who had enlisted as a private and been commissioned in the field after service in Greece and with the 2/3 Independent Company in New Guinea. In 1944, he transferred to Z Special Unit and fought behind the lines in Borneo.

Garland continued to be briefed directly by army headquarters, while Brathwaite played no part in the dialogue. This awkward command structure would cause a great deal of unnecessary friction among men temperamentally unsuited to any ambiguity in the chain of command. However, both officers were closely involved when on 10 November 1964 Menzies announced the resumption of National Service training the following year and, most pertinently, the decision to expand the SAS Regiment to four frontline squadrons plus a base squadron permanently at Campbell Barracks. It was an exciting time. Brathwaite was caught up in the immense task of raising the new squadrons, while Garland developed training and deployment plans for the Borneo engagement.

In March, he had arranged the attachment of one of his junior officers, Lieutenant Geoff Skardon, to a British commando unit operating in Sarawak. In his debriefing back at Swanbourne, he was able to report that the British were secretly crossing more than four kilometres into Indonesian Kalimantan, where their Gurkha forces were ambushing Indonesian military patrols. Prime Minister Harold Wilson cabled Acting Prime Minister John McEwen on 15 January 1965, confiding that he had extended their cross-border intrusion to eight kilometres and sought an increased commitment from Australia.

McEwen withheld a decision on the request, no doubt until the Cabinet resumed deliberations after Menzies' summer vacation, but his response revealed the rather simplistic government view of the communist threat from the north. 'It seems to us,' he said, 'that more and more the two conflicts in Vietnam and against Indonesia are coming to form part of a common pattern and a common threat.'[1] Wilson then encouraged the Malaysian Government to make a direct appeal to Australia for SAS troops (and two infantry battalions) to be sent to Borneo. Cabinet responded at the end of the month with the commitment of 1 SAS Squadron and a single infantry battalion: 3 RAR.

At Swanbourne Alf Garland gathered a unit of 100 men, including a Base HQ, for a six-month deployment on the front lines. On 13 February, he led the advance party of five, all in civilian clothes, to Perth airport, where they boarded a regular Qantas flight to Singapore. Three days later, the entire squadron and their HQ staffers climbed into another specially chartered Qantas aircraft at Pearce RAAF Base. At 4.45 pm it lifted off and set a course that would circumvent Indonesian air space by curling around the northerly tip of Sumatra en route to Singapore. For the first time, the SAS was going to war.

By then Garland and his advance team were ensconced in quarters at Brunei Town, where the British were developing their Land Forces HQ for the conflict. However, the director of Borneo operations, Major General Walter Walker, remained on Labuan Island, 50 kilometres across Brunei Bay where, 20 years before, the local Japanese commander had surrendered to the head of Australia's 9th Division, Major General George Wootten. A second HQ had been established at Kuching, the capital of Sarawak.

When the main SAS body arrived, they were immediately sent south to Tutong in Sarawak, where the British SAS instructors were waiting for them. Troop leader Lieutenant Trevor Roderick says, 'When the British SAS got hold of us, that's when the emphasis came on "shoot and scoot", the rendezvous system and the finer points of moving in the jungle.'[2] Another officer, Lieutenant Peter Schuman, says, 'The techniques that they had of guiding scouts and then moving in bounds, their security in harbouring, their cooking techniques – all the little things for survival – we were taught down at Tutong.'

The Australians were then assigned to the Central Brigade, commanded by Brigadier Tuzo, the CO of the 51st Gurkha Brigade. His specialty was artillery, which played only a minor role in jungle warfare, so Garland was not above appealing to officers further up the chain when he felt Tuzo was unable to appreciate his special operations proposals. The Australian OC had been forewarned about the cross-border operations – codenamed 'Claret' – and was keen for his lads to participate. For the moment, however, they were required to spend four weeks acclimatising themselves on the Malaysia side before they could venture into enemy territory. They used the time to get the feel of the topography and make friends with the locals. If they happened to run into an Indonesian patrol, they were to follow the 'shoot and scoot' tactic.

By early April, 12 patrols had been deployed for various periods, usually based near native settlements, where they conducted regular sick parades. They were very popular. Each day almost the entire village reported sick, especially when pills were on offer. The patrol medic would give strict instructions that the pills – for 'head pain' or 'shitty-shit' – had to be taken each morning and evening. However, according to SAS historian David Horner, 'They invariably believed that by taking the whole lot at once they would be cured a lot quicker ... [that] must have led to some awful cases of constipation.'[3] The Australians had their own share of sick parade regulars, and Garland ordered patrol leaders to ensure all water was sterilised, scratches treated immediately and anti-malarial paludrine tablets taken regularly, and not all at once.

It was tough work in rotten conditions. Schuman says, 'It was absolutely horrendous. We would start our patrolling at a place called "The Gap". The maps were absolutely atrocious; some were just white with "no reliable data because of cloud cover all year round" ... I was a million miles away from home, all by myself, in command – it was bloody lonely, it really was.'[4]

It was also dangerous. On April Fool's Day 1965, Sergeant Chris Pope fell more than ten metres from a rocky ledge into a swirling river below. The impact knocked him out, and he was only saved from drowning when Private Les Murrell dived in to rescue him. Heavy rain, painfully poisonous foliage, and venomous insects and reptiles were constant hazards. One patrol, led by Sergeant Arch Foxley, remained in the field for a record 89 days about 20 kilometres from the border. When he finally emerged from the jungle on 26 June, he was miffed to discover that in the meantime his mates had completed their Malaysian apprenticeship and been let loose across the Indonesian border. That was where the action was, and every SAS operator wanted to be part of it. That, after all, was what they had trained for.

They had a friend at court in the person of Major John Slim, son of the governor-general, who had played such a significant role in the creation of the unit. He was formally commander of 22 SAS Regiment, but in the British military hierarchy he commanded the attention of his nominal superiors, not least the new director of operations, General George Lea. In a strategy briefing on 14 May, Slim recommended that the Australian SAS contingent supply no fewer than eight patrols in the East and West Brigade areas, leaving nine in Central Brigade with the Gurkhas. He also proposed that the 'Claret' cross-border incursions be extended to between 13 and 18.5 kilometres, and that they actively engage the Indonesians.

'We fully realise that you want us primarily in the reconnaissance role,' he told General Lea, 'but we hope you will let us "off the hook" occasionally. It is important to "blood" the Australian . . . SAS.'[5] Lea concurred, but suggested that the engagements be against 'soft opportunity targets during the last 48 hours of a patrol'.

That was good enough for Garland and his team. They decided that the four-man patrols would operate for about 14 days, and since all supplies had to be carried through hostile country, patrolling would be limited to six hours a day. At night they would make camp in thick jungle with their hammocks slung between trees, the only lights permitted were for essential radio contact; and all rubbish would be buried in plastic bags to contain the smell. They would rise before dawn, shave (on Garland's strict orders), dress and set out for half an hour before stopping for breakfast. Water would be collected in pairs, and the location was never repeated. No tracks or vines could be cleared or cut, and where possible all footprints were obliterated. They were, in short, to become 'phantoms of the jungle'.

Peter Schuman says, 'Our squadron was spread over hundreds of kilometres along the border doing surveillance. We would fly from Brunei into a forward base called Pensiangan, which was a fairly large airstrip, and from there we would transfer into a single-engine short take-off [Canadian] aircraft called a Beaver, and then go into a place called Sapulot. This was the last forward airstrip before the border ridge with Kalimantan. And then we would fly in RAAF Wessex Whirlwinds up onto the border.'

When all were assembled, the four-man patrols would set out into Indonesian territory, their only cover the 105-mm Howitzer artillery based on the border. 'The Gurkhas used to take the pack Howitzers apart and carry about six rounds of ammo, and they would lug this into the jungle above some Indonesian fortresses, which were usually on the other side of a river,' Schuman says. 'They would throw a few 105 shells at them and knock off any moving targets and then come back across to the other side.'[6]

To a large extent they were successful. The knowledge and discipline acquired during this period would become standard operating procedure for the Australian SAS in the years ahead. Nevertheless, the incursions, which began on 1 May 1965 and lasted for the next four months, were not without their casualties. The first, in the early days of June, was so incongruous that it could never have been anticipated.

A patrol headed by Sergeant Roy Weir, a very experienced soldier, was tasked with discovering whether Indonesian patrols were travelling towards Sabah from Labuk on the Sembatung River. They flew by helicopter to a landing zone (LZ) near the border and struck out into Indonesian territory. They were six days into their patrol when on 2 June they noticed elephant tracks. Later they spotted the three-metre-high Asian pachyderm travelling parallel to them about 200 metres away. One patrol member, Corporal Bryan Littler, dug out his camera and climbed onto a ridge and headed towards it. The elephant spotted him and, according to the patrol report, 'threw its trunk in the air and charged straight at him'. Littler shouted, 'Run, he's charging!'[7]

Camera in one hand, rifle in the other, Littler raced down a track until confronted by a massive fallen tree. He tried to climb over but had just reached the top of the log when the elephant hit. 'The next thing I knew,' he says, 'I was flying through the air; I landed on all fours about seven metres away.' His rifle barrel was clogged with mud and he hastily tried to clean it with a thin stick. Just then, Roy Weir fired from the ridge above and the elephant went down on its front knees, but only momentarily. It regained its feet and, unseen by Littler, bore down on the patrol's radio operator, Paul Denehey. At this point, Weir was unsighted, but the fourth patrol member, Lance Corporal Stephen 'Blossom' Bloomfield, the medic, opened up on it point blank, his rounds striking the lumbering creature behind the ear. However, he was too late. The elephant had already gored Paul Denehey under the rib cage and was now heading into the jungle making fearful screams.

They gathered around their wounded comrade. Blossom administered tetracycline as an antidote to blood poisoning, as well as morphine for the pain. They quickly assembled a stretcher with two poles and a poncho. 'We have to get away from here before that bastard comes back,' Roy Weir said, but it was easier said than done. Paul Denehey was a big, powerful man and as they struggled through the thick undergrowth he bumped against jagged ridges and hidden stumps. He pleaded with them to stop. Though they didn't know it at the time, two of his ribs had been torn away from his backbone. They abandoned the stretcher, and Littler and Blossom took turns carrying him piggyback as they sought a defensible position should the elephant return.

At a rest stop they tried desperately to get the radio working. The elephant had crushed the receiver but the transmitter looked serviceable. They rigged an aerial and sent a message: 'Patrol attacked by rogue elephant; one member seriously injured; send help LZ.' They repeated it several times but had no way of knowing whether it had been received. In fact, not only had it reached 1 Squadron HQ in Brunei Town but it was also picked up back at Swanbourne. The operators puzzled over the coded translation of 'rogue elephant' until they realised no code was involved.

Alf Garland took charge of the rescue mission. It was a high priority, not only because of Paul Denehey's condition but also because of the patrol's location, which was at least ten kilometres inside Indonesian territory. This had the potential to expose the top-secret incursion policy to the enemy and the world at large. A helicopter set out from Sapulot to the last known grid reference from the patrol, but because of the broken terrain and sudden stormy weather it was unable to make contact.

Next morning, Weir decided to leave his medic with the wounded man and head out with Littler to the border. They made good time, and by 1 pm they had almost reached their goal when suddenly they spotted the elephant about 200 metres away to their right front. According to Horner, 'They both turned left and bolted over the side of the ridge and ran full pelt down the mountain and into the river.'[8] How long they remained there is not known, but at 9 am the next day they arrived at the helicopter LZ to find it deserted. They waited two hours before a chopper arrived and they were able to fly to a clearing on the Indonesian side closer to where the elephant had attacked.

Weir left immediately with several Gurkhas, while Littler followed the next day. Both patrols became disoriented, and it took until the following day before Littler happened upon a rough camp and a swinging hammock. It seemed deserted. 'Paul had left his hammock and begun to crawl,' he wrote later. 'He had moved about 20 feet, half dragging his trousers off as he went before his strength gave out and his arms were not strong enough to move his body. But he had continued trying, slowly wearing his fingers away as he dug at the earth, trying to get away from the terrible pain deep inside him. Paul's Owen gun was scattered everywhere; every piece of gear that he could reach was torn or broken; and the last scream of agony was on his face. The scene – a nightmare come true – and where was Blossom?'

They had also lost contact with Weir, but after firing several shots into the air they spotted the sergeant and his party in the distance heading towards the sound. Once they joined up, they carried their compatriot's body to a clearing, and with the Gurkhas' help they prepared a helicopter LZ. Next morning two helicopters lifted them out to Sapulot.

By then Blossom Bloomfield had made his way to the border LZ. He told Garland that, after Weir and Littler had departed, he remained with Denehey until he was running out of medication for his mate. Denehey began pleading with him to put an end to his suffering with a bullet. And by now it seemed that Weir and Littler must have come to grief. So he made his patient as comfortable as possible and set out for the border to get help.

Clearly, he was no longer thinking straight, because he took the radio with him rather than leave it with the radio operator; but, finding its weight impeded his mobility, he abandoned it shortly afterwards in a hollow log together with the patrol code books.

A month later, he led a patrol back to retrieve them. Garland had disbanded Weir's patrol and re-formed it with different personnel. By then for the first time the SAS was making contact with a viable opposing force.

11

KONFRONTASI

The first major SAS operation began on 21 June 1965, when a patrol led by Corporal John Robinson helped guide a company of Gurkhas under the command of a British officer, Captain Ashman, to attack Lumbis, a village about ten kilometres inside Indonesian territory. After three days walking, they reached the target undetected. Indonesian soldiers were active within the village, and Ashman deployed his forces around the settlement. Mortars and machine guns were in place by 6 am the following morning. However, Ashman waited until a gong sounded at 9 am to summon the troops to breakfast before ordering his men to aim their weapons. According to the official history, 'A group of about ten men gathered and started to eat and only then was the order given. Four to six enemy were killed in the first machine-gun burst and the Gurkha mortars quickly adjusted their fire onto the village. The second salvo went through the roof of the eating hut.'[1]

Though the Indonesians were 'slow to react', they eventually answered the fire with machine guns and a mortar. However, they were ineffective, and at 9.50 am Ashman ordered the company to withdraw, and a British 105-mm Howitzer about 10,000 metres to the north-west began to shell the village. According to an observer, 'One shot landed a little over a metre from the enemy's radio shack whose roof lifted then settled again.' The attacking force returned to the border, reaching it just before last light.

On 1 July, the Australian unit planned its own attack on an Indonesian airfield well inside the border at Long Bawan. Garland sent Warrant Officer Alan 'Blue' Thompson with his patrol to complete the reconnaissance. Four days later, they had reached a position about three kilometres from the airfield and set up a lay-up position (LUP) when they spotted an Indonesian patrol, travelling in single file, coming up behind them. They quickly took up ambush positions near the track, and when the leading Indonesian was only four metres away they opened fire. According to the operational report, the leader was struck by eight rifle and six Owen gun rounds, the second by ten rifle and six Owen gun bullets. Both died instantly. Their compatriots took cover and returned fire, but by then the Australians were on the move out of the area. The airfield attack never eventuated.

Further ambushes by 1 Squadron followed, and on 3 July Sergeant John Pettit took his patrol south into Indonesian territory, reaching the Salilir River the following day. There they established an overwatch position, and on 5 July they saw boats travelling up and down stream with paddlers stripped to their shorts, but in each case apparently commanded by a figure in an olive-green shirt. Suddenly a downstream craft turned towards the Australians' position on the bank, where they apparently planned to beach their boat.

When they were ten metres from the shore, Pettit and his patrol opened fire. According to their report, 'In less than a minute the patrol poured 81 rounds of [rifle] and 26 rounds of Owen gun into the boat. Not one enemy was able to return fire with the submachine guns they were carrying. Most were either knocked overboard or jumped into the river.'[2] Pettit estimated they had killed seven and seriously wounded two. Later intelligence suggested one had been killed instantly, while three died of wounds.

On 21 July, another patrol spotted a *prahu* powered by an outboard motor with six men in white T-shirts and blue shorts. As it approached the Australians' position on the bank, a Bren-gunner, Lance Corporal Chris Jennison, saw 'rifles, webbing and kitbags' on the bottom of the boat. He opened fire. Three rounds struck the man in the bow. The force of the bullets threw him into the water; three others were killed before they could move but two others leapt into the water. However, when they reached the shore and began to scramble up the bank, they were gunned down. The patrol withdrew without loss, and by 24 July they had returned to Brunei Town.

When Garland's men completed their mission after five months in country, they had killed 17 enemy with only one fatal casualty – Paul Denehey. However, by any reasonable measure it was not the most propitious beginning for an outfit that aspired to be the best of the best, operating at the highest levels of military endeavour and from its most lofty principles. It had secretly invaded the territory of another country, one that represented no particular threat to its Australian homeland. It had operated as a puppet to a colonial power whose motives remained the assertion of its own interests in a post-colonial world that no longer accepted its presumptions. Indeed, the first director of Borneo operations revealed the underlying motives nine years later, when he wrote that the mission illustrated 'the art of hitting an enemy hard by methods which neither escalate the war nor invite United Nations anti-colonialist intervention'.[3]

Nevertheless, the unit had been 'blooded', and it had learnt some hard lessons in the process. It had been exposed to the unvarnished reality of Special Forces warfare, where the unexpected was the norm and the need for initiative and versatility was paramount.

Tactically, it had confirmed Garland's belief that insertion by helicopter followed by a hard walk was far more effective than parachuting into action. And strategically there was a growing realisation that Australians operated best when given outright responsibility for an area of operation, then left to devise their own methods to achieve an agreed outcome. And nothing that occurred during the remainder of the unit's time in Borneo would contradict these conclusions.

After 1 Squadron returned to base, there was a five-month hiatus before 2 Squadron under Major Jim Hughes was considered battle ready. Hughes had won a Military Cross in Korea, fought with the British in the Malayan Emergency in the late 1950s and had been an instructor at the Royal Military College, Sandhurst. Short and slight, he was nevertheless as tough as leather and a natural leader of men.

By the time they arrived in January 1966, the strategic situation had changed totally. The attempted coup in Jakarta on 30 September 1965 had not only diminished Sukarno's authority but it had also undermined support for *konfrontasi* within the military. But while most of the regular army forces had been withdrawn, there remained a number of militia groups trained by their Special Forces, later known as Kopassus.

By now the Allied operation was dominated by Big Army personnel, and Hughes was unsettled by his reception in Brunei. 'I always remember the indifference to our arrival shown by the staff of HQ Australian Army Force, as if we were an embuggerance factor – you know, "We got rid of 1 Squadron last year, now you buggers are here!" I had a feeling I might be interfering with their golf or something.'[4]

However, at least the Brits were pleased to see them when they reached their Kuching HQ. '[When] we got down to B Squadron 22 SAS who we were replacing, they all bent over backwards,' he says. 'The difference was chalk and cheese.' Sergeant Ian Conaghan said the training at nearby Matang with their British colleagues was first rate. 'We did a tremendous amount of live firing,' he says, 'and because it was under operational conditions the normal safety limits were reduced to the absolute bare minimum. We had Iban border scouts attached who taught us tracking and they were very good. And we were introduced to Claymores there.'

The Claymore, an American invention, was a flat, rectangular mine that stood just above the ground on two folding legs. When detonated, it propelled 700 deadly steel balls in an arc 60 degrees wide, two metres high and 50 metres deep. A 22 SAS officer, Captain Angus Graham-Wigan, promoted a technique of linking an array of the mines with an electrical cord to be fired when ambushing the enemy. On the first occasion an Australian troop from 1 Squadron employed the Graham–Wigan technique, the array failed to explode. There is no record of the device being used in this fashion by 2 Squadron. Indeed, according to Jim Hughes, the emphasis of his mission was different from that of his predecessor. 'Our [aims] were firstly reconnaissance, secondly hearts and minds, thirdly border scouts for the 3rd Division, fourthly air rescue. I was a bit worried about doing that because I found the parachutes sitting on pallets on a dirt floor covered in dust and cobwebs in a shed.'[5]

In the event, they would not be needed.

The first taste of battle came early in 2 Squadron's deployment, when three of the NCOs – Sergeant John Coleman and Corporals Frank Styles and Jeff Ayles – joined B Squadron in a cross-border operation. Commanded by Major Terry Hardy, they deployed into Kalimantan with 50 British SAS soldiers at last light on 3 February, planning to attack an enemy camp at dawn. Visibility was reduced by a heavy downpour, and at 10.30 pm they stumbled into an enemy position. Coleman was with the leading troop, and they turned away quickly and began to clamber up a steep track towards a clearing. The militia opened fire with a .30-calibre machine gun. The attackers took shelter in a flimsy hut and responded but quickly retreated.

On the way out of the shelter, one patrol member threw a phosphorus grenade, but it struck an upright, rebounded and exploded. Coleman later wrote, 'We were not in a good tactical position, with our hut burning and a few of the blokes on fire, me included.'[6] Pinned down, Coleman found himself 'well alight and hurting', while the rest of the force had departed. 'This wasn't the best news I'd ever received,' he says. Major Hardy ordered distant artillery to target the camp. As the shells struck, flaming SAS operators raced for the river and jumped in. Coleman and several others joined them and drifted downstream.

When they came ashore, according to the official history, 'It was a nightmare journey for Coleman. For two hours they crawled on hands and knees along wild pig tracks and then rested before first light. They then came across a long house which could have been a base for local [enemy] scouts and then turned sharply towards the border.' During the morning they arrived at a Gurkha patrol camp and the first thing Coleman's medic did was offer him a cigarette. 'Before this I had never smoked,' he says, 'but with the burns and such I sucked the bloody thing inside-out and from that day to this, I smoke.'[7]

It was the last time 2 Squadron members were part of a British force. After this, they carried out their own operations, albeit within their non-offensive limitations. This was 'exceptionally frustrating' to Hughes and his men. 'We had honed our fighting skills to a very sharp edge and were unable to put them into practice,' he says.[8] Nevertheless, they did venture across the border several times early in their deployment. There were no contacts with the enemy, but the terrain itself proved a hazardous opponent. On 3 March,

Lieutenant Ken 'Rock' Hudson led a four-man reconnaissance patrol into enemy territory and discovered footprints of what appeared to be a militia patrol. They followed the tracks until they came to the flooded Sekayan River. Hudson resisted the urgings of his men and decided against risking a crossing. On their return, Hughes backed his fellow officer. However, on 17 March they returned to the area, and on this occasion Hudson spotted what seemed to be an enemy base across the river. Though it was raining lightly, he decided to make a night crossing for a closer look.

They left their overwatch position at 3 am, with Hudson leading. When they reached the river, Hudson entered first and behind him, with each man holding the belt of the man in front, were privates Bob Moncrieff, Frank Ayling and Bruce Gabriel. The current was moving very fast, and as they waded at chest height there was a sudden fall in the riverbed that broke their hand-holds. All four were swept into the current. Ayling, a strong swimmer, found Gabriel in the darkness, and they floated about 500 metres downstream together before they were able to scramble to the bank. There was no sign of Hudson or Moncrieff.

The two survivors made their way back to their OP, and when their compatriots failed to return they headed for the emergency rendezvous, reaching it at 7.15 am. There they tried unsuccessfully to make radio contact with base before striking out for the border. They reached it at 5.30 that evening, and once again tried to call base, but without success. Finally the next morning they got through, and a helicopter arrived at midday.

Hughes was then faced with the terrible difficulty of mounting a search for his men without alerting the enemy – or indeed the world at large – that they had trespassed into Indonesian territory. This meant they could not use helicopters, fixed-wing aircraft or large ground parties in the search area. So on 23 March, Corporal Jeff Ayles, with Gabriel as his guide, took a patrol into the area.

They searched for the next five days but in vain. The army released the names of the two casualties but no details of the incident at the time.[9]

Meanwhile, on 25 May 1966 a party of senior Indonesian officers flew to Kuala Lumpur to start negotiations to end *konfrontasi*, and three days later orders reached British SAS headquarters in Labuan that all 'Claret' operations across the border were to cease immediately. On 21 July, 2 Squadron was relieved by D Squadron of 22 SAS, and five days later they flew out of Kuching for the Australian RAAF base at Butterworth. They were given a short R&R in Penang, and all were returned to Swanbourne by 15 August. By then the peace agreement had been signed between Indonesia and Malaysia.

It was the last time the British would seek to assert their military force in the region. The fading imperial ambition to regain their colonial power was finally put to rest. For Australia, it meant a recalibration of its defence ties, with the new emphasis heavily weighted towards America. And with the intervention in Vietnam turning into a major war on the Indo-Chinese Peninsula, Australia's Special Forces would be driven very firmly into the American camp. But while Borneo had taught many valuable lessons in jungle warfare, there was still much to learn. And before they were deployed to Vietnam it became routine for the SAS to undergo a final training operation in Papua New Guinea.

There they were free of certain restrictions placed on Australian operations at the Canungra Jungle Training Centre in Queensland. Claymore mines, for example, were only detonated in strictly controlled environments on the mainland, while in Papua New Guinea they could be used in situations that more closely resembled contacts with an enemy force. Major Reg Beesley, the OC of 3 Squadron, says, 'Some of my blokes had never seen jungle, let alone fired a shot in it, so it allowed me flexibility in regard to live firing.'

The training exercises typically involved SAS patrols of five or six men in opposition to soldiers from Papua New Guinea's PIR in a variety of locations, not least the border with their new neighbour, Indonesia. It provided equally valuable training for the PIR soldiers and revealed a substantial military presence to any Indonesian observers. It also gave the squadron commanders the chance to gauge the quality of their men since only three of their four troops would be required for the Vietnam engagement. This was yet another factor in the recalibration of Australia's forces to correspond with their American ally. Jim Hughes says, 'The four troops would be in competition. First rate people got left behind but collectively they weren't the best troop.'[10]

Most of the SAS operators relished the training. According to a former regimental NCO, 'Operators had to become acutely familiar with one another's skills and idiosyncrasies to the point where they almost knew what each member was thinking. The aim [was] to hone jungle skills, acclimatize to a tropical environment but more so for each patrol member to bond.'[11] Lieutenant Bill Hindson says, 'We worked up from small patrol activities to long-distance patrols. It was essential to get the patrol working together under very difficult conditions. I think eventually we came to respect one another.'

They also learnt to take advantage of all available means to get the job done. For example, when faced with a trek over mountainous country where ridges became rock climbs and the jungle between them almost impenetrable, they were not above hiring local bearers to carry their heavy packs. This was not always successful, as even the locals demurred at some of the peaks. Others accepted payment and then departed the scene.

Back in Australia, there was a further period of fine-tuning before the final selection was made. By now, according to Jim Hughes, 'They were jumping out of their skin. They wanted to go.'[12] The trainers worked their men hard, determined to prepare them for combat following the old army dictum of 'train hard, fight easy'. But accidents were inevitable and a Silver Star swimmer, Private Tom Irwin, drowned during a crossing of the Collie River.

The first to deploy would be 3 Squadron and its final training was done in and around Swanbourne under the watchful eye of its new OC, Major John Murphy, who had served with US Special Forces in Vietnam. He quickly replaced a number of Borneo veterans whom he regarded as insufficiently flexible to adapt to the new American-style regime.

After negotiations at High Command, it had been agreed that the unit would form part of the 1st Australian Task Force with 5 and 6 RAR battalions in Phuoc Tuy Province, its designated AO, in combination with the 173 US Airborne Brigade. The Australian plan was to establish a base at Nui Dat, a small, sharply rising hill about five kilometres from Baria, the provincial capital. When Murphy arrived on the afternoon of 16 June he immediately made contact with the Task Force CO, Brigadier David Jackson. Jackson approved the SAS to go into action immediately, and on 30 June five separate patrols set out through the Task Force perimeter and into hostile territory.

Now they were in a real war.

VIETNAM – FIRST CONTACT

They were in hostile contact almost immediately. A patrol led by Sergeant Jack Wigg was attacked by three Viet Cong soldiers at 8.30 the next morning. They returned fire and withdrew, only to be targeted by four enemy fighters two hours later. They called in helicopters and within minutes an Iroquois from 9 Squadron RAAF arrived and extracted them for the return journey to base. Two other early patrols led by Sergeants Tony 'Pancho' Tonna and Alan 'Curly' Kirwan also had contacts with the enemy, and on each occasion a firefight resulted in the death of Viet Cong fighters and helicopter extraction. Since the Australians had so far escaped without casualties, morale in the SAS unit was high.

The extractions had been practised many times in training exercises in Papua New Guinea, and were the beginning of a deeply valued relationship between the two Special Forces units. The RAAF based their squadron at Vung Tau, a more secure area about 25 minutes' flying time from Nui Dat, and their ranks were supplemented by a group of seven or eight New Zealand pilots from the Royal New Zealand Air Force (RNZAF). The airmen were also on call to resupply patrols in the field, an exercise that required speed and precision to avoid giving away the location of SAS operators deep in hostile territory. Crewman Terry Pinkerton says they were constantly practising to reduce the time involved. On one occasion, they completed a resupply of 115 kilograms of water, rations, ammunition and spare batteries over a rendezvous in only 15 seconds. 'Our training was very detailed,' he says. 'Sometimes you would go down into the trees and have to manoeuvre backwards and forwards to get under the canopy.'[1]

An equally important supporting unit was the 547 Signal Troop, whose role was to provide signals intelligence to the Task Force and the SAS in particular. They were based at Nui Dat in their own secure compound with the highest top-secret classification. At first they were regarded as a 'post office', receiving and passing on signalling from the big American operation, but through their own ingenuity they were soon producing localised intelligence of enormous potential value to the Task Force.

Their principal resources were stationary intercepts of enemy radio signals through their Nui Dat receiver, which they greatly enhanced with a towering aerial made from star pickets; and high-frequency airborne radio direction-finding (ARDF) equipment that flew over the Australian area of responsibility in Cessna 180s of the 161 Reconnaissance Squadron. The radio chatter, collected by operators in a steamy galvanised-iron 'set room', was decrypted and translated by the troop's experts on site. The ARDF operation – where up to 100 sorties were flown each month from nearby Luscombe field – was able to track down enemy radio operators in the field and direct SAS patrols to the source.

The troop had worked with the SAS in Borneo and were constantly refining their operation. In Vietnam, individual members frequently joined patrols and took responsibility for a continually increasing range of communications. 'They were tremendously helpful,' an SAS Vietnam veteran said, 'but on patrol we had to make sure the Sig guy wasn't captured by the enemy. He knew too much.'[2]

Brigadier Jackson had decided to establish a defensible tactical area of responsibility with a perimeter ranging from five to eight kilometres from the centre of Nui Dat. One of his battalions would defend the home base, while the other – 6 RAR – would deploy on offensive operations beyond the perimeter, particularly in the hill country to the south-west. The SAS patrols would provide them with essential intelligence prior to their departure.

One patrol in particular would have important repercussions. Early in July, Sergeant Terry Nolan led his men into the Long Tan village area about five kilometres to the west. There was a lot of activity in and around the village, so he left his men in an LUP and moved forward to an OP in a tall tree overlooking the settlement. He saw a number of armed Viet Cong moving about the village, but what struck him most forcefully was the relaxed manner of the enemy soldiers. 'They showed no sign of having walked a long distance,' he reported. It appeared that their base camp was nearby.[3]

Further sightings and some sharp contacts were made by 3 Squadron in the area over the next several weeks. A patrol led by Lieutenant Peter Schuman, who would later be awarded the Military Cross, discovered an old military camp in the area. A few minutes later, he and Private Sam Wilson were moving stealthily forward when Schuman glanced to his right. 'I saw a VC sentry taking careful aim at Wilson,' he says. Before he could fire, Schuman dropped him with a single round from his self-loading rifle (SLR) and as they retreated all hell broke loose.[4]

They returned fire, joined with the rest of the patrol and retired to the camp, which they secured. There they stuffed their packs with documents and radios before setting fire to the flimsy buildings and signalling to be extracted. Just then a small party of Viet Cong attacked. They had only just fought them off when the

9 Squadron helicopter came clattering overhead and took them out. 'Thus ended a day's work,' Schuman says.[5]

The contacts continued in the area, particularly as the unit attempted to silence a Viet Cong radio operator they nicknamed 'Fred', who was reporting patrol movements. Clearly, all this enemy activity meant that a major effort was needed from the Task Force to clear the area of a well-entrenched opposing force. However, the Australians were unprepared for the size of the battle when it unfolded at Long Tan. According to the official SAS history, the unit 'had provided little solid evidence that the enemy was massing for an attack on the Task Force'.[6]

Recently divulged information reveals that the Signal Troop 547 not only located the major attacking force, the 275 Regiment, but the troop's OC, Captain Trevor Richards, had warned Brigadier Jackson of its approach to within five kilometres of the Task Force base.[7] At the time, however, the Australian signals interception team had yet to establish the reputation that would eventually have the Americans coming to it for its latest intelligence product.

On the night of 16–17 August, the Viet Cong fired a barrage of shells into Nui Dat, wounding 24 Australians. The next morning D Company of 6 RAR went out in search of the aggressors and at about 3.15 that afternoon contacted a small group and opened fire. The Viet Cong fled, leaving one man mortally wounded. The company continued their patrol until just after 4 pm, when they were hit with the full force of the Viet Cong's 275 Regiment of an estimated 2,000 fighters with blistering mortar, machine-gun and rifle fire.

By now it was pouring rain, and the Australians returned fire and called in artillery from base as well as a resupply of ammunition. Two RAAF Iroquois helicopters that happened to be carrying a concert party to Nui Dat dropped their passengers and flew at treetop level into the battle area, where they delivered the precious ammunition. Though D Company were taking casualties, by sundown the battle had swung in the Australians' favour. Meanwhile, their compatriots in A Company were moving in to support them mounted in armoured personnel carriers. They engaged a substantial enemy force and after a sharp firefight the Viet Cong withdrew. As darkness fell, the enemy melted back into the jungle. In the morning, 245 Viet Cong bodies were found in the battle space. The Australians had lost 18 soldiers, with a further 24 wounded.

The fact that they had been surprised by the massive Viet Cong force cast a shadow over the SAS Squadron's reputation for high-quality reconnaissance and surveillance. Controversy swirled around this aspect of the battle for several years, with some former SAS soldiers claiming the unit had warned HQ that the enemy were about to mount a major attack on the Task Force only to have it ignored by Brigadier Jackson. Others have quoted Major John Murphy specifically refuting the claim that his unit had located the Viet Cong regiment. The official record contains no evidence to back the claims of the dissenters. Instead, it is now clear that the warnings came from 547 Troop, but security classifications have prevented the truth from emerging. Significantly, after the battle, 547 Troop strength was doubled.

The eagerness to blame the SAS is another example of the perennial tension between Special Forces and the Big Army. The distinctive nature of the Special Forces 'club' was underlined early in 3 Squadron's deployment when the US Army commander, General William Westmoreland, requested the transfer of an SAS officer to his staff to advise on 'Australian techniques'. This was followed by a visit from the deputy commander of their Special Forces Team Delta Unit seeking instructors for a contingent of South Vietnamese soldiers they planned to send on clandestine missions into North Vietnam and Cambodia. Murphy said his men could not be spared from their intensive patrolling program but instead proposed an exchange of four to six senior NCOs and soldiers between the two units. His proposal was accepted and added a new dimension to the cooperative links with US Special Forces.

The original deployment of 3 Squadron was for six months, ending in December 1966. But because the regular army tours were for a year, it was decided to avoid 'unfavourable comparisons' and retain the unit in country for a similar period.[8] This ignored the relative intensity of SAS patrolling and caused unrest among the squadron's hierarchy, particularly since the men had been on a war footing in Borneo in the months prior to Vietnam. Major Murphy suggested an extended handover period to resolve the problem, and while 3 Squadron remained in country well into 1967, 1 Squadron would arrive in February and relieve them of some of their high-pressure operations.

Meantime, they did a parachute jump into a dry paddy field using gear borrowed from the US, an operation Murphy described as 'largely a sporting gimmick'. But on 17 January there was nothing sporting about a contact with a Viet Cong force some nine kilometres from base. The patrol, led by Sergeant Norm Ferguson, was fired on from the rear, and the medic, Private Russell Copeman, was hit. Private John Matten went to his aid, threw a white phosphorus grenade and, using its smoke as cover, manoeuvred the wounded man onto his shoulder and staggered into the cover of the undergrowth. There he discovered that what he thought was a bullet to the arm was much more serious; Copeman had taken a round to the stomach and the pain was horrendous.

Matten signalled for an emergency extraction and tended to his mate's wounds as best he could. When the chopper arrived, he helped Copeman onto the winch as the door gunner covered them from above with his machine gun. They were then joined by the rest of the patrol, who followed the wounded man up the winch as two Viet Cong tried unsuccessfully to pick them off from below. They flew directly to Vung Tau, where Copeman went onto the operating table immediately. He was later repatriated to Australia, where he was expected to recover fully. However, complications arose and he died three months later.

In the handover period, 3 Squadron also took the newcomers out on patrol to show them the ropes. Sergeant Nev Farley, a 1 Squadron patrol commander, says, '[It] was good value going out on the handover patrol. Everybody got briefed and we had lectures and the blokes were all talking to each other. The Diggers down at the boozer were talking to each other; everybody was sucking everybody's brains on how you did things.'[9]

Murphy and his team quietly departed by the end of March after 27 contacts resulting in 46 Viet Cong killed, with only Russell Copeman subsequently lost to enemy action. Brigadier Jackson said the OC had been 'an excellent squadron commander and very clear-headed about the use of the SAS in prevailing conditions'.

His successor, Major Dale Barnett, arrived in an advance party of 1 Squadron and would continue the process of integration with the American military. A Duntroon graduate, he had spent six months on a ranger training course at a leading US Infantry School. However, he had no prior SAS experience and had replaced the seasoned 1 Squadron commander, Major Jack Fletcher, who had injured his back. Moreover, his operations officer, Lieutenant Bob Ivey, at 24, was equally inexperienced in Special Forces operations.

There was a severe shortage of trained signals operators despite orders for the formation of an SAS signals squadron, and the 547 Troop were themselves stretched. Pressure on recruitment to the Sabre squadrons of the SAS meant that selection standards slipped. National Servicemen were included in the pool, and a touring selection board chose candidates for a six-week cadre course followed by a parachute qualification and specialist training as medics, assault pioneer, signals, weapons handling or language (Malay, Pidgin or Vietnamese).

The main body of the squadron arrived in March, and after briefing adopted similar tactics with one major difference: the five-man patrols were encouraged to take more aggressive action in setting ambushes and seeking out contacts as opposed to the earlier emphasis on reconnaissance. They deployed multiple Claymore mines to devastating effect on Viet Cong parties; and they tried repeatedly (but unsuccessfully) to capture an enemy soldier for interrogation. The reconnaissance and surveillance operations also formed a significant part of their mission, and battalion intelligence officers invariably departed the SAS base on Nui Dat hill with valuable guidance in planning their operations.

The Task Force also had new leadership in Brigadier Stuart Graham, whose command was notable for his folly of constructing a minefield barrier of 20,000 'jumping jack' mines east of the base. According to the official website of the Department of Veterans' Affairs, 'There were a number of injuries and deaths during the mine-laying operation and casualties continued after its completion. The minefield's security was ineffective and the Viet Cong breached the barrier fences, lifted the mines and re-used them against the Australian [and South Vietnamese] troops . . .

'In 1968 Australian engineers began the dangerous task of sweeping and clearing the "barrier minefield" . . . it took nearly two years to clear them; by then [they] had contributed significantly to the Australian casualty rate in Vietnam.'

Graham was replaced in October 1967 by Borneo veteran Brigadier Ron Hughes, who wanted to use the SAS even more aggressively than his predecessor. Barnett disagreed, believing 'this contravened the basic infantry doctrine of recce patrols v. fighting patrols and could have led to our interest in a particular area being given away (for the sake of body count), which could in turn jeopardise the success of Task Force operations being planned for that area. Patrol commanders must know if they are recce or fighting patrols.'[10]

However, Barnett had no problem with SAS personnel being used in major offensives such as Operation Santa Fe – a combined US, Vietnamese and Australian mission in the foothills of the Mao Tay mountains. Three SAS patrols used Claymores and airstrikes to inflict substantial casualties on enemy units. But the growing American obsession with 'body counts' was causing dissention within the SAS. Patrol leaders were told that after a successful contact they should delay being extracted but 'remain in the jungle and try for a few more kills'. The commanders regarded this as 'an unsound policy which they tried to avoid'.[11]

Nonetheless, when 2 Squadron took over from Barnett, its OC, Major Brian Wade, immediately declared himself more than willing to engage his unit in the offensive role. Though only 31, Wade had joined the SAS Company in 1957 and had been an exchange officer with the 17th Gurkha Division in Malaya. He had then completed a range of courses with US Special Forces, trained with the British Royal Commandos, and had already spent time in Vietnam with the Training Team in 1962–63. He welcomed what he called patrol 'recce ambushes' similar to the British Borneo template where they engaged in silent reconnaissance for the first part of the operation and then went 'head hunting' over the final 48 hours.

Each patrol produced its share of excitement, and the effect of close combat on individual SAS operators was often totally unexpected. Lieutenant Sam Simpson, for example, had shown very little commitment to offensive warfare training in Australia but, once in Vietnam, according to Wade, he emerged as 'the most aggressive and best patrol commander' in the unit.[12] On

6 April, his patrol in thick jungle encountered signs of enemy activity and the following day they located a major camp. They crept into the encampment and set two white smoke grenades with time fuses to guide an air strike; but at the appointed time the grenades failed to explode, and they had to call the strike in by voice. Enemy soldiers scattered and Simpson's patrol was on hand to mop them up.

Although primarily operating out of Phuoc Tuy, the Task Force was called to broaden its operation in the lead-up to an expected offensive during the Tet New Year celebration in January 1968. However, as with Long Tan, the size and strength of the enemy offensive was completely unexpected. And again Australian covert operators warned their superiors but were ignored.

On this occasion, the Australian command was fortunate in having Major Peter Young in a key military intelligence role in Saigon. Young had served as a troop commander in 22 SAS during the Malayan Emergency, and in 1962 had worked for the CIA as part of the Australian Training Team in Vietnam. His links with American intelligence and ASIS, and his own contacts as assistant military attaché in the Australian Embassy, were unparalleled, as he worked closely with the CIA's deputy station chief in Vietnam, the legendary Ted Sarong.

Young prepared a paper in July 1967 that not only foretold the offensive and the strategic reasons behind it but clearly indicated its size, strength and time frame. Today he remains irate that 'like other major warnings it was rejected'. The case, he says, 'became a battle between military [signals] analysis and the Department of External Affairs' political aims, relying on their predominantly human sources'. At the time these favoured the optimistic mirages of 'light at the end of the tunnel' and 'all over by Christmas'.[13]

In fact, his warning was treated with disdain in the embassy. The counsellor wrote, 'The Ambassador saw your paper in draft.

He would have many comments. My own general comment is that it still contains many questionable assertions. I do not see what the enemy could seize and hold in order to force negotiations on his own terms. At points in your paper you seem to believe that the seizing of ground, even temporarily, is of importance to him. My guess – nothing more – is that his intention is to inflict as many losses as possible, while keeping his own as low as possible – for as long as possible – in the supposition that we will all get tired and settle . . . I'd like to keep this to read again in six months or a year's time – or two years.'

Young's warning went no further.

Sparrow Force leaders Major Bernard Callinan, Captain Geoff 'Bull' Laidlaw and Captain Rolf Baldwin. (*AWM P00707.023*)

The men of Sparrow Force with a local catch. (*AWM P00707.023/ Damien Parer*)

Five members of the North Australian Observer Unit (NAOU) or 'Nackeroos', pose with their rifles in the bush. (*AWM P06166.003*)

Major William Stanner, commander of the North Australian Observer Unit. (*AWM P04393.001*)

Originally named *Kofuku Maru*, the MV *Krait* was commandeered by the Services Reconnaissance Department in 1942. (*AWM P01483.001*)

Z Special Unit members Andrew Huston, Ivan Lyon, Kevin Cain and Horrie Young aboard the *Krait* during Operation Jaywick. (*AWM 045413*)

A motorised submersible canoe or 'Sleeping Beauty' such as those taken on the disastrous Operation Rimau. (*AWM P00908.003*)

Soviet spymaster Vladimir Petrov defected and was granted political asylum in 1954, along with his wife Evdokia Petrova. (*Newspix*)

G. R. Richards (*left*), deputy director-general of ASIO, and Brigadier Charles Spry (*right*), director-general, appeared before the Petrov Royal Commission. (*State Library of NSW/Ern McQuilllan*)

Doc Evatt (*left*) appeared at the Petrov Royal Commission.

(*State Library of NSW/ Ern McQuilllan*)

Nui Dat, South Vietnam, 1971. Members of 2 Squadron, Special Air Service (SAS), climb on rope ladders from a hovering Iroquois helicopter.
(*AWM P00966.028/Donald Barnby*)

ASIO chief Peter Barbour gives evidence to a Senate select committee in 1973. (*Fairfax Media*)

Reporter Greg Shackleton paints the word 'Australia' and an Australian flag on the outer wall of the house in Balibo. (*Fairfax Media*)

Sir Edward Woodward, director-general of ASIO from 1976 to 1981. (*Newspix*)

February 13, 1978. Police officers at the scene of the bomb explosion outside the Hilton Hotel in Sydney during the Commonwealth Heads of Government Meeting. (*AFP/Newspix*)

IN THE THICK OF IT

When the Tet offensive began on 30 January 1968, the SAS joined with the major units of the Task Force in Operation Coburg defending the approaches to Saigon. The initial attacks stunned the US and South Vietnamese armies, and caused them to temporarily lose control of several cities, but they quickly regrouped to beat back the offensive, inflicting massive casualties on Ho Chi Minh's forces. During the battle for Huế intense fighting lasted for a month and resulted in the destruction of the city by US forces. At the Khe Sanh US combat base, fighting continued for two more months.

Tet also affected Phuoc Tuy Province, and although stretched thin, the remaining Australian forces there successfully repelled an attack on Baria, as well as spoiling a harassing offensive on Long Dien and conducting a sweep of Hoa Long, killing 50 Viet Cong and wounding 25 for the loss of five Australians killed and 24 wounded. But the casualties continued to mount, and by the end of the action 17 Australians had been killed and 61 wounded.

Tet was a turning point in the war, and although a tactical disaster for the communists, it was a strategic victory for Hanoi as public support for the war in the United States collapsed. It had a similar effect on Australian public attitudes and caused growing uncertainty in the government about the determination of the United States to 'stay the course'. Prime Minister John Gorton reflected the public mood when he declared that, despite American requests, Australia would not increase its military commitment to the war.

The North Vietnamese forces continued to pressure the Allies with 'mini-Tets' over the next few months, and the SAS was plunged into the fray. June and July were remarkably successful for 2 Squadron, with 34 patrols recording more than 50 Viet Cong killed in action. They also provided bodyguard support for Prime Minister Gorton on his visit to Nui Dat.

In June, Lieutenant Sam Simpson's patrol was inserted deep into Bien Hoa Province four kilometres south of the main Task Force. In the next 17 days, they would have three successful contacts. Simpson says, 'As we gained experience we became more aggressive and cocky. I personally thought there was much more we could do in eliminating minor VC elements by direct means rather than acting as the eyes and ears of the Task Force.'[1]

A few weeks later, his wish was granted when his expanded patrol was inserted into the Nui Dinh hills, where they discovered an enemy camp. Having observed the encampment for several hours, they took up position and opened fire, sweeping the target back and forth with M60 and automatic rifle fire. Then Simpson and three other patrol members advanced in extended line. Simpson says, 'The assault was great fun. We killed about six in the first round and grenaded all bunkers on the western perimeter ... I stumbled across the radio roughly in the centre of the camp.'

On 5 July, Simpson and his six-man patrol were having a 'smoko' before setting an ambush when they were surprised by about 30 Viet Cong heading down the road towards them. 'They saw us first,' he says. 'In fact they saw Paul Duffy who was urinating against a tree. The firefight that followed would have enthralled

John Wayne. It was like a rabbit shoot complete with hysterical rabbits.' Then more enemy soldiers appeared. 'The end of the column of VC – estimated at about 80 plus – decided to roll up our flanks,' he says. 'I decided there were far too many for any further heroics and withdrew to a pre-planned LZ.'[2]

Eight days later, Simpson and an aggressive seven-man patrol were inserted into enemy territory with no attempt made to conceal their presence. Within minutes they had several contacts. They killed at least three Viet Cong and were joined by an infantry company of 1 RAR. After an overnight bivouac, the patrol moved out with the company following. They reached an old paddy field with an abandoned hut near the edge of the jungle. While Simpson paused on the track to decide which direction to take, 'there was a flash and a bang' from an anti-personnel mine. Simpson had been badly wounded – one foot and lower leg had been blown off and the other shattered. At about 10.45 am as his patrol members, themselves wounded, came to his aid, Simpson asked them to check that his testicles were still there.

They were.

By 11.15, an American helicopter arrived, and half an hour later he was on the operating table at Vung Tau. By 1.30, both his legs had been amputated below the knee. His loss was not just a shock to the squadron; 'It was a real blow,' says then Corporal Terry O'Farrell.[3]

At this time squadron OC Wade introduced a new helicopter extraction technique: the aircraft would let down six hanging ropes of about 30 metres each. With carabiner hooks, the patrol members would each attach their own 'Swiss seat' – a lightweight pattern of cotton ropes – to a loop at the end of the rope. The chopper would then lift off with the soldiers dangling 30 metres below. They tested it in combat on 29 July, and six SAS operators were extracted in less than two minutes. They were then carried at altitudes of up to 2,500 feet (760 metres) for 20 kilometres. The technique was effective but not particularly popular with the SAS operators. One retired corporal, Stuart 'Nev' Bonner, says, 'We used to train to do these extractions a lot in the 1990s. The sensation of being carried through the air was exhilarating, but the novelty soon wore off when the harness started to cut off circulation to your legs and blokes started to call out in agony.

'It was used successfully numerous times in operations, including Timor, but hanging suspended in a tape harness for too long can be fatal. One time in Vietnam, one bloke got stuck in the limb of a tree on extraction and had to be lowered again to get out. On a separate occasion, another guy failed to hook up correctly and fell to his death.'

Meantime, the 547 Troop were also dicing with death. Corporal Dick Schafer was seeking out enemy radio operations from a Cessna 180 when the engine stopped and he and the pilot were forced to crash land in a paddy field 20 kilometres north of Nui Dat. According to a colleague, 'Dick scrambled from the broken aircraft to face an encircling patrol dressed in black. Dick and the pilot, Lieutenant Steve Tizzard, drew their guns and prepared for a desperate stand. The tallest member of the patrol suddenly put his hands into the air, shouting, "Don't shoot, I'm an American adviser!"' Schafer, Tizzard and their highly classified equipment were extracted under the protection of helicopter gunships and an SAS patrol that arrived within minutes of the forced landing.[4]

October 1968 saw the arrival of another experimental direction-finding device known as a 'single-station locator'. It was erected within the Nui Dat perimeter, but away from the troop's main operational base. Called 'the Cell', it was based on a World War II German system, which used four aerials in a circle. The Cell pinpointed the source of a Viet Cong radio wave by measuring the phased time and angle difference between two incoming radio waves striking the antennas and calculating the angle of deflection from the ionosphere. Once it was bedded down, the results were outstanding, and some of the technical innovations were shared with the Americans. The methodology, developed by Australians, is now used worldwide.

As the Task Force HQ deployed forward in operations, the troop developed a portable radio direction-finding (DF) system mounted in an armoured command vehicle to give rapid replies to operational planners. However, most of the more hazardous operations of the troop were airborne. Early in 1969, for example, Corporal Garth Brown was returning from an ARDF mission in heavy weather. Since there were no navaids at Luscombe field, the pilot, Captain Daniels, tried four times to drop below the cloud cover to land but each time missed the runway. As fuel was running low, he diverted to Vung Tau, which did have navigational aids.

'As we were letting down,' Brown says, 'the rain intensified and visibility was zilch; the turbulence was horrific. Then in a series of split seconds the sky lightened, visibility increased to about 100 metres, and there dead in front of us was a Chinook helicopter! The crew chief was standing on the ramp; his look of absolute terror as he saw us is embedded in my brain forever. Captain Daniels threw us into a violent "wing over" manoeuvre to starboard. I don't know how our port wing missed the rear rotor of the Chinook but somehow it did.'

Daniels changed course to Tan Son Nhut on the outskirts of Saigon. 'On our approach the port engine cut out due to fuel starvation,' Brown says. 'By toggling the fuel tanks, Daniels was able to restart the engine and then got an emergency clearance into the strip. We touched down safely but both engines had cut out before we finished our landing roll.'[5] However, their aerial operations were remarkably successful. A senior Task Force officer says, 'The enemy was largely inhibited from widespread use of radio by his knowledge that our intercept capability and technical expertise . . . were just too good to take risks with.'[6]

By contrast, Brigadier Sandy Pearson, who succeeded Hughes as Task Force commander in October 1968, was no fan of the SAS. 'My first contact [with them] was on one of our big exercises on the Colo-Putty area,' he says. 'The SAS had been given several days to reconnoitre a route for 1 RAR. This they botched. My own intelligence people did in two hours what the SAS claimed could not be done . . .'

Pearson's attitude affected patrolling operations as he was unwilling to provide as much helicopter support as his predecessor. In response, Wade encouraged his patrol leaders to remain on the ground for longer periods, and this caused resentment among them. Nevertheless, they conducted a series of highly successful patrols and though they provided valuable intelligence on enemy movements the tension with the Task Force CO Pearson persisted. Wade says, 'There were a number of occasions during the squadron tour that I recommended follow-up action after a patrol was extracted, but the problem generally was the non-availability of an infantry company to conduct the task.'

Then, on 17 January 1969, tragedy struck when Corporal Ron 'Harry' Harris, one of the few Aboriginal SAS operators, was accidentally shot by one of his own patrol members during a contact with the Viet Cong in thick jungle. An investigation found that no blame could be sheeted home to the man who fired the fatal shot. The investigating officer, Major Brian Lindsay from New Zealand's 4 RAR, reported that, '[Harris's] direction of movement and sudden body movements combined with the colour of his skin and no camouflage paint indicated him to be enemy in a situation where reflex action was required.' According to the official history, 'Where men lived on their nerves in constant danger from the enemy, it is remarkable, and a testimony to their training, that there were not more accidents.[7]

Nevertheless, it was a blow to squadron morale, and there were only a few more contacts – and no casualties – before 2 Squadron ended its tour on 21 February 1969. By then they had handed over to 3 Squadron, which was supplemented by a New Zealand SAS troop already in place and yet to be integrated into the system. And the new OC, Major Reg Beesley, was confronted by the same implacable attitude of the Task Force CO Brigadier Pearson.

At their first meeting Pearson told Beesley he wanted the entire squadron deployed on 'fan'-type patrols. Beesley countered that he had trained his patrols to be inserted separately from Nui Dat and to stay in their target areas for an extended period. And that's the way he wanted them deployed. Faced with a determined SAS leader, Pearson compromised. He gave Beesley six weeks to produce results.

In fact, Beesley agreed with Pearson's overriding emphasis on intelligence gathering over ambush and other aggressive contacts. This, after all, was the foundation of the unit's traditional modus operandi. And when Pearson allocated an area to the north of the province for special attention, the OC was happy to work within his guidelines.

He was less pleased by the attitude of the Kiwis, who had not only established a little camp of their own but were also tasking their own patrols. He tackled the issue head on, putting all New Zealand vehicles under his control. While he was impressed with their dedication, sense of purpose and professionalism, he felt that their leadership 'lacked maturity'. Within weeks, his 'tough love' approach worked; the integration had been secured and the new Anzacs operated as a single unit.

While the reconnaissance role greatly improved the quality of intelligence from the target area, it was inevitable that the

SAS patrols would encounter the enemy on the ground. In early April, Sergeant Tony Tonna's six-man patrol observed a series of small Viet Cong patrols over several days, until on 5 April one of them advanced on their OP. Private Barry Williams fired four well-aimed shots, and Tonna ordered a quick withdrawal from the scene. The next day, they crossed a well-used track and then followed it to a suitable ambush area. Within half an hour, four more enemy soldiers approached and the patrol opened fire, killing all four. They immediately signalled for extraction and the helicopter reached them an hour later.

By this time, Beesley's six-week 'probation' was up. Pearson was more than happy with the results and made no further demands for a tactical change. Typical of their subsequent patrols was an operation led by Sergeant Ned Kelly into the Long Green area of Phuoc Tuy. The men observed a total of 175 enemy who appeared to be establishing a supply dump for an incoming combat unit. When the intelligence was received at HQ, the Task Force commander responded with a major infantry insertion to clear the area.

Beesley used his free hand to increase further the duration of the patrols and – unique among SAS squadron commanders – to lead patrols himself. Seven days into the first one, they made contact with three Viet Cong and dispatched them without loss. Beesley then remained in the area with his men for two further days before being extracted by rope. The OC also increased the size of the patrols, and by now Pearson had become an advocate of ambushing the enemy if the opportunity arose.

In mid-May, a 17-man patrol under Lieutenant Terry Nolan established a five-man OP near a track and observed 61 Viet Cong. However, before he could set up an ambush, more and more enemy personnel were passing through, some of whom had been wounded in a battle with American forces to the east. Nolan decided the best course was for a company of infantry to be inserted and he radioed his message to HQ. Twenty-four hours later, the order came back that he should mount the ambush himself.

His second-in-command, Tony Tonna, was concerned about the size of the opposing force. And when Nolan injured his knee and had to be evacuated, he found himself in charge. The odds worsened when his OP reported another 97 well-armed enemy passing through; then half an hour later another 118. Tonna decided his best option was to spring the ambush on one of the smaller groups coming in from the east. So, on 24 May, he set a Claymore array near the track and detonated it as four Viet Cong approached. Three were killed outright, but when the team went forward to do the obligatory body count the fourth opened fire on Private Ray Mickleberg. Fortunately the rounds struck his pack and knocked him to the ground, and he was otherwise uninjured. The wounded Viet Cong escaped and the patrol was extracted the next morning.

The intense activity in the area indicated a build-up of enemy forces designed to overwhelm the Australian operation. Pearson responded aggressively, deploying the newly arrived 6 RAR into the area. The North Vietnamese Army (NVA) hit the Task Force HQ with rocket attacks, but most landed in the Nui Dat rubbish dump. However, one exploded above an SAS tent and severely injured Corporal Bob 'Buff' Lorimer. He was evacuated to hospital and made a complete recovery. The engagement lasted a full month, and at the end the enemy force withdrew to neighbouring Bien Hoa Province.

The battle represented the end of major actions in Phuoc Tuy for an extended period. The SAS turned their attention to 'pacification' roles within the province, and expanded patrols into Binh Tuy Province until Pearson handed over to his successor, Stuart 'Black Jack' Weir, in September 1969. Weir supported the dual SAS role of reconnaissance and contact when the opportunities arose.

It was during this period that, in a rope extraction, 23-year-old Private David Fisher fell at least 30 metres into the jungle. That afternoon, OC Beesley himself led a nine-man patrol into the area to search for him. Next morning they were joined by a company from 9 RAR, but to no avail. They sighted three Viet Cong and killed one before being relieved by another company. His body was not found and recovered until 2008.

Another casualty of the roping extraction technique occurred shortly afterwards, when a helicopter lifting out a five-man New Zealand patrol went out of control soon after take-off because of the swinging pendulum, and crashed; the patrol was dragged 60 metres by the aircraft before the ropes were released. Amazingly no one was killed.

On 18 February 1970, 1 Squadron returned to Vietnam on its second tour, to replace Beesley's unit. The new OC, Major Ian Teague, realised immediately that his mission would be very different from the tours to date. By now the war was winding down. Brigadier Weir told him, 'You will have to be flexible and adapt to a number of different tasks.' In fact, while the contacts were less frequent, the recce–ambush format of the patrols remained the same. Ironically, while the Americans were losing the war, Phuoc Tuy, Teague discovered, was 'far more subdued'.[8] This meant the SAS was freed to extend its operations further and in May four patrols embarked on a US Navy patrol boat that inserted them down the coastal strip in a Gemini assault craft. The patrols were relatively uneventful, but they reinforced the cooperative nature of the US and Australian Special Forces units.

After almost five years of SAS operations, the Viet Cong had become familiar with the unit's insertion and extraction techniques. The lead-up usually involved airborne reconnaissance and this gave the enemy an indication of the insertion locations. The result was that patrols were often in contact very shortly after deployment.

New techniques were tested, such as 'cowboy insertions', where a second patrol followed quickly to reinforce any initial contact before being extracted once the threat was neutralised.

In December, Major Teague returned to attend a staff college and was replaced by the OC of 2 Squadron, Major Geoff Chipman. The new incumbent's first task was to deal with objections from the New Zealand Special Air Service (NZSAS) troop, who wanted to confine their operations to long-range reconnaissance, where contacts with the enemy were unlikely. This caused some friction in the command structure, and in December 1970 the New Zealand troop was given permission to withdraw. However, it was still in the country in February 1971, and joined with 1 Squadron in its final contact when the troop killed two Viet Cong.

Chipman welcomed a new Task Force commander, Brigadier Bruce McDonald, at the end of the month, and immediately established a good working relationship, rapidly deploying his SAS troops to the eastern sector. They were followed by infantry operations acting on the intelligence they gathered. The pace of operations was maintained through the early months in country and, while the contacts were few, they were always dangerous.

In April, Lieutenant Brian Jones led a patrol into an area of jungle and high grass, where an engineering party was trying to locate an underground Viet Cong bunker system. In a shocking mix-up, Jones was mistakenly shot by an Australian soldier as he walked through the long grass. He was the last SAS casualty of the war.

14

GROWING INTELLIGENCE
STRENGTH

It was now clear that, while the North Vietnamese forces were pressing home their strategic advances elsewhere, they had abandoned Phuoc Tuy Province as a viable battlefield. And while this was a compliment to the Australian Task Force, it forced a reorganisation of SAS operations. Brigadier McDonald received permission to extend his AO into Long Kanh Province, and this allowed the SAS to revert to the long-range reconnaissance that had been so much a part of its training in Western Australia from its inception.

However, Chipman's 2 Squadron was suffering the effects of five tough years in the front lines. Its 95 personnel now included 21 from the previous squadron and 25 National Servicemen. Properly qualified officers were particularly scarce; it took more than a month to find a replacement for Lieutenant Jones. Nevertheless, the squadron maintained its strong working relationship with the US Navy SEAL teams operating in the Mekong Delta and conducted patrols seeking to release captured American and Vietnamese prisoners. In this, the commander of US Naval Forces in Vietnam told McDonald, the SAS displayed 'superb examples of professionalism'.[1]

The squadron also conducted successful long-range patrols, with a series of minor skirmishes, before the arrival of a signal from Canberra on 12 September that it would cease operations on 6 October and return to Swanbourne four days later. While this was welcomed by Major Chipman, there was an unexpected kick in the tail: on its return the squadron would be disbanded. 'This had a very natural adverse effect on the morale of the unit,' Chipman says. 'The future of every man was at stake.'[2] It was not until a week later that a further message reassured the professional soldiers that 'all members of the unit would be absorbed into the regiment'.

On 10 October 1971, the SAS soldiers flew to Vung Tau by Caribou before boarding a C-130 for Australia and ending more than six years in continuous operational service in Borneo and Vietnam. In that time, they had established vital working relationships with their supporting forces, particularly 9 RAAF Squadron, 152 Signals Squadron and 547 Troop. By now the signallers were responsible for the SAS's communications from the base station, monitoring and cipher facilities, advice on communications, liaison with other signals units and accompanying SAS personnel on patrols. They were remarkably effective. Brigadier Hughes says, 'The intercept unit at Nui Dat was a wonderful source of intelligence and it achieved its greatest success when, as a result of their information, I was able to send an SAS patrol to destroy a VC logistics element.'[3]

The SAS squadrons and their leadership had all distinguished themselves in every aspect of their operations, from reconnaissance and surveillance to fighting patrols. So much so that some SAS officers believed they could have accomplished a great deal more if they had been given their head. Retired SAS major Jim Truscott says, 'The tragedy of course is that SAS were never committed on strategic missions. One wonders if there would have been a different outcome if these men had been pitted against the North Vietnamese regime. It is only in more recent times that the Australian Government has understood the political and psychological utility of the SAS in addition to its military skills.'[4]

They would exploit these elements during the next big operational outbreak from 1999 to 2013, but in the interim they would confront a very different problem: peace. After the initial let-down that always follows a period of intense operational activity, the regiment welcomed the chance to review the lessons learnt and plan for future contingencies. But the SAS thrived on the sense of challenge, and in an inactive operational period that becomes increasingly difficult to maintain. In its absence, the unit could easily find itself looking backward to its Vietnam triumphs, particularly as veterans of that conflict rose through the ranks to become senior officers and NCOs. As we shall see, the regiment was not immune to that operational malaise.

However, the other Special Forces pillars were not similarly burdened, since their involvement in the war, while significant, was not so all-consuming. The commandos, for example, made a measured contribution. Many of the professional cadres – and three trainees – were deployed to Vietnam with the Australian Army Training Team, working for the CIA, and with US Special Forces at Danang. On their return, they used their experience to train commando recruits. The most senior of these was Major Harry Smith, the commander of D Company in 6 RAR at the battle of Long Tan. According to commando historian Peter Collins, 'He returned to Georges Heights [Sydney] with a wealth of knowledge and practical ideas about staying alive in combat.'[5]

In 1969, commando company commanders had attended a meeting of all Australian Special Forces hierarchy at Swanbourne, where they were told that any of their men prepared to serve in Vietnam were virtually guaranteed a position in the SASR.

Several took up the challenge. But, despite these losses, the units maintained their training regimes and at the end of the war were well placed to incorporate veterans who wanted to retain their military connection. They made the transition from war to peace by introducing new skills training in small craft handling on the coastline and climbing ventures, particularly at Mount Arapiles in Victoria's Grampians mountain range. While 2 Company ran the climbing courses, 1 Company developed diving courses in Sydney Harbour. The standards were maintained at a very high level; in the mid-1970s virtually every member of the commandos who sought to transfer to the SASR passed selection with flying colours. Both companies' annual exercises were usually held in conjunction with the SAS. And in March 1972 the OC of SAS 3 Squadron, Major Royston 'Bill' Billett, was transferred to command 2 Commando Company in Melbourne.

Billett was well placed to expand the links between the two Special Forces units with some joint training operations. Then, in July 1973, they were consolidated in a historic 'round-up' of Australia's fighting Special Forces in Appian Way, the first major joint exercise conducted by the Australian Army. Extending over two months, it involved both commando companies, 3 Squadron SAS and 126 Signals Squadron in the vast Kimberley ranges in Western Australia.

Starting from a bush airstrip, it began with a long hike over a mountain plateau at night with a sharp descent from an escarpment to a distant rendezvous. Once they reached the mustering point, they flew by Caribou to a second staging post and finally by helicopter to the insertion area. 'From this point,' Billett says, 'there were many nights hard marching along the approach to the objective with my old squadron from the SASR keen to "put us in the bag".' He was pleased when, 'with the loss of only one CSM and one patrol, we had successfully passed through the screen of SAS patrols covering the approaches to the final objective'.

The Outback provided its own surprises. 'For the first time in my military career,' he says, 'I was distracted while giving orders to my troops by a flock of brolgas who seemed totally unaware of our presence as they hunted for food right alongside our position. This briefing covered the final approach to the objective. By now our food had almost run out, [but] on the plus side, our loads were lighter for the night descent from that plateau. Beyond the cliff the ground was strewn with shin-high boulders hidden in long grass, resulting in many impromptu somersaults. About two in the morning after a short halt I passed one of the signallers. I asked what was wrong and he replied that he couldn't go on. My reply was that was fine but we would have to leave him – and we would not be coming back.'

The delay caused by the rough ground meant that they missed the end of the exercise. As they approached the final rendezvous, the 'enemy' on the other side of the river was decamping by helicopter. 'Soon it would be our turn,' Billett says, 'so we went non-tac and had a brew.' When he looked back up the slope, 'with the halo from the morning sun highlighting him, there was the signalman who couldn't go on! He received a rousing welcome.'[6]

The exercise was so successful it was repeated with variations the following year when the commando companies raided the Albany area against SASR defenders, finishing with an exhausting night march accompanied by SAS Vietnam veterans and a US Navy SEAL petty officer. But as time passed, the initial post-Vietnam enthusiasm began to wear thin among CMF volunteers. A government defence review by Dr Tom Millar noted that, 'The minimum annual training requirement for commandos is 63 days and this limits the potential intake to a select few. Strengths are difficult to maintain and the turnover is high. It is extremely difficult to find Citizen Force officers with the necessary time, dedication and physical fitness to join these units particularly when they cannot progress beyond the rank of captain . . .'

The intelligence agencies had similarly bumpy roads to negotiate in the mid-1970s. The turmoil in ASIO after the Murphy raids and the sacking of Peter Barbour subsided for a time under the steady hand of Frank Mahoney, a senior officer of the Attorney-General's Department when Prime Minister Whitlam tapped him for the caretaker role. An amiable and courteous man, Mahoney was a good judge of character and impervious to the flattery that is an occupational hazard of his position. While his leadership lasted for little more than a year, he at least kept a firm grasp on the tiller through the political cyclone of 11 November 1975.

When the Whitlam Government was dismissed by Governor-General John Kerr, there were wild accusations from the PM's office that the CIA was implicated and that somehow ASIO was associated in the plot. Mahoney had inadvertently added a little fuel to the fire by (quite properly) showing the prime minister a cable from the CIA expressing their concern about Whitlam's revelations in parliament of the association between their former director of the CIA-operated Pine Gap facility near Alice Springs and the Australian Country Party leader Doug Anthony. The message threatened that, 'If this [exposure] problem cannot be solved [we] do not see how our mutually beneficial relationships are going to continue.'

Whether John Kerr was influenced by the Americans remains a moot point. He had long been associated with the intelligence community, and might well have been privy to CIA concerns. But it is much more likely that domestic (and egotistical) considerations played the major role in his decision. In any case, by the time Justice Edward Woodward took up the permanent appointment as director-general of ASIO in 1976, Malcolm Fraser was prime minister and the agency was deeply involved in the first Royal Commission on Intelligence and Security being conducted by Justice Robert Hope.

Judge Woodward had been born in Ballarat in 1928, the son of an army officer who would become governor of New South Wales in 1957. He earned a Master of Laws Degree at the University of Melbourne, took silk at an early age and was appointed to the bench in 1972. The following year he was appointed to the Aboriginal Land Rights Commission in the Northern Territory and established a close and enduring relationship with the Aboriginal people. He had a reputation as a patient listener and a firm, collegial administrator.

Justice Hope's findings set Woodward some immediate challenges. The intelligence community, Hope reported, was 'fragmented, poorly coordinated and organised'. And that was just the beginning. Behind the scenes, as revealed in an unpublished section of the Hope report, the situation in ASIO was dire. In 2008, the secretary of the commission, George Brownbill, revealed for the first time that they formed the following damning judgements: 'poor management, poorly resourced, poor personnel practices, authoritarian, [and] hierarchical'. Brownbill says, 'My own opinion is that the ASIO created in 1949 up to the time of Petrov and perhaps beyond was reasonably well resourced. But I think beyond that, a lot of Cold War claptrap got mixed up with genuine concerns about security and I think it went downhill from there.

'We found a security service that had been badly politicised. It would have been much more serious if the ASIO operatives had been more competent, but as it was, their scattergun approach to the investigation of "subversion" resulted in an equally scattergun approach to the fulfilment of their true function as the fourth arm of the defence of the realm.'[7]

Woodward instituted a clean-up campaign assisted by his deputy, Harvey Barnett, a former deputy head of ASIS. Born in Albany, Western Australia, in 1925, Barnett had travelled to Britain and Europe after World War II, and taught school for a time in the Black Forest area of West Germany. 'One of my main duties,' he says, 'was to give special tutoring to students newly escaped from the East Zone. The firsthand stories related by the girls and boys I taught, of life under the Leninist–Marxist system caused me to revise thoroughly any idealistic notions I may have had about Marxist theory and practice.'[8] When he returned to Australia he was recruited into ASIS in the 1950s, and later ran stations in Singapore, Cambodia and Vietnam. He became the ASIS deputy director for operations in 1973 and under Woodward was in charge of ASIO's operational arm.

Another important member of Woodward's executive was Leslie McBride, one of Justice Hope's assistants. It was his task to reform an administration that, according to the commission, had become 'wracked by nepotism, favouritism and probable unethical behaviour'. He introduced a formal administrative structure to encourage promotion by merit, while minimising the internal bureaucracy. He also encouraged the formation of a staff association to air grievances and to develop a collegial ethos.

His approach was not universally appreciated within the agency. According to one critic, John Miller, 'at a headquarters meeting attended by all staff, and at subsequent mini-meetings in regional (state) offices, officers were told that a line had been drawn underneath their personal history and performance: they were recommencing at a new Year One.'[9] These claims are disputed by ASIO members of the time, not least because Miller never worked for the organisation except for a period during the 1970s when he assisted the agency with some administrative and financial matters. However, the senior ASIO agent, Colin Brown, was transferred to London, while a recruitment drive garnered a new crop of operatives untainted by the past. Barnett says more than 1,000 applicants responded from a wide range of academic disciplines. 'Of these, I recall, we took a total of twenty-one officers, male and female.'[10]

Miller says, 'They were given intensive training and placed on a merry-go-round of postings designed to smash specialisation in favour of generalisation.' New open-plan offices were instituted and the changes were not well received by the old hands. The qualifications for advancement, they claimed, were now 'a Diploma in tasting boot polish, a Bachelor's degree in buck-passing, a Master's in writing the new government-speak and a PhD in sycophancy, mismanagement and dress sense'.[11] These claims are strongly disputed among the new recruits themselves. In fact, while they were graduates, some had also worked in private industry, while others had served in Vietnam. And before they were eligible for promotion they had to 'earn their spurs' in field operations. Moreover, the 'old hands' were given time and funding to undertake university courses and most took advantage of the offer.

Woodward himself was regarded universally as a very fair and decent man, if rather aloof and judicial. In combination with his executive, he re-established the agency's standing within government. His relations with Malcolm Fraser were formal and professional and the prime minister requested Justice Hope to conduct a protective security review that ASIO insiders believe was as significant as any of the royal commissions into the security services.

Hope found that the arrangements between the states and the Commonwealth were 'chaotic and unworkable', with no clear lines of responsibility. His overriding recommendation was that one agency should be responsible for threat assessments, and that ASIO should accept the task. The agency has maintained that responsibility to the present day, with state police forces and the Australian Federal Police (AFP) at the operational level when necessary.

Funding was increased and by 1980 ASIO would have a budget of $13 million, almost three times its subvention at the beginning of the decade. Its operatives found new targets for surveillance in the Palestinian community of Sydney, particularly among the Al Fatah organisation and its spokesman Ali Razak. The new graduates did not mix well with the 'exotics' from the Middle East and there was some resistance to engaging the demimonde that an earlier generation had relied upon for their human intelligence (HUMINT) among target groups. However, by the late 1970s they had access to a new range of electronic spyware, from listening devices to visual aids and increasingly sensitive cameras. A technological revolution was on the horizon and the spy agencies would be quick to exploit it.

Nevertheless, when the first terrorist attack on Australian soil erupted on 13 February 1978, ASIO was caught flat-footed. Just after midnight a bomb exploded outside the Sydney Hilton during a session of the Commonwealth Heads of Government Meeting (CHOGM). It killed two garbage collectors and a police officer, with 11 others injured. Malcolm Fraser called out the army, and they remained in overwatch throughout the rest of the meeting.

It sent a shockwave through Australia's Special Forces. For the first time since the withdrawal from Vietnam six years previously, they were called to the front line. In June, a police informer implicated members of the Ananda Marga religious sect, who were said to have targeted the Indian prime minister, Morarji Desai, in retaliation for his jailing of their leader, Shrii Shrii Anandamurti. There followed a decade of legal controversy, and the fine points of the case remain unresolved. All attempts to institute an inquiry into the matter were vetoed by the federal government. But while

ASIO was quite properly the first in line to take the blame for not preventing the outrage, the international nature of the threat also brought its sister organisation ASIS into the frame, front and centre.

BALIBO

ASIS had a good war. The Vietnam conflict focused official attention on the South-East Asian bailiwick of the agency and provided unprecedented opportunities for cooperation with its American counterpart. While the agency declined special operations in the field in favour of the army training team and later the SAS, the service became ever more active in the Indochina peninsula.

Indonesia remained its top priority, and under Harvey Barnett it was much less coy about 'dirty tricks' in that country. The leadership authorised six operations in the 1960s, including propaganda campaigns, medical assistance to Sukarno's opponents and 'more direct' attempts to engineer the president's political demise. An example of the interlocking nature of Special Forces is the revelation that the 'foot soldiers' used by ASIS in those special operations were members of Sydney's 1 Commando Company.[1] Indeed, for several decades 1 Commando was 'two-hatted' – one was conventional army, but under the other it undertook special operations for ASIS.

Prime Minister Harold Holt in his 1966 'pivot' to Asia had authorised new or expanded ASIS posts in Manila, Rangoon, Bangkok and Saigon. The agency maintained its radio listening station outside Darwin and the training facility at Swan Island on the western tip of Port Phillip Bay. An ASIS office was opened in Port Moresby with the responsibility of reporting on Papua New Guinea's newly independent government and on Indonesian activities across the border in Irian Jaya.

Holt's long-serving foreign minister Paul Hasluck continued the Asian engagement after the prime minister's untimely death in December 1967 with another office in the Cambodian capital Phnom Penh occupied by Frederick Stuart Fry, a former languages teacher at Sydney's Scots College. Fry would be involved in a CIA operation to undermine the Cambodian leader, Prince Sihanouk, but would rise through the service to become acting director of ASIS in the 1980s.

From 1968, the agency's director was Bill Robertson, one of the founding fathers, who had twice been passed over for the leadership but finally got the nod when Cawthorn retired. The following year, Hasluck was 'kicked upstairs' by his successful rival for the Liberal Party leadership, John Gorton, to become governor-general.

The new foreign minister, William 'Billy' McMahon, knew little and cared less about ASIS. The sentiment was reciprocated and Gorton was equally uninterested in the agency's operations. The result was that, until his retirement in January 1971, the de facto ministerial head of the organisation was deputy prime minister and Country Party leader John McEwen, who had vetoed McMahon's prime-ministerial ambitions on the death of Harold Holt.

However, once McEwen departed, McMahon found himself confronted by a request from the CIA that caused him 'to dance three times around it', according to a participant at the meeting. The Americans wanted ASIS to provide three officers to act as proxies in Santiago in case the Chilean president, Salvador Allende, cut diplomatic relations and forced the withdrawal of the CIA.

At the completion of his nervous jitterbug, McMahon approved the postings, though later denied all knowledge of them. In fact, two ASIS operatives were sent to Santiago where they worked with the CIA to destabilise Allende's government, leading to his overthrow and suicide.[2]

When McMahon, having succeeded Gorton as prime minister in 1971, lost the 1972 election to Whitlam, Robertson was quick to brief the incoming prime minister on the Chilean misadventure. The Labor leader was appalled, and Robertson, a politically savvy bureaucrat, had come armed with a draft order to rescind the postings. Whitlam would take the matter to Cabinet but the men would not be withdrawn until the following year.

It was not a good start. However, the prime minister was perfectly prepared to support the expansion of the agency's operations in Vietnam, where they recruited agents from their Saigon base. When diplomatic relations were resumed after the war an ASIS operative was posted to Hanoi where he worked under embassy cover. There was, however, continuous pressure from elements in government to remove the special operations capacity of the service.

Head of the Joint Intelligence Organisation (JIO) Gordon Jockel and the deputy secretary of Foreign Affairs, Lewis Border, reviewed the agency at Whitlam's behest and delivered their report in June 1973. 'There seems to be little justification now for the ... Director [of ASIS] to conduct "special operations",' they wrote. 'It is difficult to envisage a situation, particularly in our area of interest, in which our people could be effectively employed in a clandestine role.' Instead, they suggested, any such activities would best be carried out by the military.

Whitlam postponed any change, and instead appointed Justice Hope to undertake his much wider inquiry. His only move to prune back the agency's operations was a decision to close the Tokyo office, since the quality of the ASIS product from that station was trivial at best. But when word of the intended closure leaked, the CIA came to the rescue and fed the Australian representative such 'juicy' material that the prime minister reversed his decision.[3]

In 1974, a coup in Portugal against its right-wing regime – the so-called Carnation Revolution – meant that its exploited and neglected colonies were to be set adrift. Once again Australia's defence planners turned their attention to the island of Timor. The Portuguese territory occupied a strip on the east of the island and an enclave within the former Dutch colonial area that had reverted to Indonesia after its postwar independence from the Netherlands. On 20 December, Gordon Jockel contacted ASIS seeking action to upgrade their intelligence from East Timor and soon afterwards delivered a series of questions on the economic, social and military situation there.

ASIS turned to ASIO for help, and Harvey Barnett, now deputy director-general of the sister agency, referred them to an Italian–Australian, Frank Favaro, who had offices in Darwin and a hotel in Dili. He was a willing recruit but, according to ASIS sources, '[He] was found not to meet ASIS' normal desiderata for its agents. His movements were irregular, and this left him the initiative of making contact with his case officer. He repeatedly failed to do so. He appeared willing to help but his business interests intervened.'

Nevertheless, the agency persisted.

Many East Timorese who had suffered under colonial rule for almost four centuries harboured ambitions for independence. But they were divided on ideological grounds between the left-wing Revolutionary Front for an Independent East Timor (Fretilin), APODETI, which favoured integration with Indonesia, and the Timorese Democratic Union (UDT), which sought continued links with Portugal. The latter two briefly combined, but then split into warring factions, and some UDT leaders held meetings with BAKIN, the Indonesian military intelligence organisation.

The 'communist' Fretilin group was anathema to the Suharto Government, which began an international diplomatic campaign for the incorporation of the territory within the larger Indonesian polity. And when civil war broke out in the tiny colony in 1975 following an attempted coup by the UDT, Indonesia redoubled its efforts, with notable success among Western governments, including the US and Australia. Fretilin unilaterally declared independence on 28 November 1975, and thereafter the die was cast: Indonesia decided to invade.

Meanwhile, ASIS continued to have problems controlling Favaro as its principal HUMINT source. Now he wanted to become the Australian consul in Dili and asked his case officer for support. The ASIS official declined and was then staggered when Favaro took his request to a Foreign Affairs diplomat and declared his ASIS connection. That was the final straw. The director, Bill Robertson, decided he should be cut loose after one more meeting to 'tie off the loose ends'. Unfortunately, events intervened and the meeting never took place.

By October 1975, an Indonesian Kopassus unit had already made cross-border incursions in preparation for the invasion. On 16 October, one operation would have tragic repercussions. A group of five newsmen, including two Australians, reporter Greg Shackleton and sound recordist Tony Stewart, as well as New Zealander Gary Cunningham and two British television journalists, Brian Peters and Malcolm Rennie, had taken up position in a house on the outskirts of Balibo near the East Timorese border. It was an excellent vantage point. All were in their 20s and had rejected the advice of more experienced correspondents to stay out of the firing line. But they had taken the precaution of painting an Australian flag and an 'AUSTRALIA' sign on the house.

When 'Team Susi' of Kopassus reached the area, they were on full alert and shocked to discover that their presence had been discovered. A team member, Colonel Gatot Purwanto, admitted some 35 years later that they signalled Jakarta for orders on how to deal with the discovery.

'Our position (at that moment) was extremely difficult,' he says. 'If they were allowed to live, they would have said this was an Indonesian invasion. If they were killed and it was left at that, there would have been evidence they were shot in an area controlled by Indonesian guerrillas. To make things easy, we got rid of them completely. We said we didn't know anything. That was a spontaneous reaction at that moment.'[4]

Another eyewitness revealed that four of the journalists surrendered and were standing outside the house with their hands in the air when they were shot. The fifth had locked himself in a bathroom but was stabbed to death when he emerged.

In Canberra, ASIS's problems with its loose cannon in Dili were coming to a head. Favaro's activities in East Timor were attracting Indonesian attention as newspaper reports suggested Australia's 'Honorary Consul' was a Fretilin spy. On 16 October, as Team Susi advanced on Balibo, the secretary of foreign affairs advised his minister, Senator Don Willesee, to 'knock the idea on the head'. Willesee arranged for a friendly 'Dorothy Dix' question to be asked in parliament and responded that Favaro 'did not represent the Australian Government in Timor in any capacity'.

Five days later, Robertson fronted the prime minister and admitted that Favaro was still officially employed by ASIS. In a towering rage, Whitlam sacked Robertson on the spot, even threatening to deny him his superannuation. His uncontrolled fury could be heard in the corridor outside. In 2002, Whitlam said, 'Sure I sacked the head of ASIS. I had to tell him twice to put an end to the work his agents in our embassy in Chile were doing to undermine Allende on behalf of the CIA. Earlier his agents had worked with the same ambassador to undermine Sihanouk in Cambodia on behalf of the CIA. In 1975, he employed an agent in Dili without my authority.'

Clearly, Whitlam was unnerved at the time by the political crisis that would see his government dismissed three weeks later. The defence minister of the day, Bill Morrison, later said he had deliberately kept news of the deaths of the Balibo Five from the prime minister for five days, since 'it was on pain of death to go anywhere near his office at that stage'.

Robertson says, 'When I left the meeting, I was shocked and disgusted. I was shocked as I realised that I had been summarily and unfairly dismissed without any investigation of the facts, for an incident – [the Favaro connection] – which had caused no political embarrassment; I was disgusted that anyone in Mr Whitlam's position could act in such an undignified manner in front of senior public officials.'[5] It was an ignominious and thoroughly unwarranted end to a distinguished career. However, he would be warmly embraced by Justice Hope in his subsequent royal commission deliberations.

For many years the Indonesian Government, backed by Australian Foreign Affairs officials, claimed the Balibo Five were killed in 'crossfire' on the border. However, there is evidence that the DSD monitored the radio message from Balibo to Jakarta. Partly to protect its DSD operation and partly to excuse its own failings, the Australian government steadfastly maintained the cover-up, even after another Australian journalist, Roger East of AAP Reuters, on a mission to investigate the killings, was captured in Dili by the Indonesian military on 7 December 1975, the day of the full-scale invasion. He was executed by firing squad the next morning, with his body being disposed of in the ocean. He has been referred to as the forgotten sixth member of the Balibo

Five. Calls for an inquest into East's death have been rejected by successive governments.

Indonesia declared East Timor its 27th province on 17 July 1976. However, the UN Security Council opposed the invasion and, despite a massive investment by Jakarta in infrastructure, education and health, the territory's nominal status in the UN remained incongruously 'a non-self-governing territory under Portuguese administration'.

This provided the Portuguese Catholic Church and other neo-conservatives with the formal cover to encourage and support resistance to the Muslim Indonesian administration. The Indonesian military responded and in time this meant that the province became an economic stronghold of the Indonesian Armed Forces (TNI) and Kopassus in particular. At the same time, the Fretilin leadership conducted a guerrilla war from mountain redoubts and sought international support in a long-running diplomatic offensive.

•

The new ASIS director, Ian James Kennison, had been Robertson's deputy, and by general consensus he would be one of the very best of the agency's heads. Little is publicly known about his background, but in office he was highly regarded and respected by his peers, while able 'to keep his feet on the ground'. He refined the training regime of his operatives to the point where MI6 officers, who until 1972 had trained some 80 ASIS personnel, were now coming to Australia themselves for specialist courses.

He retained a 'close but discreet' relationship with the CIA chief of station in Australia. One of his first actions was to post an ASIS officer to Jakarta with the express purpose of establishing a direct liaison with BAKIN 'to improve regional and counter-intelligence matters common to both countries'. Kennison also re-energised the New Zealand connection, and from time to time would use the NZ Security Intelligence Service (their ASIO equivalent) for 'traces' on the background of persons of interest.

Kennison also had to deal with the backlash from an extraordinary decision by Whitlam to accept a massive election campaign donation of $500,000 from the Ba'ath Party of Iraq, the power base of Saddam Hussein, who would take the formal title of president of Iraq less than four years later. In the heightened political drama of the time, the new prime minister, Malcolm Fraser, was concerned that as a quid pro quo Whitlam would either alter Labor's pro-Israel policy or supply the Iraqis with classified information. And while there is no evidence that either response was undertaken, or even contemplated, ASIS could not avoid being drawn into the imbroglio behind the scenes.

Fraser asked the secretary of foreign affairs, Alan Renouf, to post an ASIS officer to Baghdad to investigate the matter, despite the fact that Australia had no embassy in the Iraqi capital. Kennison resisted, fearing that the agency was being drawn into a party political issue. Indeed, he quietly conspired with Renouf's deputy and successor, Nick Parkinson, to find reasons to delay the operation. In the event, they opened an embassy at great expense, appointed an ASIS operative, but then withdrew him to Cairo after only 12 months with no notable revelations. It is to Kennison's credit that the agency emerged politically unscathed.

When the Sydney Hilton bombing took place in 1978, ASIS's role in the investigation was two-pronged. The agency's mainstream unit gathered intelligence from its contacts worldwide, while a rehabilitated Bill Robertson was appointed by Fraser to head a new Protective Services Coordination Centre that greatly improved ASIS facilities, including an airfield on Swan Island. Most significantly, he oversaw the development of a counterterrorist capacity within the SAS. This would include a mock aircraft at Swan Island, where they could practise anti-hijack exercises – a facility they would later duplicate at their training area at Bindoon, an hour's drive north of Perth.

The new association with the SAS would allow Kennison to devolve much of the special operations action to the regiment. Indeed, he cut the budget for this area to only 1 per cent of the agency's total expenditure.[6] For its part, the SAS became increasingly involved in counterinsurgency exercises with American and Philippines Special Forces on the main island of Luzon, and on one occasion in Western Australia. Operation Lion's Den on the coast north of Perth included parachute and submarine landings, and both an abduction and the rescue of a notional VIP.

This reordering of priorities allowed Kennison to increase ASIS's intelligence-gathering efforts in the economic and trade areas, as well as nuclear proliferation and safeguards, particularly as China developed its atomic weaponry. The economic information was shared from time to time with selected Australian companies, notably 'The Big Australian', BHP, in its negotiations with Japan and other regional and international entities.

The company had established a Canberra presence in the 1930s led by James Menzies, father of the future prime minister Robert Menzies, to lobby support among politicians for tariff protection of the company's steel production. BHP's Melbourne headquarters facilitated a warm association, one that would continue unabated and under cover of the Foreign Affairs mantle to the present time.

Kennison tried to improve relations with the department through joint seminars and the assignment of a senior diplomat to ASIS's ranks for a 12-month tour of duty; and he attempted to find 'an appropriate balance' in the agency's relations with the other key departments of Treasury and Prime Minister and Cabinet (PM&C). He also had to deal with a new entry into Australia's Special Forces landscape, the Office of National Assessments

(ONA), created in response to Hope's findings that Australia's spy force was uncoordinated and disorganised.

Under the direction of a former ambassador to Indonesia and director of the Defence Department's JIO, Bob Furlonger, the ONA exercised an uncomfortable degree of control over ASIS's operations. Furlonger's authority was bolstered by ONA's location within the prime minister's own portfolio. Ian Kennison was not alone in resenting ONA's incursions on his turf. And when Furlonger's misreading of the 1979 crisis between China and Vietnam exposed ONA's shortcomings, the wrath of Canberra's most hardened and unforgiving mandarins descended upon the personally charming but professionally overbearing bureaucrat and his fledgling cohort.

16

CHOPPY WATERS

While the fate of the Balibo Five has been proclaimed a scandalous failure of Australian officialdom, and Australia's Special Forces in particular, a far more serious mishandling of national responsibilities has been swept from the pages of history. Incredible as it may seem now, Australia not only turned a blind eye to the horrors of the Pol Pot regime in Cambodia from 1975 to 1979; it also condemned the Vietnamese forces when they overthrew the murderous Khmer Rouge cabal that had turned the tiny nation into a killing field. It even sided with the Chinese, who declared war on Vietnam in retaliation.

Australia cannot plead ignorance; throughout the period its Special Forces ensured that the government was aware of the genocidal horrors being perpetrated within Cambodia. And even after they were publicly exposed, and the Khmer Rouge deposed, the government continued to back Pol Pot and his government in exile.

The United States was also morally bereft, though their attitude was more understandable. As the world's superpower, they were still smarting from their defeat at the hands of the Vietnamese. And with their massive illegal bombing raids on Cambodia they had created the conditions that enabled Pol Pot's rise to power in the first place. In March 1970, Marshal Lon Nol, a Cambodian front man for the CIA, staged a successful coup to depose Prince Sihanouk as head of state. At this time, the Khmer Rouge's army was led by Pol Pot. Two years later, he was also leader of the Communist Party, and with help from the Vietnamese his forces gained supremacy on the battlefield. The Vietnamese then withdrew. This was the starting gun for President Nixon's and Henry Kissinger's 'secret war' on Cambodia, during which they dropped half a million tons of bombs on the tiny kingdom. Casualties reached an estimated 300,000, and the Cambodians responded by rallying to the Khmer Rouge. On 17 April 1975, Phnom Penh fell to the communist forces.

Then the real horror began. Starting the calendar at 'Year Zero', the Khmer Rouge banished two million people from Phnom Penh and other cities into the countryside. Thousands died during the evacuations. They then abolished money, free markets, normal schooling, private property, foreign clothing, religious practices and traditional Khmer culture. Public schools, pagodas, mosques, churches, universities, shops and government buildings were shut or turned into prisons and re-education camps. There was no public or private transportation, no private property, and no non-revolutionary entertainment. Everyone wore black.

The regime arrested and killed thousands of soldiers and civil servants. Over the next three years, they executed hundreds of thousands of intellectuals, city residents, minorities such as the Cham, Vietnamese and Chinese, as well as many of their own soldiers and party members. By 1977, the biggest prison in Cambodia, known as S-21, held 14,000 prisoners; one year later only 12 had survived.

In December 1978, Vietnamese troops fought their way into Cambodia and captured Phnom Penh on 7 January 1979. The Khmer Rouge leaders then fled to the west and established their remnant forces in Thai territory, aided by China and Thailand. The United Nations, with American and Australian support, voted to give them a seat in the General Assembly. From 1979 to 1990, it recognised them as the only legitimate representative of Cambodia.

In 1980, Foreign Minister Andrew Peacock had threatened to resign if Australia continued its recognition. Peacock was the recipient of ASIS and DSD reporting on the situation, and was appalled. He'd had an early experience of Cambodia. 'I had first gone there with my mother when I was a teenager,' he says. Twenty years later he was in the capital on a study tour with fellow coalition frontbencher Ian Sinclair when the Khmer Rouge encircled the city. 'The Khmer Rouge weren't letting any food in, so the population was starving,' he says. 'It was a horrifying experience to witness what was happening to people there.' When Phnom Penh fell, Peacock and Sinclair sought help from the US ambassador, who arranged for them to join the last American flight out.

Four years later as foreign minister in the wake of the Pol Pot genocide, he confronted Prime Minister Malcolm Fraser on the issue. By now the Vietnamese forces had overthrown the Khmer Rouge; the de facto leader Hun Sen had been appointed deputy prime minister and foreign minister. China had intervened with a short, sharp war against Vietnam in February and March 1979, resulting in a humiliating defeat for China's People's Liberation Army (PLA).

Both ASIS and DSD were on the ground in the area. The man in charge of the operation, who would later become deputy director of ASIS, had been based in Thailand for several years, and when he heard from intelligence sources that the Chinese invasion was about to take place he travelled to the area to observe. An associate says, 'China, the US and Australia couldn't handle that the Vietnamese were doing a good thing. They were supplying stuff to Pol Pot. We had a covert assistance program . . . a ghastly and terrible position we took at that stage.'[1]

Unfortunately, Furlonger's ONA was not passing the ASIS information through to the policymakers in PM&C. Upon learning this, the secretary of the Prime Minister's Department, Sir Geoffrey Yeend, delivered a 'rocket' to the ONA, and one of his deputies savagely rejected ONA's claim that the Americans had 'blacked out' the information flow from the area.

In his July 1980 Cabinet submission, Peacock said, 'I believe the domestic revulsion against the atrocities of the Pol Pot regime is a factor which should properly be reflected in our foreign policy stance on Kampuchea.' He recommended that the government back UN acceptance of the deposed regime's credentials for the forthcoming meeting of the UN General Assembly but agree in principle to withdraw Australian recognition thereafter.

Cabinet rebuffed his submission and he offered Fraser his resignation. The PM refused to accept it. In September, he asked Fraser to relist the issue for Cabinet, but he declined. When Fraser decided to call an election the following month, Peacock again threatened resignation. Fearing the electoral consequences Fraser agreed to a position similar to the one Peacock had recommended in July: Australia would continue to recognise Pol Pot but only in the short term.

After the election, Peacock sought a change of portfolio, and he was replaced as foreign minister by Fraser's old school friend Tony Street. The government continued to support the Pol Pot exiles in Thailand. As in the earlier conflicts in Malaysia and Vietnam, Australia found itself playing follow-the-leader in the Anglosphere of the day. The development of a truly independent regional foreign policy was as distant as ever.

Britain also provided assistance to the Khmer Rouge. On 25 June 1991, after two years of denials, the UK Government finally admitted that their SAS had been secretly training the Pol Pot 'resistance' since 1983.

A report by Asia Watch filled in the detail: the SAS had taught 'the use of improvised explosive devices, booby traps and the manufacture and use of time-delay devices'. There is no record in the official history of any Australian SAS involvement; however, it is known that the ASIS Bangkok station was active in the area with a small unit patched around 72 Electronic Warfare (EW) Signals Squadron providing covert communications support to Australia's ASIS operatives.

With the arrival of the new foreign minister came a new head of ASIS: John Ryan, a deputy secretary in the Foreign Affairs Department, whose most recent overseas posting had been as Australia's high commissioner to Canada. Born in 1923, Ryan had fought in the 2/7 Independent Company during World War II, and had retained his taste for special operations. One of his first innovations was to establish a Directorate of Covert Action and Emergency Planning within the agency. This decision would eventually bring about his downfall.

Meantime, he had the firm support of Commissioner Hope, who declared in his report, 'ASIS exists to conduct espionage against foreign countries and . . . to do so successfully ASIS must probably infringe the laws of those countries . . . The service's job is to break those laws without being caught.' Hope was also much in favour of increased cooperation between ASIS and DSD, particularly in electronic eavesdropping. While ASIO would 'run' the operation, he encouraged them to work together to bug diplomatic premises and the accommodation of visiting delegations. DSD should provide the technical equipment, he said, while the ASIS operatives should install the bugs. ASIO would monitor the product. The Fraser Government accepted the recommendations.

Soon afterwards, the Labor Party under Bob Hawke – the last-minute replacement for the long-suffering Bill Hayden – won the federal election of March 1983. Hayden became foreign minister in the new government and very quickly endorsed Ryan's activist approach. His Special Operations directorate – referred to internally as 'The Project' – recruited personnel with a liking for James Bond-style derring-do and trained them at an expanded Swan Island facility. There they learnt 'offensive driving', weapons handling, close combat and waterborne insertions.

It was within this aggressive mindset that a special, tightly held training exercise began at Swan Island on 11 November 1983 under the formal responsibility of the commander of Sydney's 1 Commando Regiment.[2] Ryan himself attended the course, and on the weekend of 26/27 November the trainees were briefed on their scenario: first they would conduct surveillance of a 'foreign defector' whose brother might also be planning to join him. However, the nature of the exercise would change when the defector was 'abducted' by two 'foreign intelligence officers'. The trainees were to stay on his track and report regularly to the project head.

What followed was a farce bordering on criminality. First the trainees lost the abducted defector and had to be tipped off by a member of the army instruction team that he was located at Melbourne's Sheraton Hotel. Then at 4 pm on 29 November the project head told the team leader that the operation had changed again: now they must rescue the defector using 'minimum force necessary'.

At about 8 pm the trainees gathered in their tenth floor hotel room – inevitably numbered 007 – all equipped with party masks or balaclavas, six Browning 9-mm automatic pistols and four submachine guns (two of them silenced) plus a sledgehammer. The abducted defector was being held along the corridor in suite 004.

Their first plan was for one team member to dress as a waiter and try to enter the suite on the pretext that a signature was required for a parcel. However, the ploy failed when the 'foreign intelligence officers' refused to open the door. Not to be denied, the team then attacked the door with nine blows of the sledgehammer and burst in with their deadly weapons. They discovered the defector naked in the bath pretending to be drugged. Undeterred, they handcuffed his 'guards', and dried and partially dressed the defector, while the team leader returned to the corridor and pressed the button to summon the elevator.

Meantime, a bona fide guest at the hotel had heard the commotion and seen the masked men smashing down the door. He called the manager, Nicholas Rice, and when the lift arrived at the team leader's summons the doors opened to reveal a deeply perturbed hotelier. The team leader entered, and as the lift descended the two men 'jostled each other' on the way down. When they reached the ground floor, Nick Rice called for someone to ring the police.

The team leader took the lift back up to the tenth floor, where the 'foreign intelligence officers' were still handcuffed, but the rest had departed using another lift. The team leader followed and caught up with his team on the ground floor, where he found them surrounded by Nick Rice wielding a night stick and a group of hotel-employee reinforcements summoned by their manager. When the ASIS men brandished their weaponry, the hotel staff retreated sufficiently for the masked intruders to reach the back door in the kitchen, from where their pre-arranged 'getaway cars' picked them up and drove off.

The Sheraton's assistant manager took the number of one of the cars, and the police intercepted it in Melbourne's CBD. Despite their protests, the police took its five occupants – including the semi-nude defector – to headquarters for questioning. According to a current senior intelligence officer familiar with the events,

'They were very lucky that no one was shot dead. The police were armed and these guys gave every impression of being terrorists. The police would have been justified in opening fire.'

At headquarters they were soon joined by the project head, who had told other police in the hotel foyer that it was a 'Defence Department' matter, and offered to pay any damages. The Victorian constabulary were unimpressed; and when the ASIS head, John Ryan, arrived on the scene and refused to cooperate the farce turned into a political imbroglio.

Justice Hope was then conducting a royal commission into an ASIO operation and Hayden asked him to add an investigation of the Sheraton shenanigans to his terms of reference. In the interim, he accepted Ryan's resignation and appointed his deputy, Stuart Fry, to the post of acting director until a more permanent director-general could be found. Justice Hope's inquiry sheeted the blame home to Ryan, the project head and the team leader. Eventually it would lead to the withdrawal (at least temporarily) of covert operations from the ASIS arsenal. By then, however, the issue had been subsumed – at least in the public mind – by the even more sensational aspects of Hope's principal investigation: the alleged attempt by the KGB to turn a former ALP national secretary, David Combe, into an 'agent of influence' within the upper echelons of the Australian Government.

Combe's downfall is only marginally significant in the progressive development of Australia's Special Forces; however, it shines a light on the mindset of ASIO in setting the nation's security priorities. It reveals that, as recently as the mid-1980s, with the collapse of the Soviet Union only half a decade into the future, the leadership in the agency was obsessed with the threat posed by Moscow to Australia's security. This derived partly from ASIO's history, partly from its close association with the American espionage establishment, and not least from the background of its director-general, Harvey Barnett.

In his 1988 memoir, *Tale of the Scorpion*, Barnett relives his 1981 anguish in accepting the post rather than director-general of ASIS, which had also been offered to him with Ian Kennison's departure. Though he was already ASIO's deputy director-general under the retiring Judge Woodward, and 'the head of ASIO is more senior in the Public Service hierarchy', he says, 'I resisted the ASIO call to the end ... walking lonely along the beach; discussing it with my wife and sons; thumping the piano in the hope perhaps that some bright light of inspiration might provide me with an answer ... The truth was that I really wanted to go back to ASIS ... However, in the end I capitulated and on 5 September 1981 I entered on my inheritance. It did not take me long to get my feet under the table.'[3]

Less than two years later, however, those feet would carry him into the jaws of a political crisis that could so easily have undermined the credibility of the country's premier security agency. The return of Labor, albeit under the moderately centrist leadership of Bob Hawke, was always going to present difficulties. The party's left wing was intractably hostile to ASIO, and Barnett could reasonably expect choppy waters to be navigated before his agency found a comfortable berth within the new regime. Inevitably, this played its part in his decisions surrounding the David Combe affair.

The big, bluff South Australian Labor apparatchik had come to Barnett's notice when on Christmas Eve 1982 the head of his counterespionage branch reported that Combe had recently returned from a trip to the Soviet Union as a member of the Australia-USSR Friendship Society. Barnett says this caused him 'no special alarm' at the time, even though he knew the society was used by the KGB to identify 'soft touches'. However, he says, 'We had observed Combe's developing relationship with Valeriy

Ivanov, First Secretary at the Soviet Embassy in Canberra.' And they had assessed Ivanov to be a KGB operative.[4]

Barnett says that he issued orders that Combe was not to be regarded as an ASIO 'target', and that this was a 'kid gloves' case; the real target was Ivanov. But while pursuing the KGB spy via the latest eavesdropping technology in his suburban Canberra residence, they happened upon an extraordinary dinner conversation on 3 March 1983. At the time, Combe was working for a Melbourne businessman, Laurie Matheson, who by chance had been personally involved in the search for Harold Holt when the prime minister was lost in the surf at Cheviot Beach. Matheson, with the support of Deputy Prime Minister and Trade Minister John McEwen, was developing an import/export business with the USSR.

During the dinner at Ivanov's Curtin home, as Combe became progressively drunker and more boastful, he appeared to ASIO to lay himself open to recruitment (or entrapment) as an 'agent of influence'. Barnett says, 'David Combe appeared to be impaling himself on the KGB hook.'[5] He also agreed to a more discreet meeting with the Russian at a Canberra hotel.

Barnett readily agrees that one of his options was to quietly approach Combe 'in order to warn him of the danger we believed him to be in'. He chose not to, he says, because, 'We had taken counsel separately of several contacts of ours who knew Combe well, and the unanimous opinion of each individual was that not only would Combe reject such an approach but also that he was likely to be entirely hostile to ASIO.' Instead, he went to the other extreme and confronted the new prime minister directly, taking with him a recommendation that Ivanov be publicly expelled.

'I realised that the decision to see the prime minister could land me in hot political water,' he says, 'for I thought he might well eject me from his office when David Combe's name was broached. But I believed I still had to act without fear or favour because Australia's national security was at stake.'[6]

This was unquestionably special pleading. In fact, Barnett was perfectly aware that Combe was in bad odour with Hawke following his involvement with Whitlam in the attempt to raise election funds from Saddam Hussein's Ba'ath Party in 1976. He knew of Labor's electoral sensitivities still reverberating from the Petrov Affair. And he was well aware that a new government, desperate to assert its centrist credentials in contrast to its Whitlamesque predecessor, would be eagerly compliant to the recommendations of its chief spycatcher.

This is not to suggest that Barnett took his action only to protect his agency. He harboured an almost ungovernable fear of Soviet intentions for his native land. Indeed, writing only one year before the 1989 collapse of the Soviet Union, he says, 'According to the Soviet planners, Australia will become a Soviet base in South-East Asia and throw a "half-circle of steel" around the Soviet Union's mortal enemy, China.' This would be achieved by first subverting the trade unions, then 'infiltrating the Liberal and National Country Party and compromising their leaders . . . with the final aim to subvert the military forces, so that when the revolution comes they will remain neutral and not join in any reactive attack on the revolutionary left'.[7]

In fact, within the agency there was a strong movement, powered by the young graduate intake, that felt the 'old guard' was overly concerned with the USSR threat and pressed for a more wide-ranging counterintelligence regime. But whatever weight may be applied to Barnett's several motivations, the ploy was totally successful. Ivanov was expelled to Moscow, where he subsequently 'disappeared'. Combe was disgraced but not jailed; he was later rehabilitated as an Australian trade commissioner and in time became a power in the South Australian wine industry. ASIO not only expanded its operations but also moved to Canberra where in 1986 it occupied 'a splendid new Central Office building' that Barnett helped to design.

He did not, however, have the pleasure of occupying its spacious corner office overlooking Lake Burley Griffin. In 1985, he retired to Melbourne where until his final illness he enjoyed 'cycling, skiing, tennis, music, birdwatching and MG sportscars'. He died in June 1995.

His 1988 reflection on the Combe affair says much about his somewhat overblown frame of reference. 'I did not then, nor do I now, regard David Combe as having already been recruited by the KGB,' he says, 'but to my mind he was within a hair's breadth of entering the grand gallery of KGB spies, along with Philby, Burgess, Maclean, Fuchs, Walker, Prime, Pathe, Paterson and Arne Treholt.

'I like to think ASIO saved him from such a fate.'[8]

It was, and remains, perfect nonsense. David Combe might well have found himself under pressure from Ivanov to go beyond the usual limits of the lobbyist's bag of tricks. But there is no reason to believe that he would have compromised his country or even the political party he had served so loyally since his teenage years. And there is every reason to believe that if Barnett or one of his lieutenants had taken him aside for a quiet 'word to the wise', he would have dropped the Russian like the proverbial hot potato.

Instead, Barnett preferred to deploy a bureaucratic powerplay in defence of his agency. And he judged Hawke's psychological vulnerability to such an approach with the precision of a brain surgeon. Combe's reputation was eviscerated on ASIO's operating table.

INTELLIGENCE SPREADS ITS WINGS

Australia's senior intelligence service emerged from the second Hope Royal Commission if not triumphant, then certainly vindicated. ASIO would now be permitted to collect foreign intelligence and carry out operations against foreign interests within Australia on behalf of ASIS, thus blurring the lines with its sister agency.

Barnett's successor Alan Wrigley reoriented its approach from his predecessor's Soviet obsession, and a year later had identified 'about three dozen' foreign intelligence officers from ten different countries working against Australia's best interests.

On the other hand, the government would pass amendments to the ASIO Act to place more emphasis on politically motivated violence rather than simply subversion of the state. It required the agency to monitor ethnic migrant groups intent on perpetuating hostilities against each other in Australia – for example, Serbs and Croats, and Arabs and Jews – and to pass its information to the police as flashpoints threatened. Other legislation introduced an inspector-general of intelligence and security, and established judicial, administrative and parliamentary oversight.

By contrast, ASIS remained under a cloud. Its special operations function was removed, except when specifically ordered by government. On 27 February 1984, Stuart Fry stepped aside for the new permanent head, 57-year-old Brigadier Jim Furner, who since 1982 had been the director of the JIO.

A country boy from Warragul, Victoria, Furner graduated from the University of Melbourne shortly after World War II and began his career as a schoolteacher. In 1952, he enlisted in the army and earned his commission at the Portsea Officer Cadet School. He served overseas in South Korea in 1955–56, and on his return transferred to the Intelligence Corps. He was the senior intelligence officer with the Task Force in Vietnam in 1967–68, and rose through the ranks to become deputy director (military) of JIO before retiring from the army to facilitate his promotion to the director's post.

By now ASIS had followed ASIO to the national capital, where it occupied a well-partitioned floor of the Foreign Affairs building. The move meant the loss of some experienced staffers unwilling to forgo Melbourne's gracious charms for the raw 'bush capital'. Furner inherited an operation in serious difficulties, and despite the firm support of his minister, Bill Hayden, the pressure was unremitting. Within months rumours abounded that one of his senior field officers in Jakarta had been caught in a compromising homosexual relationship by the Indonesian counterespionage agency BAKIN. It was alleged that, in return for their silence, the officer had agreed to provide intelligence on sensitive issues such as Australia's developing policies on East Timor and West Papua. While nothing emerged publicly, it was a serious blow to the agency's standing within government.

On 6 April 1984, ASIS suddenly found itself in the international spotlight when the Soviet Embassy in Bangkok accused a counsellor in the Australian Embassy – presumed to be an ASIS operative – of seeking classified documents from one of their officials in exchange for cash plus residency in either Australia or the US. Hayden called the accusation 'a feverish concoction' and gave a 'categorical assurance that no Australian was involved in any way in Bangkok with any other security agency'.[1] It was yet another body blow.

However, in this respect Justice Hope was very firm in his belief that Australia needed an overseas spy agency, and that ASIS was a genuine asset to the nation's security. Moreover, it had scored some notable successes and had even uncovered intelligence 'diamonds'. 'For example,' he says, 'in September/October 1965 following the coup in Indonesia, ASIS was able to continue its intelligence production when other agencies, Australian and Allied, had some difficulties.' Others included Indonesian papers on the 1972 Law of the Sea Conference, and 'the Soviet manual obtained from Indonesian Air Force sources on MIG-21 fighters'.

He recommended that ASIS play a greater role in counter-intelligence operations, which presently accounted for only 9 per cent of its resources. 'Both the US and UK would very much welcome an expanding role for ASIS (and for that matter ASIO) in CI work,' he said. 'ASIS liaison with CIA is harmonious and effective but different in nature from the ASIS/SIS [MI6] relationship. CIA is much more a "foreign" intelligence service and thus treats ASIS with some professional reserve. The Americans expect a more exact quid pro quo from ASIS than does SIS.'

By now ASIS was liaising with all Association of Southeast Asian Nations (ASEAN) intelligence services and with the Japanese Cabinet Research Office. This permitted the agency, Hope said, to handle 'delicate political matters over the intelligence channel'. Liaison services, and some foreign ministers, know that information given to ASIS will not be sourced to individuals and therefore no embarrassment can be suffered as a result of records being released to the public or the media.

'Throughout history,' he said, 'the idea of a secret intelligence service has been over-shot with notions of hostility and has carried undertones of enmity. There is, however, another way of looking at the matter.' The agency might well uncover corruption and nepotism in overseas organisations that might otherwise be the recipients of Australian aid. 'ASIS is also the channel through which the intelligence services of friendly countries may pass to us information they believe we shall find of value,' he said. Indeed, the commissioner said ASIS should actually expand its operations to additional countries, in the collection of economic intelligence and 'in counter-intelligence generally, both defensive and offensive'.

The minister secured the agency a 25 per cent increase in its 1985 budget, and this helped the embattled Furner to reorganise his forces and restore a measure of morale among the troops. It also permitted him, as suggested by Hope, to expand the range of ASIS activities to include economic intelligence, providing insights to government on trade negotiations. And while some senior bureaucrats dismissed ASIS product as marginal, the economic and commercial insights were eagerly sought by Australian industry, particularly that perennial governmental hanger-on, BHP.

By the mid-1980s, under the guiding hand of its highly respected Western Australian CEO Brian Loton, the miner was engaged in a series of international acquisitions, not least the massive Escondida copper mines in Chile. In 1987, the company formalised its alliance with the American Utah corporation to create one of the biggest mining and minerals operations in the world, with major holdings in Australia, Japan, Europe and the Americas. Its Canberra representatives – by now frequently former senior public servants – requested and received regular briefings.

Nevertheless, in the early years of his tenure, Jim Furner was constantly obliged to defend his agency against influential public servants and politicians who remained highly sceptical about its usefulness. They regarded ASIS input to Foreign Affairs reportage to government as marginal at best. Indeed, one Foreign Affairs department head demanded that the ASIS element be separately identified to demonstrate how little originated from that source. A former defence minister, Bill Morrison, was scathing. 'They had curious characters floating around putting in top-secret reports that you could read in the *Far Eastern Economic Review*,' he said. Former secretary of foreign affairs Alan Renouf said, 'I don't see why the government shouldn't seriously consider scrapping the organisation entirely.'[2]

Hope acknowledged the problem, noting that a genuine atmosphere of mutual trust between ASIS and Foreign Affairs 'has been sadly lacking'. 'ASIS has suffered from prejudice and ignorance on the part of not a few officials and some ministers over the years,' he said. He recommended that ASIS officers spend more extended periods in the department prior to and on return from postings abroad.

He also noted the special difficulties of officers having to lead double lives and congratulated the agency in giving women 'a large percentage' of professional positions. 'I found ASIS to be a singularly well-run and well-managed agency,' he concluded.

This would have given Furner the encouragement he needed to struggle on. He would remain at the helm for a record eight and a half years, during which he would guide his agents into other non-traditional areas such as the South-East Asian drug trade and the massive money-laundering of the drug lords to legitimise their ill-gotten gains.

But his freedom of action was inhibited by the operations of a rehabilitated ONA following the departure of the controversial

Bob Furlonger. His successor, Michael Cook, a highly regarded diplomat on the rise, had the ear of Prime Minister Bob Hawke and set the agenda for the intelligence-gathering agencies, particularly ASIS and through the Defence Department, the Defence Signals Directorate (DSD).

ONA spread its net very wide, including projecting future Soviet and Chinese policies, analysing communism in Europe, the flow of boat people from South-East Asia, peacekeeping in Africa, developments in the Middle East and Australia's stake in Antarctica. It was the recipient of American and British intelligence, including some input from the Joint US–Australian facilities at Pine Gap near Alice Springs in the Northern Territory, and Nurrungar in South Australia. While Nurrungar was designed mainly to detect the launching of Soviet Intercontinental Ballistic Missiles (ICBMs), Pine Gap was – and remains – one of the cornerstones of the American defence surveillance program.

It is ideally located in a valley providing a natural, electronically quiet environment. Leaseholders of the surrounding grazing properties had undertaken to keep 'visitors' away; an ASIO office in Alice Springs remained on watch for suspicious strangers; and the local air traffic controllers monitored any unusual light aircraft movements. Codenamed MERINO, Pine Gap is now one of the biggest satellite ground stations in the world. It is a CIA espionage operation originally under the direction of the super-secret National Reconnaissance Office (NRO). It directs the activities of many of America's spy satellites collecting photographic and signals intelligence, including the interception of communications, telemetry and radar. In 1970 it began monitoring the output of a series of Rhyolite geostationary satellites spying on Soviet nuclear activity.

The 'birds' were repositioned to monitor the battle space in Vietnam several times, and in 1971 the India–Pakistan War. However, their principal task was to capture a wide spectrum of military and diplomatic communications and then beam them down to the ground station. In the 1970s and '80s, the telemetry element – electronic reportage from a missile or warhead during a test flight – was top of the CIA's priorities. But increasingly their receptors were adjusted to sweep up telephone calls, radio transmissions and the communications of other satellites.

By the late 1980s, Pine Gap consisted of eight large radomes, a huge computer room and more than 20 support and service buildings. It employed almost 600 personnel, about half Australian and the rest American. However, the CIA officers occupied all the key roles and a great many of the Australians were engaged in unclassified positions as cooks, gardeners, labourers and clerical staff.

The agreement with the US Government meant that 'information derived from the . . . programs conducted at the facility shall be shared by the two governments', in Australia's case via the Department of Defence. ONA in turn received briefings from Military Intelligence and established a demanding schedule with the Australian espionage agencies to supplement the input of the 'cousins'.

The Defence Signals Directorate was also in the process of moving its HQ to Canberra from Melbourne's Albert Park Barracks and was entering a period of exponential expansion. It had been directed for a remarkable 28 years from 1950 by Ralph Thompson, when he succeeded the founder, 'Teddy' Poundler, an Englishman who had retired from the Royal Navy. Thompson had served as a major in the Middle East in World War II with the army's main signals intelligence unit, No. 4 Australian Special Wireless Section. After the war, he joined the Australian Mint as head of the refining department and moved to run the Department of Defence's Communications Group in 1950. He had overseen the development of a highly professional operation with technical innovations that led the world. He had positioned DSD to increase its civilian personnel by almost 50 per cent from 1981 to more than 650 employees in 1990, with an annual operating budget of about $80 million to run their ground stations.

Its oldest signals interception base, HMAS *Harman* on the outskirts of Canberra, was established in 1939–40, but it was continually upgraded to intercept diplomatic traffic to and from the capital's foreign embassies as well as other transmissions emanating from South-East Asia. *Harman* also had an Adcock radio DF system for ocean surveillance. Plans were under way for an $80 million facility in the Riverina at Morandah and Lyndoch designed to complement *Harman*.

New facilities coming on line included the $100 million base at Kojarena near Geraldton in Western Australia, formally designated the Australian Defence Satellite Communications Station (ADSCS), where massive satellite dishes swept up data that provided insights on the activities of governments and individuals of interest. The ADSCS monitored signals from satellites in geostationary orbits over the Indian Ocean and South-East Asia, intercepting data from Russian, Japanese, Chinese, Indonesian, Indian and Pakistani sources. It also captured INTELSAT, COMSAT and MARISAT messages from maritime communications satellites. The new Geraldton facility was followed by upgrades to the Pearce Air Force Base outside Perth to monitor naval and air signal traffic over the Indian Ocean.

On the eastern side of the continent, DSD had developed new facilities at Cabarlah, near Toowoomba in Queensland, designed to monitor high-frequency (HF) transmissions across South-East Asia and the South-West Pacific. In 1988, a detachment from Cabarlah established a new $25 million station near Bamaga at the tip of Cape York. Its primary purpose was to monitor communications in Papua New Guinea and the Pacific Islands. The signals interception facilities at Shoal Bay near Darwin had been upgraded to monitor the activities of the Indonesian military and would play a key role in the uprising in East Timor towards the end of the century. And plans were underway for an $80 million HF network for the Defence Department near Wagga Wagga. When completed, it would be known (incorrectly) as DSD Riverina.

As well as its Australian bases, DSD had joint operations with the British in Hong Kong to spy on the Chinese mainland, and highly sophisticated intercept equipment (codenamed Reprieve) at its embassies in Jakarta and Bangkok. It coordinated with the three arms of the military, which also ran intercepts from ships, aircraft and the army's 72 Electronic Warfare (EW) Signals Squadron at Cabarlah.

The sheer volume of this product required highly sophisticated computer analysis to decode and extract the nuggets of usable information from the ocean of dross, and skilled analysis to join the dots of suspicious activity. Since much of it was encoded, ASIS operatives were tasked with obtaining access to the code books and other devices in classic espionage operations. They achieved some notable successes. But paradoxically this contributed to their conventional HUMINT material being overwhelmed by signals intelligence. Moreover, the loss of the agency's special operations arm provided an opening for another of the Special Forces pillars – the SAS – to step into the breach. ASIS officers would continue to be trained in close combat skills and the black arts of 'break and enter', and sophisticated tradecraft, but on special operations the regiment would increasingly supply the frontline operatives.

The Defence White Paper of March 1987 focused on the defence of continental Australia and areas of direct military interest in the region. Shortly after the white paper's release, a military coup in Fiji tested the limits of the new doctrine. The SAS deployed a squadron in an operation to rescue and evacuate Australian personnel. However, the situation stabilised before their intervention was required. Similarly, a civil outbreak in Vanuatu brought the regiment to the brink, but it subsided before they went into action.

By then a new and influential CO had taken up his post at Swanbourne. Lieutenant Colonel Jim Wallace, at 36, was the first leader of the regiment with no war service in his record. He had graduated from Duntroon in 1973 and had served as a troop and squadron commander. He had also deployed with the UN as an observer in Syria and Lebanon in 1980.

Wallace was a devoted Christian and, while popular with the men, he brought an unusual dimension to the regiment. On retirement, he would become leader of the conservative Australian Christian Lobby, but even while CO he was able to divine at least one 'happy miracle' when, in his view, a healing service conducted at HQ saved a soldier injured in a training exercise from either dying or becoming a quadriplegic. Instead he survived as a paraplegic.[3]

One trooper who served under him says, 'He was the complete professional. He made a point of spending time where he could with the men. I recall we were in Darwin after a CT [counterterrorism] exercise and we all went to the Vic Hotel for a beer. Jim came in and bought the whole squadron a drink, talked to the boys and left us to enjoy ourselves.

'He was a guy who really invigorated a lot of things, and initiated the remuneration tribunal to come and reassess the pay.'[4]

Wallace and his immediate predecessors had also expanded the range of training programs to provide interest and excitement among soldiers without a war to fight. They were encouraged to develop their parachuting expertise, and a mountain-climbing wing was formed to conquer Mount Everest. In their first attempt, they were turned back by bad weather. Individual members then joined expeditions or formed small teams to tackle peaks around the world.

Captains Pat Cullinan and Tom Moylan climbed Mount Kilimanjaro, while Captain Jim Truscott conquered the formidable Ganesh IV in the Himalayas, despite losing his climbing partner in an avalanche. Captain Tim McOwan scaled the Matterhorn in Switzerland. In 1986, ten members of the wing made it to the summit of Mount Victoria in Papua New Guinea. One team member, Trooper Clint Palmer, says, 'When we got to the top, there's a rock cairn and a little tin with notes in it. We discovered that we were only the seventh group ever to be up there. We had taken our weapons and full packs up but left them at base camp at 11,500 feet. On the way back down, the weather started closing in. The clouds started to build up and going back across this ridge it was clear and then quite suddenly, whiteout. Instantaneously we all had vertigo, loss of balance and disorientation so I dropped and stayed down on my hands and knees for about 30 seconds and pop, it was clear as a bell again.

'It was basically a shakedown exercise, getting to know each other, going through certain procedures but just spending time together for a week or so.'[5]

Finally, in 1988, the leaders of the wing felt they were ready for another assault on the ultimate challenge. When they discovered that the Australian Alpine Climbing Club had booked Everest for that year, they joined with them to form the Australian Bicentenary Everest Expedition. And being the SAS, they decided to make the assault that little bit harder by spurning the assistance of high-altitude porters.

Of the 18 expedition members, four were either current or ex-SAS serving members. Majors Cullinan, Truscott and Rick Moor were SAS, with Cullinan now in 1 Commando Regiment, while Sergeant Norm Crookston was a leader of the SASR climbing wing. Cullinan actually reached the summit with a civilian companion, Paul Baynes, in the first successful assault from Nepal without porters.

By 1990, the SAS had been in the counterterrorism role for more than a decade and, while they had continued to develop their warfare skills, there seemed little prospect that they would have to deploy them anytime soon. The end of the Cold War in 1989 had demanded a fundamental change in their priorities, and they turned their attention increasingly to the Asia-Pacific area. When UN peacekeeping missions arose, the SAS hierarchy used the opportunity to deploy small teams to familiarise the unit with conditions in potential hotspots where they might well be needed in the future.

The new CO, Lieutenant Colonel Don Higgins, says that when he took up his post in 1993 he found 'a unit with a wide range of regional training activities as well as ongoing counterterrorism functions. Peacekeeping operations were trickling in, although we could never seem to get enough to please everyone. The unit contribution to the UN missions in Cambodia, Somalia, Rwanda and Iraq were largely positive experiences and our contingents were widely praised.'[6]

Against the usual opposition from traditionalists, the ADF hierarchy accepted the need for a reorganisation of its Special Forces. In February 1990, they established new Special Forces Headquarters in Canberra, with Colonel Chris Roberts as its first commander. Roberts had fought in Vietnam as a troop commander of 3 Squadron SAS. He then served in a number of regimental and training appointments including officer commanding 1 SAS Squadron and brigade major 1st Task Force before taking over as the CO of SASR.

His new command incorporated the SAS and 1 Commando Regiment under the chief of the general staff for training and administration, but reporting directly to the chief of the Defence Force (CDF) for operations including counterterrorism. It was a major step forward in the development of an integrated Special Forces command. And, at the same time, DSD was on the move from Melbourne to Defence headquarters at Canberra's Russell Offices 'to facilitate a closer relationship with Defence, other intelligence agencies and key government departments'. The move would be completed by Christmas 1992, when another piece of the Special Forces jigsaw now fitted neatly into place.

SPECIAL FORCES EVOLUTION

Australia was not alone in appreciating the growing importance of Special Forces within its defence establishment. The US had created its own Special Operations Command in 1986, incorporating 16 battalions from various Special Forces units as well as three air force wings, 165 dedicated aircraft and 89 navy boats. Its commander-in-chief was a three-star general with headquarters at MacDill Air Force Base in Tampa, Florida. By comparison, Australia's Special Forces command was small beer indeed.

While the SAS had established a strong record in the field, 1 Commando Regiment had been created only in February 1981 by combining the two reserve commando companies from Sydney and Melbourne, and 126 Signals Squadron. The first CO, Lieutenant Colonel Peter McDougall, was ordered to establish a headquarters 'and a framework for the support of counter-terrorist training on the Australian east coast'.[1]

McDougall and his HQ team leant heavily on the SASR and the Directorate of Special Action Forces in Canberra under Colonel Michael Jeffrey for support in the early stages. 'I had expected some resistance to the previously independent units being brought under a new Headquarters,' he says, 'but thankfully cooperation was generally good and we worked together well. I was most impressed by the enthusiasm and capabilities of the average army reserve commandos and the many long-serving "characters" who were the backbone of, and the repository of, the specialist skills.'[2]

Later that year, he moved the HQ from a small office at Moore Park Barracks to a more permanent site in a Defence Department building in Randwick recently vacated by the Australian Services Canteen Organisation. From there he initiated a series of counter-terrorism operations involving the SASR, the AFP and state police forces.

In 1983, the regiment was given responsibility for Special Warfare Development, with the task of writing the Australian Army's training manual for close-quarter fighting and counter-terrorism training. The SAS leadership was not impressed as they had previously held responsibility in this area. But on 7 February, Captain Greg Mawkes, a Vietnam veteran who had risen through the ranks at SASR to become senior instructor of its Tactics Wing, transferred to 1 Commando Regiment to develop and formulate the Special Warfare doctrine at the Swan Island facility in Port Phillip Bay.

'There was a greater emphasis on company and regimental strength raids as opposed to the small scale raids [in the SAS],' he says. 'Individual training gave more emphasis to infantry battle skills.'[3] It was a trend that would increasingly come to distinguish the commando unit from the SAS. The following year, Mawkes was promoted to major and given command of 2 Commando Company within the regiment.

Over the next five years 1st Commando, often in conjunction with SASR, conducted large-scale training exercises in most Australian states and Papua New Guinea. The 126 Signals Squadron broke new ground with the recruitment of women signallers – their first appearance in the Special Forces front line. The commandos were enthusiastic mountain climbers and ran a highly regarded mountain warfare course in the snowfields of Perisher Valley, Charlotte Pass and the wintry peaks of Tasmania. They became the repository of snow and high-altitude warfare skills in the ADF, and these would be called upon in future actions in Afghanistan.

In 1989, Lieutenant Colonel Allen Valentine, a former SAS squadron commander, was appointed CO. He immediately began preparations for Exercise Kangaroo 89, a major Special Forces operation in northern Australia. An American unit, 1 Special Forces (Airborne) Group, from Washington State, participated, and the highlight was a night raid when four members of 126 Signals Squadron boarded a USAF MC-130 Talon aircraft, black as a starless night, and flew beneath the radar towards the 'defenders' of RAAF Tindal airbase.

As they approached, the Talon used its electronic counter-measures to render it virtually invisible to the radar operators. When they landed, they lowered the ramp to discharge the signals team, all wearing night vision goggles (NVGs), in a specially refitted Land Rover. They sped towards the control tower with guns blazing and then turned their weapons on the aircraft parked nearby.

The troops defending the base – facing each other across the tarmac – opened fire in the total darkness, causing mayhem to their own forces as the Land Rover returned to its aircraft and was flown off into the night. The whole raid had taken less than five minutes.

The exercise provided a welcome boost to morale, and it was followed in 1990 by a recruiting drive that, for the first time, included Brisbane-based reservists. But as the training commitment was becoming ever more demanding, the personnel turnover was reaching crisis point and the northern capital was unable to stem the tide. Moreover, officers were now required to pass a selection course based on the SAS model – a physical and mental ordeal that many found daunting. Throughout the 1990s this would be a perennial problem.

Major Jim Truscott, whose mountaineering feats had singled him out from his SAS colleagues, was appointed OC of the Melbourne unit in 1990. He did his best to keep his troops fully engaged, and in his enthusiasm for mountain warfare he devised a raid by ski-borne troops on the Snowy River hydroelectric power station at Guthega, New South Wales. 'The patrol commenced with a river crossing,' he says, 'and they continued upwards for nearly 1,600 metres through unconsolidated snow and horizontal scrub.

'From here on in it was necessary to ski by night to evade detection from patrols around the network of power stations and pondages in the Snowy Mountains. After several nights, the group was in a position to make a close reconnaissance of the power station nestled at the bottom of a deep valley. They chose to abseil [and enter] through ground level glass windows to achieve surprise. Timed demolition charges were placed on the governors without which the turbines would accelerate and seize. This was an operative's dream and the team raced through the night to await pickup from an old construction camp airfield downstream. The Mountain Warfare capability was proven.'

The 126 Signals Squadron was also spreading its operational wings. Having won the coveted Mountbatten Trophy for Special Force excellence in 1992, the squadron provided key personnel to the hazardous peacekeeping force in Somalia. There they worked for more than a year with the US 5 Special Forces Group. One of the team members, Corporal Geoff (Chips) Rafferty, says, 'These guys had a vast array of the latest and greatest military equipment: the best body armour, armoured Humvees and the best weapons. They pretty much had access to Black Hawk helicopters as they wished for their patrols.'[4]

It was the shooting down of two of these aircraft that resulted in the tragic 'Black Hawk Down' incident. Some of the wounded survivors were able to escape to the US compound, but others were isolated near the crash sites and surrounded by a vicious mob throughout the night. Early next morning a combined force of American, Malaysian and Pakistani soldiers in tanks and armoured personnel carriers reached the first crash site and rescued the survivors. But the second site had been overrun by Somalis, who killed two men and captured the American pilot Michael Durant. American gunships responded, and, at best estimate, several hundred Somali militiamen were killed. Durant was released and the incident formed the basis of a popular Hollywood movie starring Australia's Eric Bana.

When President Bill Clinton withdrew the American forces, the SAS sent ten members of 3 Squadron to protect the 67 Australian aid workers attached to the Australian Services Contingent (ASC). Known as J Troop, under Sergeant Gary Kingston, they used UN armoured personnel carriers as well as their own Land Cruisers. They commandeered an operating base at the airport, which quickly became known as Camp Gerbil after the small rodents that infested Mogadishu. Firefights were continually breaking out in the city, and when a new ASC team arrived on rotation the SAS operators guarded their disembarkation with overlapping arcs of fire.

In May, a Canadian civilian helicopter crash-landed 20 kilometres from the city, and an armed mob threatened a replay of Black Hawk Down. Eight 'Gerbils' took a chopper to the crash scene, and they flung open the doors to reveal a fully armed Special Force with weapons primed for action. The Somali gunmen in the crowd melted away.

Somali gangs surrounded a three-vehicle UN convoy of Malaysian, New Zealand and Italian personnel headed to the airport. The convoy commander surrendered to the gunmen, and all were bashed and threatened with execution. They were released only after prolonged talks with the local warlords. The Australians then intervened and escorted them safely to the airport. The Gerbils withdrew with the ASC in November, their work highly commended by HQ command.

By then command of 1 Commando Regiment had passed to Lieutenant Colonel Graham Ferguson, formerly with the SASR. 'Prior to assuming command my views on the regiment were not very flattering,' he says. 'My arrogant prejudices were similar to those harboured by other regular Special Forces soldiers who had limited exposure to 1 Commando Regiment. Not long after assuming command I found my preconceived views were baseless and so very flawed.'[5]

In 1994, former SAS commander Jim Wallace, now a brigadier and director of Special Forces in Canberra, proposed relocating 126 Signals Squadron to Holsworthy, the main army base in New South Wales. It was the first step in a long-term reorganisation that would eventually involve the transformation of the commando component of the nation's Special Forces. During the mid-1990s, the army was fully engaged in developing a 'vision statement' for the next century titled Army '21. One of the most significant decisions was to transform a Holsworthy-based battalion, 4 RAR, into a commando unit under the banner of HQ Special Operations. All training for this new professional unit would be undertaken by a cadre from 1 Commando Company under Major Hans Fleer and Captain Chris Wallis.

The role of the SAS also came under review, and its new CO, Lieutenant Colonel Mike Silverstone, set up a team of majors to devise new approaches and objectives. They organised trials to discover whether Sabre squadrons could be recast to focus on particular countries in the region rather than the traditional water, vehicle and air insertion specialties; and they put greater stress on foreign-language training. They were well placed to arrange the trials since, over the previous decade, they had established good working relationships with Special Forces from Thailand, Malaysia, Singapore, Brunei and Indonesia. Some had conducted counterterrorism training in Australia with special emphasis on countering aircraft hijacking at the SAS Bindoon facility and at oil platforms offshore.

The regiment was struck a savage blow in 1996 in a night exercise at Townsville with the 5th Aviation Regiment in Black Hawk helicopters. On the evening of 12 June, six helicopters were approaching a 'defended area', with the pilots wearing NVGs. Four of the six were carrying SAS troopers, the other two providing fire support on each flank.

As they approached the target, with the three leading aircraft carrying the assault force, the left forward helicopter unaccountably veered right, into the path of the centre aircraft. When they collided, one fell from the sky and all 12 troopers aboard were killed. The other, piloted by Captain David Burke, made a crash landing but burst into flames on impact and six other soldiers died. Burke, whose professionalism in landing the wounded 'bird' earned him great respect, says, 'There were rounds going off, there was ammunition flying in the air, there were explosions in the back of the aircraft going off and these men, both SAS and air crew, were going into the flames and cutting people out and bringing them out.'

The SASR was devastated by the tragedy. The 18 killed and the others wounded were intimately connected within the tightly knit SAS community. Mike Silverstone acted swiftly to assist the families, while at the same time triggering a standby plan to re-establish the regiment's counterterrorism capability. But he was not able to stem the resentment from many of his men towards the Big Army, which seemed to be unfairly blaming the regiment for the accident. This was exacerbated when the army's board of inquiry, headed by the chief of staff at Land HQ, Brigadier Paul O'Sullivan, recommended that charges be laid against Major Bob Hunter, OC of 1 Squadron, his operations officer Captain Sean Bellis and Major Chris Jameson of the 5th Aviation Regiment.

A year later the charges were dropped but the resentment remained. Chris Jameson, who by then had left the army, was 'disgusted' by some senior officers. 'The hierarchy has been able to damage reputations with relative impunity and the accused have had no opportunity to clear their names,' he says. 'I would have been more than happy to stand my ground so the real faults could have been exposed. They have slunk out of it and left a sour taste in everyone's mouth.'[6] Bob Hunter and Sean Bellis also left the army.

In the aftermath, as part of the reorganisation of Special Forces, the Special Forces Headquarters was moved from Canberra to Sydney and lost its direct link with the CDF. Henceforth, it would answer to the land commander and the commander Australian theatre. Only on special operations would it have direct access to the CDF.

The restructure took a year to complete. From 1998, the Special Forces Group comprised SASR, 1 Commando Regiment (Army Reserve), 4 RAR (Commando) and 126 Commando Signals Squadron. Forward planning provided for 4 RAR to take over the SAS's counterterrorism role. In the meantime, the SAS remained the front line of Australia's counterterrorist force.

Other elements of Australia's Special Forces structure were also undergoing relocation and expansion at this time. A relative newcomer, the defence aspects of Australia's space activities, was coming into focus. Pine Gap remained the cornerstone of the operation, and Australians were taking a greater role in the management and analytical demands of the facility. Australia also benefited from the US Defense Satellite Communications System (DSCS), with ground terminals around the world providing 'high-quality secure voice, high-speed data between automated command and control centres, high-resolution graphics and imagery, and rapid transmission of sensor data'.[7] As well, the DSCS supported navy ship-to-shore communications, ground mobile forces, and the diplomatic traffic of US, British and North Alantic Treaty Organization (NATO) stations. Moreover, the progressive development of the global positioning system would transform Special Forces operations in fields as disparate as helicopter insertions and sniper rifle calibration.

Telecommunications links in virtually every geographical area of the world could be established in the time required to deploy a portable terminal. The effect was to revolutionise battlefield communications. But while it would give the US and its allies remarkable advantages in command and control, as will be seen, it was not particularly well suited to combating the low-tech enemy forces in the Middle East and Afghanistan that were already making their presence felt on the US defence radar. Indeed, it may well have contributed to an unwarranted sense of invincibility in the years ahead.

Australia's fully owned and operated satellite defence terminal, codenamed Project Sparrow, at Watsonia Barracks in Melbourne began as a 60-foot-diameter (18-metre) Heavy Earth Terminal operated by a highly classified troop of 6 Signal Regiment. It provided a communications link via the DSCS system between DSD headquarters and the US National Security Agency at Fort Meade in Maryland. According to the ANU's Desmond Ball, now professor of the Defence and Strategic Studies Centre, there has been a continuing stream of Australian space technicians undergoing training at Fort Meade and Fort Gordon in Augusta, Georgia.

The main component of the Georgia post was, and remains, the advanced individual training of the military signal corps.

Australia's satellite system grew substantially in the 1990s. The AUSSAT A-series were launched in the mid-1980s and some are still in service, having been renamed the Optus A-series. Their successors, the Optus B-series, were sent aloft from the United States in the early 1990s, while the Western Pacific Laser Tracking Network (WPLTN) was launched in 1998 and is owned by the Canberra-based Electro Optic Systems (EOS). EOS remains pivotal to the operation, with highly classified units within the astronomical observatory of Canberra's Mount Stromlo, in nearby Queanbeyan and in both Singapore and Tucson, Arizona.

The ADSCS at Kojarena near Geraldton would be upgraded to four satellite tracking dishes, allowing it to refine its interception of communications from Russian, Chinese, Japanese, Indian and Pakistani satellites. It would be jointly manned by Australian and US personnel. All would feed into Australia's Special Forces capability.

•

In 1994, Major Jim Truscott led an expedition to recall and honour one of the outstanding Special Forces operations of World War II on the 50th anniversary of Operation Rimau. While Rimau ended tragically, it had been conducted in the best traditions of the commando units and the death of all team members had left many questions unanswered. Truscott's six team members – all former and serving officers and men from SASR and 1 Commando – followed the original escape route from the islands off Singapore to the southerly tip of Indonesia's Lingga Archipelago. Paddling two-man kayaks they planned to cover some 240 nautical miles in conditions similar to those experienced by Lyon, Davidson, Page and their compatriots.

Jim Truscott says, 'The debilitating effect of the arduous conditions, lack of food, 35 degree heat and humidity combined with being wet 24 hours a day cannot be overstated.' The wind and currents meant that they actually paddled more than 500 kilometres through Indonesian waters without major incident or illness. They returned via Bukit Timah, where the last of the Rimau men were so barbarically executed 50 years previously. No sign or memorial stood to record their passing.

Coincidentally, it was at this time that another tragedy from the past returned to haunt the Special Forces community: the Balibo Five. By now it was 20 years since the Indonesian takeover of East Timor, but a combination of the Catholic Church and Portuguese reactionaries had supplied the anti-Indonesian fighters with guns and materiel. The Indonesian Government had turned the province into a virtual Kopassus protectorate. This was a recipe for violent upheaval and in 1991 following the cancellation of a Portuguese parliamentary delegation to Dili – and in the presence of a British cameraman – Indonesian troops opened fire on a crowd of protestors at the Santa Cruz cemetery. The graphic footage caused outrage around the world and growing support within the United Nations for East Timorese independence.

In November 1992, the Fretilin guerrilla leader Xanana Gusmão had been arrested and the following year he was sentenced to 20 years' imprisonment. By then Shirley Shackleton, widow of one of the Balibo Five, had become an effective spokesperson for Timorese independence coupled with demands for an inquiry into the circumstances surrounding the death of her husband and his colleagues. That year she joined with several hundred European activists and a big Australian media contingent in an oceangoing Portuguese ferry, the *Lusitania Expresso*, setting out from Darwin to run an Indonesian naval blockade surrounding the island.

When the ferry reached Indonesian waters and was confronted by naval ships with Indonesian sailors manning the guns, the vessel halted. Despite attempts by some of the activists to provoke a confrontation, the ship then turned tail for Darwin.[8]

However, the campaign was bolstered in 1996 when the Nobel Peace Prize was awarded to Fretilin spokesman José Ramos-Horta and the East Timorese Catholic bishop Carlos Belo 'in the hope that the award would spur efforts to find a diplomatic solution to the conflict in East Timor based on the people's right to self-determination'. The effect was to increase international pressure on Indonesia and give free rein to anti-Indonesian sentiment among some members of the Australian political and media establishment. It also put added pressure on military planners and the intelligence agencies, notably ASIS and the Defence Signals Directorate. But no one anticipated the political missteps and racist excesses that would lead to a violent implosion in the years ahead.

REFERENDUM IN EAST TIMOR

The raising of 4 RAR (Commando) was proving more challenging than expected. Brigadier Jim Wallace, as director of Special Forces, found himself confronted by Big Army traditionalists. 'It soon became clear,' he says, 'that to get the infantry "mafia" behind the proposal we needed to re-raise 4 RAR and make it a commando regiment.'[1] According to historian Peter Collins, a former OC of 1 Commando Company, 'The shape of the Australian Army and the process of change was – and remains – in the firm grip of those trained in the mainstream of conventional warfare, based on the solid infantry skills developed and practised by the RAR since its inception in 1947.' Moreover, he says, 'Not everyone in 4 RAR welcomed the prospect of converting from the core business of infantry to Special Forces and quite a few transferred to other RAR battalions. Not everyone who "gave it a go" succeeded in passing the more demanding Special Forces tests. The conversion was not simply a renaming exercise. It was a rigorous and demanding improvement of certain standards.'[2]

In fact, so demanding was the process that by 2000 they had raised only two commando companies; so it was decided that the counterterrorism role should remain with the SAS. By then, however, the regiment had begun the most intense operational decade in its history, and counterterrorism was only one of the many demands on its thinly stretched resources.

By 1997, another of the pivotal COs of SASR, Lieutenant Colonel Mike Hindmarsh, had taken over from Silverstone. A Duntroon graduate, he had been both a troop and squadron commander in SASR and had also served at the headquarters of Britain's and Australia's Special Forces commands. He directed the SAS deployment to Bougainville as part of the Truce Monitoring Group when Australia took command of the operation in 1998. And when the Cambodian co-prime minister Hun Sen the same year led a violent coup d'état against his non-communist coalition partners in government, Hindmarsh directed a short, sharp operation to airlift almost 500 Australians and other expats from Phnom Penh. He sent Major Jim Truscott to Butterworth in Malaysia to liaise with the US forces planning to evacuate their people from Cambodia across the Thai border.

Truscott had benefited from Silverstone's decision to enhance the regiment's language skills and says, 'By now I was feeling quite confident in conversing in the Indo-Malay language whenever the opportunity presented itself. As it turned out, I did little more than sit in a hangar in a Royal Malaysia Air Force base.' However, he too was concerned at a sense of drift in the SAS and considered writing a book designed, he says, 'to drag the regiment into the twenty-first century'.

'Operations aside, something had to be done to propel SAS forward. It was languishing from the lack of any contact with terrorists, despite maintaining one of the world's most sophisticated counterterrorist forces for over twenty years. We needed another role, and the majority of my time was spent in operational research to identify the nature of futuristic special operations.'[3]

Hindmarsh had the first taste of operating with the Americans in the Middle East when the Howard Government in 1998 decided to deploy the SAS to Kuwait in support of proposed US actions against the Saddam Hussein Government in Iraq. The CO, his logistics officer, Major Brad Rickerby, and Major Truscott arrived in Kuwait on 15 February and set about organising 1 Squadron and a New Zealand SAS contingent into an Anzac unit that he hoped would be 'the force of choice' for the US commander of Special Forces missions.

While he welded his force into a viable unit the crisis was quickly defused as Saddam parried diplomatically. The Allied build-up of Special Forces at the huge Ali Al Salem airbase turned into a frustrating wait. Truscott says, 'Within two months operation Desert Thunder had petered out into operation Desert Spring. The SEALs brought their desert patrol vehicles and the Green Berets brought their Humvees. We brought our long-range patrol vehicles [LRPVs] and the Air Force came with Talon C-130s, Pavelow and Chinook helicopters. It was a Special Forces theme park and, not to be outdone, the Kuwaitis roared around in Yugoslav M84 tanks, a direct copy of Iraqi T72s. This was all about the smell of cordite over the handset.

'Fighting to get into and out of theatre was the biggest battle for us. The only casualties were the 150 Muslims killed during the stoning of the devil when the Haj finished in early April. Witnessing a helicopter aerial shoot at night and its attendant accidental discharges was the closest thing to getting shot. For the majority of my time I worked in an air-conditioned tent scheming plans in the desert to fill in my time. When totally bored, I climbed the huge, missile-damaged aircraft bunkers at our air base.'[4]

Lieutenant Colonel Rowan Tink, chief of staff at Special Operations HQ in Sydney, arrived in April to take over from Hindmarsh and organise the withdrawal. By June 1998, all SAS forces had returned to Swanbourne but for a liaison officer who remained in Kuwait. Hindmarsh had rediscovered the lessons learnt by the Vietnam Task Force in working with the Americans. 'We have a different culture,' he says, 'more reliant on animal cunning and individual initiative born from years of having to make do with what we've got . . . the overarching lesson is the need to blend rather than replace our basic soldierly common sense and nous with their application of technology. The danger is that in taking the technology route, as we must do, we become lazy and lose over time those fundamental soldierly skills which have traditionally set us apart from the rest.'[5] It is a lesson that successive Special Forces leaders have had to reinforce.

By the end of 1998, the Middle East operations had given way to a crisis much closer to home. Portugal, despite having abandoned its neglected East Timor colony 20 years earlier, now pursued the moral high ground with a martyr's intensity, ably supported by the worldwide diplomatic efforts of the Vatican. The pressure on Indonesia was unremitting. When the South African president Nelson Mandela visited Jakarta, for example, he not only talked with President Suharto but also pointedly met with the imprisoned Xanana Gusmão and urged his release.

Suharto was losing his grip on power as the Asian financial crisis battered the economy, and his own moral authority was undermined by massive corruption within not only his administration but also his close family. In February and March 1998, there were price riots, bomb threats and bombings on Java, and soon the unrest was spreading throughout the archipelago. By May students were holding demonstrations on campuses across the country, and on 12 May at Jakarta's elite Trisakti University security forces shot and killed four demonstrators. The capital was enflamed and the military responded with unconcealed brutality. Many civilians died in burning malls and supermarkets; others were shot or beaten to death.

Suharto bowed to the inevitable and resigned on 21 May, naming the mercurial B. J. Habibie to take his place. Born in South Sulawesi in 1936, Habibie had gained an engineering degree in Germany and spent much of his adult life there working as a research assistant and later an executive in transportation companies. He returned to Indonesia in 1974 at Suharto's behest and by 1991 was overseeing ten state-owned industries, including shipping and aviation, steel, arms, communications and energy. He became a permanent fixture in Suharto's entourage and was named vice-president in March 1998.

Successive Australian governments had committed themselves to supporting Indonesia's claims to East Timor, and Habibie had frequently declared his determination to keep the province within the Indonesian fold. However, soon after his rise to the presidency he appeared to be open to negotiation for a measure of autonomy within the Indonesian polity. The Australian media, still affronted by the death of the Balibo Five, pressed the case against Indonesia. The opposition Foreign Affairs spokesman Laurie Brereton now signalled that Labor might well change its policy to support an Independent East Timor.

Prime Minister John Howard, who had supported East Timorese integration within Indonesia, now took a fateful step. On 19 December 1998, he sent Habibie a letter in which he made 'some suggestions about the East Timor situation'. Drafted with the assistance of Foreign Minister Alexander Downer, the letter emphasised that 'Australia's support for Indonesia's sovereignty is unchanged and that the interests of Australia, Indonesia and East Timor are best served by East Timor remaining part of Indonesia.' But he then opened the door for a significant revision. 'Your offer of autonomy for East Timor was a bold and clear-sighted step that has opened a window of opportunity both to achieve a peaceful settlement in East Timor and to resolve an issue that has long caused Indonesia difficulties in the international community,' Howard wrote. 'However, I fear that the boldness of your offer has not been matched with the degree of progress in negotiations which might have been expected.'

He suggested that Indonesia negotiate directly with the East Timorese leadership rather than the Portuguese. 'A decisive element of East Timorese opinion is insisting on an act of self-determination,' he said. 'Their position, with a fair degree of international support, seems to be strengthening on this. It might be worth considering, therefore, a means of addressing the East Timorese desire for an act of self-determination in a manner that avoids an early and final decision on the future status of the province.

'One way of doing this would be to build into the autonomy package a review mechanism along the lines of the Matignon Accords [with the French] in New Caledonia. The Matignon Accords have enabled a compromise political solution to be implemented, while deferring a referendum on the final status of New Caledonia for many years. The successful implementation of an autonomy package with a built-in review mechanism would allow time to convince the East Timorese of the benefits of autonomy within the Indonesian Republic . . .'

Howard then offered to talk through the suggestions with him. But the unpredictable Habibie reportedly 'brandished' the letter at an Indonesian Cabinet meeting in January 1999 and told his ministers that Indonesia should move straight to a choice between autonomy and independence for East Timor.

According to intelligence reports, Foreign Minister Ali Alatas was the only dissenting voice. Australia's former ambassador in Jakarta, Dick Woolcott, says, 'Alatas received no support. The economic ministers were glad to be rid of the cost. Some of Habibie's stronger Islamic ministers were happy "to be rid of 600,000 Catholics" as one put it. That such a major decision could be taken without full consideration and with such limited discussion by an impatient, erratic interim president can only be regarded as irresponsible.'[6]

Woolcott had played a significant role in the aftermath of the Balibo Five tragedy and was widely regarded as an enthusiastic proponent of closer ties with Indonesia. Educated at Geelong Grammar and the University of Melbourne, he became spokesman for the Foreign Affairs Department in the 1960s and gained a prominent media profile. After his Indonesian posting he would continue his rise through the ranks as Australia's ambassador to the UN from 1982 to 1988 and then secretary of the department until 1992. By the time of Howard's letter he had retired from the department but remained an active participant in regional affairs as the founding director of the Asia Society's AustralAsia Centre.

News of the Habibie Cabinet's decision – to have a snap referendum among the East Timorese within six months – provoked a violent reaction in the province from pro-Indonesian supporters. Formed into local militia bands, they rioted and attacked their Fretilin opponents. The Indonesian military not only refused to intervene; evidence would later come to light that they had encouraged and armed the militia. When Howard finally met with Habibie at a summit in Bali, he urged that a UN peacekeeping force oversee the process. Habibie rejected the idea out of hand as an 'insult' to the TNI. From that moment, Australia's intervention, with its Special Forces playing a major role, became inevitable.

The result of the referendum was predictable: almost 80 per cent voted for independence. The response from the TNI and their militia supporters was equally foreseeable: widespread violence, the destruction of infrastructure and 300,000 refugees taking flight into Indonesian West Timor and other provinces. The international community rose to demand intervention and on 12 September 1999 President Habibie bowed to unrelenting pressure. 'A couple of minutes ago,' he said, 'I called the United Nations Secretary General Mr Kofi Annan, to inform [him] about our readiness to accept international peacekeeping forces through the United Nations, from friendly nations, to restore peace and security in East Timor.'

The UN authorised the raising of a multinational military force known as Interfet, to which 17 nations contributed, with Australia providing about half of the 9,900 total and Major General Peter Cosgrove as the commander. On 20 September 1999, he and his troops deployed to the battlefield.

Cosgrove, born in 1947, was a Big Army traditionalist from a military family. His father was a warrant officer in the army and Peter was educated at Waverley College. After graduation from Duntroon, he fought with the 9th Battalion in Vietnam and was awarded the Military Cross. He later commanded the 1st Battalion RAR and, like most Big Army men, he was suspicious of Special Forces. Timor would transform his perceptions, not just of the SAS but also of ASIS, which had been very active in the province. A colleague says, 'Cosgrove told me afterwards that he'd never used ASIS before Timor and didn't think much of them; afterwards he said he'd never go into a conflict without them.'[7]

The SAS had been preparing for action in Indonesia – and particularly East Timor – since January 1999, when Lieutenant Colonel Tim McOwan succeeded Mike Hindmarsh and Major James McMahon took command of 3 SAS Squadron, which would be the first to deploy. In May, they organised a month of intensive language study, with half the squadron learning Bahasa Indonesia and the other half Tetum, the local Timorese language. McMahon had worked with Cosgrove in April, when he and his staff were planning the evacuation of Australians from Indonesia at Cosgrove's base at Enoggera. McOwan, at 41, had served with Britain's SAS headquarters and in Kuwait.

The regiment was also represented in Operation Faber – together with ASIS operatives – from June to September, monitoring the referendum and sending intelligence back to HQ. The evacuation of both Australian and UN personnel from East Timor, Operation Spitfire, began on 6 September, with SAS security teams in the front line. The regimental operations officer, Major Jim Truscott, was one of the first to arrive at the UN compound in Dili. 'It was full of local East Timorese people seeking protection from the marauding militia,' he says. 'For a month we had been poised to recover Australian nationals in case the air evacuations had turned sour and a more surgical response was required.

'We learnt that the province-wide domestic violence had been directed through covert operations mounted out of Jakarta,' he says. It was reminiscent of Operasi Komodo in preparation for the 1975 invasion. 'This time the Javanese oligarchy that really controls Indonesia's political regime was caught off guard by the United Nations' resolve to intervene.

'We began evacuating UN staff and other internally displaced people. We flew nearly thirty sorties in a week to return some 2,500 very distressed people to Darwin. It was a tiring and frustrating task. When the evacuation teams arrived each day Dili was covered in a pall of smoke. The town was in the final throes of being looted and burnt.

'We didn't appreciate the full effects of this devastation until returning a week later to stay. The people were clearly traumatised by the events and even those who managed to escape the holocaust were forced to flee into the hills and eke out a survival existence for over a month. Tragically the United Nations was later to claim that this was the disaster that had to happen. For Australia it was a clear failure of foreign policy for the last quarter of the century.'[8]

Lieutenant Colonel McOwan was appointed Cosgrove's Special Operations commander, with a force of about 200 soldiers designated the 'Response Force' to disguise their SAS identity. However, according to Truscott, 'Everyone knew who we were, including Kopassus and BAKIN.'

They could deploy up to 20 patrols structured as self-contained units able to operate in remote areas with limited support. They would gather intelligence mostly through extended reconnaissance and surveillance. They would also act as commandos to raid and apprehend militia. McOwan and his officers would secure the air and sea entry points for the main force and establish contact with the TNI leadership. They would also run interference between the militias, their covert operatives in the population and their controllers in the TNI.

It was a job tailor-made for the SASR.

INTERFET ARRIVES

The main Interfet force arrived in East Timor by sea and air with all the panoply of a hostile invasion. Sixteen warships of the RAN with US and New Zealand support advanced on Dili Harbour, while FA-18s and F-111s from the RAAF provided air cover. An Indonesian submarine was detected on the approaches but no hostile contact was made at sea. Later in the day Australian Black Hawk helicopters swept in to support the SAS and other vital units at a newly established HQ in Dili.

Many of the militia bands retreated across the border to West Timor where they planned cross-border raids, sometimes with the tacit support of the TNI. The SAS's 3 Squadron established its own discrete HQ at Dili's Komoro airport. Well before they landed, CO McOwan and 3 Squadron OC McMahon had developed a precise battle plan.

ASIS HUMINT and signals interception input was vital. But they also used their own resources. Operations Officer Truscott says, 'Before I arrived in country I made discreet contact with Dr Andrew McNaughton, a political activist from the East Timor International Support Centre in Darwin. I needed to find out how we could make contact with Falintil. Within a week I was the first man from the international force to step off the plane at

Komoro airport.' Three days later he was meeting with Taur Matan Ruak, the vice-commander of Falintil, in his bamboo headquarters at Uaimori in the foothills of the Mundo Perdido Mountains.

The village was within a steep-sided valley, a classic guerrilla stronghold. 'I got to know him quite well during the week I spent living in his temporary camp,' Truscott says. 'At 43 he was a similar age to me and, while his fighters carried a variety of weapons, old and new, Taur Matan Ruak simply carried a pistol and he passed his orders by satellite phone and email. The evenings were often interrupted by a flurry of information concerning the movements of the militia and his fighters who were responding to requests for assistance from all over the country.'[1]

Some of the Falintil soldiers in the village wore Kopassus uniforms taken from the Indonesian Special Forces operatives they had killed in action. 'Evenings would be punctuated by Portuguese television news,' Truscott says. 'It was somewhat ironic to view Australian troops patrolling the streets of Dili from this mountain camp.' Other soldiers from 3 Squadron also deployed to Uaimori.

'Joint SAS and Falintil patrols went out to search for land mines and to bring back a Falintil fighter who had been wounded for some time,' Truscott says. He was quickly flown back to Dili. 'Another group went to locate a small child who had lost his leg following an airdrop of some United Nations food directly on to their encampment. This child was soon on his way to Australia.

'It was apparent one evening that a massacre had occurred near the eastern end of the island. As it turned out a religious group, containing three priests, two sisters, one Indonesian journalist and two young people, had been ambushed by the local militia. Falintil were incensed that the international force had not been in position in sufficient strength to stop it from occurring.

'Isolated as I was in the hills, all I could do was relay the information back to headquarters in Dili. The militia had hurriedly taken some of the bodies away and the survivors had managed to place some of the corpses in the river, but two of the dead bodies had been left in place. According to some other religious people in the area, the militia was planning to return to dispose of the remaining bodies, and twelve Falintil fighters set out to prevent this from occurring. Inevitably this patrol led to an ambush in which they killed thirteen militia, with the rest of the group in that area fleeing to the port of Com further to the east. A successful SAS heliborne raid on Com village followed in quick succession and the troops detained many other militia, but it was still too late as far as Falintil were concerned.'[2]

Just before Truscott returned to Dili, a captured Indonesian Army captain was escorted into the camp. Suspected of being a Kopassus operative, Truscott questioned him indirectly and learnt that he was an infantry officer who had been abandoned by his own troops some weeks ago.

'On the helicopter flight back to Dili, I landed beside the church in the centre of Bacau to speak with Father Martinho,' Truscott says. 'It was a noisy arrival as the helicopter nestled between the buildings, and much to my dismay I had interrupted a funeral service for the religious people who had been massacred.'

He returned to Uaimori a few days later to pick up Taur Matan Ruak and take him by helicopter to visit Ular Rehik, commander of Falintil's Region Four at nearby Ermera. This guerrilla camp was sited on a bare feature, he says. 'On arrival we quickly got down to business to find out what the militia were doing, where the local people were hiding in the hills and so on. Such was the decentralised nature of guerrilla warfare that Ruak and Ular had never before met each other in the flesh.'

On this visit, he helped organise a meeting between the guerrilla leader and General Cosgrove, which he attended. The Interfet commander, he says, 'was a little taken aback on Ruak's ready offer to facilitate reconciliation. However, the East Timorese would not even consider disarming its guerrilla forces until some diplomatic arrangements had been put in place with Indonesia to guarantee its security.'

On 16 October, an SAS patrol was attacked in a series of firefights by a group of about 20 militia, five of whom were killed; the patrol was extracted by Black Hawks without casualties. 'Not long after this engagement,' Truscott says, 'a local boy named Lafu from the Oecussi enclave surrounded by West Timor arrived in Dili with a letter addressed to Cosgrove seeking his support for the local people.

'We took the courier under our wing, and a few weeks later he was inserted back into his regency in a clandestine operation from the sea. This time Lafu was equipped with a Falintil high-frequency radio to be able to send reports on the local conditions.' He provided a running report on the continuing violence in the enclave, but this intelligence was to remain secret until SAS troops raided the main town later in the month.

'We knew that many people were being killed, but the international force was stretched and the likely Indonesian reaction could not be accurately determined,' he says. It was not until late December following the discovery of mass graves that Lafu's reporting was conclusively proven. 'We assaulted the Oecussi enclave,' Truscott says, 'in a near-desperate response to the atrocities occurring there, rather than as a pre-planned venture.'

On the morning of 22 October, James McMahon and an SAS troop flew into the enclave in Black Hawks and encountered between 30 and 40 militia, who immediately surrendered when they saw the force arrayed against them. An hour later reinforcements arrived on a navy landing craft. McMahon then quickly deployed his patrols by helicopter to the main villages and towns in the area, and three days later Lieutenant Colonel Mike Crane, commander of the 4th Field Regiment, arrived with an additional platoon of Gurkhas and a mechanised platoon from 5/7 RAR. They remained for four weeks along the semicircular border to open negotiations with the withdrawn Indonesian Army and to operate a crossing point to receive refugees back into the country.

By now a company of 2 RAR had joined the Response Force, and some assaults required high skill for the pilots to navigate in the pre-dawn light, looking for holes in the mist to penetrate jungle-clad valleys and to land their teams on the outskirts of villages. The SAS command decided that the only way they could dislocate the militia from their Kopassus controllers across the border was by a series of raids around Dili and further afield.

'One day the CO decided to patrol out towards the suburb of Becora into the foothills past the local army barracks,' Truscott says. 'We passed two open Indonesian army trucks, which were full of jeering troops in mixed dress. These were either soldiers acting as militia or militia themselves, but it was not the moment to stop and check. It was necessary to get away and quickly. We had little option but to continue to drive on and up the narrow winding road and find an alternate route back, even considering the possibility of having to abandon the vehicle and walk cross-country back to Dili.

'On reaching the crest of the escarpment we saw several more army trucks coming up the road from the other side. There was no other alternative now but to head down a goat track leading to a communications tower out on a spur line. Much to our relief, we eventually found our way back down some narrow mountain tracks to re-enter Dili through another militia suburban stronghold that was all but deserted.

'There was a strong feeling that we could be ambushed at every bend in the road, but luckily this did not eventuate. That night a Dutch journalist actually came to grief, and we had driven past what must have been his band of executioners. Other SAS operators found themselves in similar circumstances as patrols came across graves and bodies on succeeding days.'

The psychological effect of directly confronting the militia was to leave its mark, not least from the raid upon the village of Com mounted in response to the religious massacre. It was launched over a distance of 250 kilometres after a 15-minute briefing. Other raids were more deliberately planned but didn't always result in contact with the enemy. It was not always possible to immediately react to the information that Falintil provided, but in the next two weeks SAS troops raided by day and night, in one case at Suai killing two militia and taking two friendly casualties in return.

But once again the inherent tension between Special Forces and the Big Army intruded. By now Cosgrove was more than willing to use his Response Force but it was difficult for the Canberra-based hierarchy to accept the kind of individual initiative that was an essential part of the Special Forces ethos. On one occasion, Truscott says, he escorted a patrol commander to Major General Cosgrove's office to establish what had occurred during a contact so he could respond to questions from Canberra. 'The Patrol Commander was still visibly affected,' he says, 'there were 120 militia at the village and they were patrolling in twenty man groups with four Kopassus controllers. These controllers flew out by helicopter the day after the contact occurred.'

Moreover, the capacity of the SAS to raid rapidly across the countryside resulted in tension and jealousy from the Australian battalions who could not emulate their battlefield mobility and ready access to Falintil intelligence. However, the effect was not all negative; a number of infantrymen decided that when they completed the mission they would apply for selection to the SAS. One in particular, Rob Maylor, who roomed with subsequent

Victoria Cross winner Ben Roberts-Smith during selection, went on to a distinguished career as one of the regiment's top snipers.[3]

By mid-October, the area was considered safe enough for Xanana Gusmão to return, and an SAS protection team whisked him from Darwin to Dili in the middle of the night. Truscott was nearby when Gusmão met up with Taur Matan Ruak in the back of an armoured car in Dili. 'Both were almost in tears, not having seen each other for over seven years,' he says. 'A few days later I was invited to the small village of Remixio in the hills behind Dili to watch Xanana Gusmão's formal return to a Falintil cantonment. We arrived in the same helicopters to a tumultuous welcome by a large crowd. Traditional Timorese warriors and children in national dress serenaded him along the road to the parade ground where a battalion of Falintil fighters marched past in review order.

'I was pleasantly surprised to be called to the dais above the parade ground when he personally embraced the wives of fallen fighters and many of the original fighters who had been with him from the beginning. Almost all were in tears. I had to return to Dili that afternoon, but the festivities continued well into the night with dancing and boiled water.'

The battleground was now changing with the focus shifting much more towards the return of the refugees. The United Nations High Commission for Refugees had begun return flights in early October and late at night on 31 October the last Indonesian troops quietly departed East Timor by ship. An Australian soldier cast off the rope.

The 3 Squadron troops needed the break as some were starting to fall asleep in open doorways of helicopters at the end of a hectic 30 days. Dili was hot, humid and debilitating. They were about to be replaced in December by 1 Squadron, which had been preparing risk assessments for the Sydney 2000 Olympics.

A patrol commander in the new unit, Stuart 'Nev' Bonner, who had also attended an intensive Bahasa course at Point Cook, says, 'We flew by C-130 to a staging area near Darwin where we met some of the departing SASR men and were briefed on our role and tasks. I soon found that my language course was a real asset. We deployed in a Hercules to Dili's airport then on to the heliport, where we were accommodated in a series of small houses and offices surrounded by low concrete walls and topped with razor wire against militia attacks.

'. . . For the first few days we had to share space with 3 Squadron's L Troop until they left. There was ammunition all over the place and they'd got used to living like that – a bit like *Apocalypse Now*.' The militia by now had been neutralised; the troops' main intruders were feral dogs. 'You'd be in bed at night and hear this thing sniffing through your pack.'[4]

After two weeks, Bonner was ordered to take his patrol to Eileu, a Falintil stronghold in the mountains. 'The five of us would replace one of the teams that had been living up there for some months, interacting with the Falintil soldiers,' he says. 'When we arrived in our Land Rovers we spent our first few weeks living in an old abandoned set of villas and then moved to a prison about six kilometres outside the town.

'Xanana Gusmão now lived in an old Portuguese villa near the centre of town and a football oval. His was the flashest house; then on a sliding scale every other commander got the next flashest house in town.' Electricity came from a local generator and running water was limited. 'We used to deliver jerry cans of fresh creek water to two of the commanders' houses near our prison each day as a gesture of goodwill,' he says. 'What we were really doing there, as well as creating a relationship, was monitoring what they were doing and planning.'[5]

By mid-November, United Nations border liaison teams had started moving into position. According to Truscott, 'There was a gradual realisation that our job was done. Kopassus had been effectively dislocated from operating in country and militia groups were making tentative moves towards a political agenda. Occasionally some Indonesian soldiers would cross the border, some foraging, some using old 1936 Dutch maps and others in individual acts of bravado.

'Even Xanana Gusmão was commenting upon the excessive size of the peacekeeping force, which was to replace the international coalition. Some of the SAS patrols with the Falintil cantonments were starting to go native.'

Stuart Bonner says that each day he was in the town he conducted English classes for the children but the patrol was often deployed to outlying villages where they held sick parades and treated injuries and illnesses. 'On any day we'd get up to 100 villagers seeking treatment for malaria, cuts and infections, even leprosy, and some other diseases we never see in Australia.

'The burns were what really blew me away. Most of them came from electrocution,' he says. 'Children would find wiring that had been ripped out of a wall and they wouldn't know whether it was live or not and the next thing, "Zap". The wounds were terrible; the child might have grabbed the wire with his hand but the charge had blown a hole in the back of his elbow. I would try to hold and console the children as the wounds were being dressed and it was heartbreaking to be unable to do anything for their pain.'

Australia's Remembrance Day on 11 November was held in the mist and rain at the World War II OP at Fatunaba in the Dili foothills. Taur Matan Ruak arrived, standing proudly beside the coalition partners. Jim Truscott says, 'The 2/2 Independent Company had originally used this post in their own guerrilla war against the Japanese. Late in November a patrol came across some old men who took them to the sites where World War II Australian commandos had encountered their Japanese enemy. One of these men was a boy in 1942 in the house where the patrol was staying, and he was an eyewitness to the contact. The Japanese had sprung a surprise attack. The Australians made a hurried departure leaving a lot of equipment, and escaping with only what they wore.

'As they withdrew west they were engaged at a river crossing where one Australian and one Timorese were killed. Further west still, the survivors were contacted again where another Australian and a second Timorese reportedly died. The third Australian was last seen moving towards the village of Grouto-Hatoudo. Apparently the Timorese with the Japanese cut an ear off each of the victims and placed them on a stick like a kebab. Such is the fate of guerrillas.'[6]

21

EAST TIMOR OPERATIONS

In its six-month deployment of almost 7,000 soldiers (including unit rotations), Australia suffered only two fatal Interfet casualties – when one soldier discharged his weapon accidentally and another serviceman succumbed to illness. Neither was from SASR. One factor in this extraordinary result was the high standard of SAS training, but it was the quality of signals interception supplied by the Defence Signals Directorate and the other signals agencies that proved decisive.

Preparations had begun long before the deployment. SAS patrols were making secret seaborne incursions from July 1999 to observe and determine the disposition of Indonesian forces; and they left sensor systems on the island to send intercepts back to Australia. By then DSD was gaining a comprehensive picture of the situation on East Timor.

The US was also monitoring the zone via CIA assets and the American Navy's Los Angeles-class submarines, which were positioning pods called Ivy Bells on underwater communication links to be regularly retrieved and decoded.

The DSD intercepts mapped out the chain of command from the local militias and covert Indonesian forces. They came from 'Secret Spoke', meaning intercepted clear-voice telephone calls, and

'Top Secret Umbra', derived from encrypted or scrambled voice communications. DSD also intercepted urgent requests from the Indonesian defence attaché in Canberra, Brigadier-General Judi Yusuf, to his ministry in Jakarta for 'clarification' of the East Timor atrocities being reported in the Australian media. He was told these were 'press fabrications'.

Australia's Special Forces knew better. On 9 February 1999, shortly after President Habibie's decision to call a referendum, DSD intercepted messages that two Indonesian Special Forces units had arrived in East Timor to supplement undercover operations by the East Timor command. They had been arming local militias to counter the unrest that had spread unchecked since the fall of Suharto.

Another major Special Forces asset was the Australian Imagery Organisation (AIO), located in Canberra's Russell Hill Defence complex, where they had access to the highly classified high-resolution satellite images from the US NRO. The pictures were so clear that they could easily identify individuals on the ground in East Timor. As well, they commissioned commercial companies to provide lower resolution pictures giving images between one and ten metres from the subject; and gathered photographs of the terrain – in colour and infrared – taken by the RAAF's F-111 reconnaissance aircraft.

According to Professor Desmond Ball, the US Navy deployed its E-P3 signals interception aircraft to the area. 'These aircraft flew for up to twelve hours each sortie, intercepting communications and sending the processed intercepts back to Australia,' he says. 'At different times during the year the United States agreed to the realignment of one of its geostationary satellites controlled from Pine Gap to provide coverage of signals from the VHF up to the super high-frequency (SHF) band.' This gave access to walkie-talkies and satphones. From April to November, US Air Force transport aircraft delivered tons of computer hardware, software and other electronic equipment to Canberra for installation in DSD, AIO and the Defence Intelligence Organisation (DIO) to upgrade their operation.[1]

However, there were differences in emphasis between the two traditional allies. Initially, Australian officials tended to downplay the possibility of a major intervention. And when the US asked for access to ASIS HUMINT material gathered from East Timor, Foreign Minister Alexander Downer refused on grounds that sources would be compromised. Nevertheless, the flow of signals intercepts and imagery continued and was undoubtedly a decisive factor in keeping Australia's Special Forces' casualties to a minimum.

According to one SAS officer with access to the DSD material, 'We knew exactly from these sources what Black Operations were occurring.'[2] And the regiment knew their opponents. They had exercised with Kopassus regularly in the past decade and knowledge of their leading figures – as well as their capabilities – was the foundation of their strategic planning. One SAS patrol leader said, 'They have quite good soldiering skills for their nation's level of expertise. They are not very well equipped but they are absolutely ruthless, and if they are told to do something and it's justified to them, they will carry it out. They will also do things that may be criminal. That dark side can come out and they are capable of some horrendous things.'[3]

Kopassus was under the command of Major General Syahrir, who would initiate a series of Black Operations using hit squads codenamed Kiper-9 to hunt down pro-independence elements and former collaborators who had changed sides. Syahrir was born in 1947 in South Sumatra and graduated from the Indonesian Military Academy in 1971. Most of his career was spent within Kopassus and in 1992 he studied at the Joint Services Academy in Weston, a Canberra suburb. He became Kopassus commander in 1998.

The most prominent militia leader was Eurico Guterres, who had been born in East Timor in 1971. His parents were killed in the long-running Fretilin rebellion and he was brought up by an Indonesian civil servant in the far east of the province. He moved to Dili to attend high school, where he was an indifferent student and an activist against the Indonesian administration. Local military intelligence detained him as a suspect in a plot to assassinate President Suharto, who visited East Timor in October 1988. During his detention he appears to have been 'turned' by his interrogators, and from that time became an informer for Kopassus.

Indonesia's top counterinsurgency officer and Suharto's son-in-law, retired general Prabowo Subianto, recruited him into Gadapaksi, an organisation providing cheap loans to young people in East Timor but which also used them in pro-Indonesian vigilante squads. By 1999, Guterres had risen to become the most active Kopassus operative among the militia forces.

Joao da Silva Tavares, a much older man, was the nominal 'supreme commander' of militia forces. A veteran of the struggle against Fretilin, he operated from Bobonaro and gained a reputation as a merciless enemy. He told a Balibo rally on 19 February that if the people rejected the autonomy option and voted for independence, 'there will be war'.[4]

A week later, DSD heard Eurico Guterres in Dili call the HQ of one of the new Indonesian units to inquire about one of his men who had been injured. On 5 May, Indonesia's Colonel Tono Suratman was intercepted phoning Guterres to ask where he was massing his militia group for a show of force in Dili. Guterres said he had 400 men waiting outside a city hotel. On 1 June, DSD intercepted Colonel Suratman telling Guterres, 'Don't deal with me directly. Contact me via Bambang.' Bambang Wisnumurti was his intelligence chief. On 8 August, they heard military HQ in Jakarta allocating radio frequencies for use by pro-Indonesian groups.

Immediately after the people voted overwhelmingly for independence, the Indonesian authorities arranged for the evacuation of pro-integration elements and Indonesian residents prior to the arrival of the Interfet. DSD was able to monitor that operation as an overblown propaganda exercise. Once the Interfet units landed and the Black Hawk helicopters arrived in Dili, they immediately began monitoring militia activity from the air, spotting and reporting suspicious activity. The intelligence officer of the Australian 3rd Brigade at Cosgrove's HQ, Major John Blaxland, says, 'This had the effect of intimidating troublemakers in town, boosting the confidence of the force, and significantly adding to the Brigade's situational awareness.'[5]

Soon afterwards the brigade, renamed Westfor, became the Western force of Interfet, with headquarters in Suai and operating from there throughout the engagement. But it received signals interception from the intelligence hierarchy as required for its 'named areas of interest'. 'Other reconnaissance platforms,' Blaxland says, 'began delivering crystal-clear vertical imagery of villages, hamlets, roads and crossing points.'

These were supplemented by field intelligence teams, including some women, who worked through the battalions' intelligence officers. They also sent daily reports to Cosgrove's HQ for dissemination to all relevant forces. The HQ intelligence officer in Dili was receiving a vast input from US and other Allied international staff. 'This was a feat never before attempted on such a scale by an Australian-led headquarters,' Blaxland says. 'Providing intelligence support to a wide range of national components while supporting subordinate units and providing the intelligence advice to the force commander and to higher authorities was quite a task ... But overall it is fair to say that the tactical-level intelligence system proved equal to its complex tasking in East Timor.'

One of the key strategic locations of the conflict was Balibo. Early in the Interfet operation, two SAS patrols inserted as pathfinders for 2 RAR, which would seize the town. They rappelled from a Black Hawk into rough country, then sought a hilltop from which to observe Balibo. One operator had landed heavily and broken his leg. He was immediately evacuated and the others pushed on through a dense tangle of scrub and prepared an LZ just before the infantry troops arrived.

It then became the headquarters of an Australian mechanised infantry unit, a communications hub and a pivotal SAS assembly point for reconnaissance operations in the border areas south of Batugade. By now it was a substantial town crowned by an old Portuguese fort that had been renovated and its defences upgraded by the Indonesians. According to one SAS patrol commander who used it as a stepping-off point several times from December to February, 'It had a cement wall about ten feet high with various small, concrete buildings inside the compound. There was a paved road that ran from the village up the hill into the fort complex.

'In the village square at the centre of the town was an old monument and the house of the infamous Balibo Five killing was close by. The border was around 12 kilometres away as the crow flies along a winding road down to the coastal areas. Quite often we saw and surprised Indonesian soldiers there. They used the border as a trade route and also supervised the mining and processing of building gravel from the river. They seemed to have their grubby hands in all manner of things.'[6]

A senior SAS officer also confirmed the pivotal role Balibo played in the pacification of the area. 'It was ironic that here we were, back operating from a base that had been a key position in the Sparrow Force operation yet had caused such enmity between Australia and Indonesia over the years.'[7]

It was this unresolved bitterness within the Australian media from the Balibo Five killings that had spilt over into the political arena to set the scene for the Howard–Habibie imbroglio. The Australian-led intervention in turn fed into the atmosphere of tension and distrust between the two countries. And there was more to come. In 2000, as the Interfet troops departed, Australian publisher Allen & Unwin released a book called *Death in Balibo, Lies in Canberra*, which not only accused the Indonesian military of deliberately murdering the journalists but also implicated a number of Australia's intelligence agencies in the tragedy.

The authors, Desmond Ball and investigative journalist Hamish McDonald, said Ambassador Woolcott had cabled the Department of Foreign Affairs advance warning of the secret incursion – codenamed Operation Komodo – three days before the 16 October 1975 Balibo attack. The next day television reports from the journalists were aired from the border, yet no attempt was made to warn them of the military assault heading their way.

DSD, still under the command of its founding director Ralph Thompson, was monitoring the situation very closely from its headquarters at Melbourne's Albert Park. While its coverage was not as comprehensive as it became 25 years later, according to Ball and McDonald their equipment gave them access to 'essentially all Indonesian radio communications reckoned to be of political, diplomatic or military significance'.

Its primary listening post was at Shoal Bay 20 kilometres from Darwin, where more than 150 personnel were engaged in signals interception work. The intercepted material was relayed to Melbourne by encrypted teletype. From there it was processed and sent to the JIO in the Defence complex in Canberra. Other signals interception came from a DSD team aboard a navy destroyer cruising close to the island.

It detected a vital message from Colonel Dading Kalbuadi, who was leading the invasion force from Atambua to his superior General Benny Murdani in Jakarta. He reminded Murdani of the presence of the journalists. Murdani responded, 'We can't have any witnesses.' The timing of the transmission is unclear. According to Ball and McDonald, by then the attack might have begun. The next intercept mentioning the journalists came from the Indonesian squad leader at Balibo, Captain Yunus Yosfiah, to Colonel Dading. It said, 'Among the dead are four [*sic*] white men. What are we going to do with the bodies?' Dading told him to do nothing until he arrived (by helicopter). Later Dading reported that 'all traces have been removed'.

For four days the Australian Government kept the tragedy 'under wraps' until the story appeared in the Jakarta press on 20 October. By then, according to Ball and McDonald, 'Officials in Canberra and Jakarta had fallen into the pattern of two parallel cover-ups of the Balibo affair. Each had something to hide. Jakarta wanted to conceal any involvement by its forces in the East Timor fighting. It also wanted to deny culpability of its Timor allies who, the Indonesians claimed, carried out the Balibo attack unaided. Canberra was trying to avoid any public acknowledgement that it had been told by the Indonesians what was going on. It also had to conceal from the Indonesians that it could follow what was happening through signals intelligence.'

Two weeks after the killings, Foreign Minister Don Willesee still maintained the fiction of ignorance, suggesting the government was only aware of 'widespread reports' of the invasion. On 30 October, he said that, if they were true, 'Australia would be extremely disappointed'. On 5 November, Gough Whitlam wrote to President Suharto, 'We are still lacking, however, final and positive confirmation that the bodies located at Balibo are in fact those of the missing newsmen.' However, by the time Suharto received it,

Whitlam's government had been dismissed by Governor-General John Kerr in the parliamentary constitutional crisis.

The cover-up continued. Though DSD at Shoal Bay heard the Indonesian military figures coordinating their stories in case of an inquiry, as late as 6 June 1976 Foreign Minister Andrew Peacock told the parliament, 'I regret it is still not possible to come to firm and final conclusions as to the circumstances and manner of the deaths of the newsmen.' Either the minister was deliberately misleading the parliament or the DSD signals interception had been kept from him.

In November 1995, a ministerial successor, Gareth Evans, commissioned an inquiry by a former chairman of the National Crime Commission, Tom Sherman, into the Balibo deaths. The inquiry would include the subsequent disappearance of AAP journalist Roger East, who remained in Dili during the acknowledged invasion of 7 December.

Sherman's report, presented to parliament by Evans's successor Alexander Downer in 1996, revealed the Indonesian officers Yunus and Dading were intimately involved, and accepted that the bodies had been dressed in uniforms and posed for propaganda photographs later burnt as part of a cover-up. Downer also asked Sherman to undertake a second inquiry, which reported in 1999, but without any new revelations. However, Ball and McDonald not only endorsed the conclusion that the Balibo Five were deliberately shot and stabbed to death; they also traced the subsequent capture and barbaric execution of Roger East.

'On Monday 8 December,' they wrote, 'he was captured and brought to the Dili wharf. At around 8 am, his hands tied behind him with wire, East was marched to the side of the pier and executed by rifle fire by Battalion 501 or 502 soldiers. His body floated in the water with those of dozens of other men, women and children associated with the Fretilin side, or just picked out because they were Chinese.'

Publication by two such well-respected figures compounded the wounds in Australian–Indonesian relations, and Downer ordered yet another inquiry, this time by Bill Blick, the inspector-general of intelligence and security. The publicly released version of Blick's report was equivocal about the authors' evidence of DSD interceptions and the conclusions that followed from them. However, it would not be the last word on the subject.

Meantime, Australia's Special Forces pillars were voluntarily pooling all their resources without a hint of restraint or inter-service rivalry for perhaps the first time in their history. And while the occasion had very little to do with the defence of the homeland, it was unquestionably an event of enormous national importance: the 2000 Sydney Olympics.

DOMESTIC CONCERNS – AND INTERNATIONAL RUMBLINGS

Security at Australia's second Olympic Games was very different from the task that faced the nascent ASIO in Melbourne in 1956. At that time, several Middle Eastern countries had withdrawn over the Suez crisis and China declined to participate when Taiwan was allowed to compete. The Soviet Union had just crushed the Hungarian revolution, and this brought the withdrawal of three more European countries. The Soviet presence in Melbourne raised the spectre of defections from the communist team and preoccupied the few full-time ASIO agents in the agency's establishment.

Tension remained high throughout the competition. It was not until a young Melburnian, John Ian Wing, suggested that during the closing ceremony the athletes abandon their national flags and mingle in the great arena of the MCG that they became the 'friendly games', and this began a tradition that has endured.

Forty-four years later the Soviet Union was no more. ASIO was a fully matured intelligence agency with total responsibility for threat assessment in the Commonwealth, and it took charge of a massive security operation. The result was an unabashed triumph. According to one of the senior operatives, the system they developed for Operation Gold would become the model for inter-agency and inter-government relations in managing the security of all subsequent big events such as APEC and international sporting competitions.

It also marked the first public airing of the convergence of intelligence agencies and the military units of our Special Forces. It consisted of a coordinating centre in ASIO's Canberra headquarters with representatives from all relevant state and Commonwealth departments and agencies, including ASIS, Defence Intelligence, DSD, Attorney-General's, ONA, AFP and state equivalents. This nerve centre was equipped with stand-alone computer networks but also linked to the various organisations' networks that provided the raw data for threat assessments within ASIO. Then, at tactical level, inside the police centre in Sydney there was an intelligence group run by the police but similarly staffed by officers from all state and Commonwealth agencies. It had direct links to the strategic centre in Canberra.

Then came the response groups within the police forces if some incident occurred. Their officials were in the police centre at Ultimo with operational support from ASIO's New South Wales office. To manage the operation upwards, there were daily briefings of potential or real risks to high-level state and Commonwealth police. The highlights went to the Special Forces commander, Brigadier Philip McNamara, who personally briefed Prime Minister John Howard each day. Indeed, Howard would participate personally in SAS emergency drills and so develop a relationship of mutual admiration with its hierarchy.

The whole operation was driven by continually updated threat assessments from ASIO headquarters. According to ASIO sources, 'No one took any action unless it was on the threat assessments issued daily.' Moreover, the military Special Forces 'had their operational group ready at a moment's notice to spring into action and kill every terrorist if necessary'. They were linked by computer and other communications but sat separately.[1]

In March, an SAS Tactical Assault Group deployed secretly to Randwick Barracks in Sydney for a month's training. They relocated to Swanbourne to analyse the lessons learnt, and then returned in May for a series of five major exercises in and around the city. An SAS officer who took a leading role in the operation says, 'We deployed to Sydney with distant memories of the terrorist acts at the Olympic Games in Munich and Atlanta in our minds. Sydney's enemies were less well defined, but the threat of carnage was greater from faceless international terrorists with loyalties to religion or the lone rogue nutcase seeking to cause massive harm.

'Terrorism is a special type of violence and combating it is a major factor in the staging of any modern public event. Numerous threats to stage major terrorist strikes at public venues in Sydney had been received.'

One man had been arrested after a three-month investigation into a series of threats received by the Russian and Turkish consulates; another was taken into custody after the Olympic Investigation Strike Force seized racist material and uncovered explosive substances in an underground bunker west of Sydney.

Australia tried to avoid a 'Fort Sydney' approach, but did not want a repeat of the bungled rescue attempt that helped seal the fate of Israeli athletes murdered during the 1972 Olympics. In fact, the Israelis sent their own Mossad unit, and according to security officials, 'The Israelis did their own thing, as they always do. We understood that.'[2]

The Americans were strongly represented. The CIA was one of 72 international intelligence agencies that had been networking and swapping notes to ensure the games were free of terrorism. By the time the games began, US warships – including an aircraft carrier – were stationed off the coast.

The SAS unit was ensconced at a temporary military camp together with 4 RAR (Commando) and the reserve 1 Commando Company at Holsworthy Barracks in Sydney's south-west, where helicopter gunships would be on standby to carry troops into action. The soldiers dubbed it 'Camp John West, the one that the Kosovos rejected'.[3] According to the SAS officer, 'We were ready for just about any problem including any ships that may have been taken by pirates while underway in the harbour or chemical, biological and radiological forms of terrorism.'

In late August, a quantity of weapons had been stolen from a navy ship in the harbour, but they were quickly recovered. The same month, New Zealand foiled an attempt by a group of refugees linked to an obscure Saudi Arabian terrorist leader, Osama bin Laden, with designs on the Lucas Heights nuclear reactor. A Turkish immigrant worker from Sydney's west, Fahim Louchi, was arrested and charged with threatening to destroy planes carrying athletes from the US and France.

The exercise was not without its gremlins. 'On an early reconnaissance of the building which was to house the National Security Committee of Cabinet,' the SAS officer says, 'I was surprised to find that any member of the public could simply walk in off Phillip Street and place a bomb in letterboxes with the member of parliament's name. It was obvious that Australia had never been confronted by bombing terror.

'Late one night we responded to a simulated siege–hostage incident on Cockatoo Island in inner Sydney in order to hone our readiness. By the time we had arrived at the Police Forward Command Post, their water police had cordoned the target. Within a few hours plans had been formulated and, on command, assaulters and snipers simultaneously approached from helicopters and rigid-hull inflatable boats in order to kill the terrorists in the multi-storey building and save the lives of the hostages held in the stronghold.

'A few days later we practised against a large commercial ship as it steamed towards Sydney. This takedown was even more complicated with maritime surveillance aircraft and two large naval vessels contributing to the task of locating and picketing the moving target. The assault had our men simultaneously roping down from six helicopters with others climbing ladders from the rigid-hull boats alongside in order to stop the ship and clear the many passageways of terrorists.

'Early on another day I was climbing The Fear, the cliff on North Head, when a high-speed catamaran emblazoned with Shell Australia was met by a barrier of about ten medium-sized fishing boats attempting to prevent its entry into the Harbour. The cat simply pushed through a small gap at speed as they pursued it into Harbour. The ambush must have been advertised, as two news helicopters were hovering in the area.'

As the spectacular opening ceremony unfolded, more than 5,000 military personnel were in position around the city, together with thousands of New South Wales state police, hundreds of federal police, scores of intelligence officers, 30,000 private security guards and tens of thousands of Olympic volunteers with powers to search, remove and detain people acting suspiciously. Brigadier McNamara told a luncheon of current and former military officers, 'We are prepared to meet any challenge.'

The operation was a complete success. The senior intelligence officer says, 'It went really well. We had some actual threats. But they were dealt with in a proper, timely way. Nothing occurred that wasn't foretold or forestalled.' The 1978 Hope Report had laid the foundation for inter-agency cooperation with ASIO at its peak. 'There aren't that many federations in the world,' he says, 'that have such functioning, well-coordinated and cooperative relations between State, Federal and Police agencies and, to their credit, the Department of Defence.' But, of course, there are not many federations so distant from the globe's traditional trouble spots and surrounded by a moat incorporating two of the world's great oceans.

While Australia's Special Forces pillars gave themselves a jubilant pat on the back, no one in the top echelon of Special Forces believed it could last; their exposure to the aggressive international groups being monitored by allies meant that 'we couldn't relax our vigilance for a second'. However, in the months that followed, Australia's political focus turned to a rising tide of refugees making the hazardous journey in leaky boats from Indonesia across the Arafura Sea and the Indian Ocean to the nearest Australian territory – either Darwin or, more often, Christmas Island.

In August 2001, Howard was facing an election campaign against a resurgent Labor Party under former Defence minister Kim Beazley. But Labor was split on the refugee issue between those favouring the 'soft' approach of accepting ever-increasing refugee numbers and the hardliners reflecting the traditional community attitude to 'illegal migrants'. When the Norwegian freighter MV *Tampa* rescued 438 Afghan refugees – predominantly persecuted Hazaras – from a sinking vessel and ferried them towards Christmas Island, Howard turned to his much admired spearhead of the Defence Force, the SAS, to board the ship and repel the 'invaders'. Use of the 'super soldiers' was politically devastating; it elevated the status of the refugees to a national security threat.

Beazley equivocated, and Howard seized the moment by introducing a Border Protection Bill with a rallying cry: 'We will decide who comes to this country and the circumstances in which they come.' His government then initiated the so-called Pacific Solution and sailed the refugees several thousand kilometres to

Nauru. It was a telling – if expensive – gesture, though almost all would eventually resettle in Australia.

While Howard had made an outrageous misuse of the SAS, his coalition government would be returned to office with an increased majority. But the issue paled into insignificance soon afterwards when, exactly one year after the Olympics, two commercial aircraft hijacked by terrorists from Osama bin Laden's al-Qaeda ploughed into New York's World Trade Center, a third slammed into the side of the Pentagon, and a fourth – targeted for the US Capitol – crashed into a Pennsylvania field after a valiant struggle by the passengers.

'That was the day that changed the world,' says one of Australia's top military security officials. 'We weren't prepared. No one was. And we could not have anticipated that the American administration would react the way it did – perhaps immediately in striking back, but not the way it panned out in Iraq.'

By chance, Howard was in Washington at the time and felt firsthand the shock, bewilderment and rage that engulfed the American people, and particularly the George W. Bush administration. 'Just as the Cold War lasted a long time and defined several generations,' Howard said, 'so the war on terror will last a long time and define other generations.' The sentiments were not only prophetic but – as embraced, distorted and propounded by the Bush–Cheney White House – also became a self-fulfilling prophecy.

The US quickly identified the perpetrators as bin Laden and his al-Qaeda organisation, operating under the protection of the Taliban regime in Afghanistan. And when they refused to hand him over to US authorities, Bush launched military action. Teams of US and British Special Forces combined with the Northern Alliance of Afghan warlords to attack Taliban forces throughout the country. In a short, sharp operation the extremists were stripped of power and the hardcore leadership fled to neighbouring Pakistan or the bare and brutal mountain borderlands.

By December, the Allies had installed a new government under Hamid Karzai and an International Security Assistance Force (ISAF) had been established by the UN. Australia was a founding signatory and its Special Forces regime was fully engaged; the SAS was preparing to deploy.

Like the rest of the world, the Special Forces soldiers had watched in horror as the great New York towers crumpled in the wake of the airborne impact. One SAS operator, Stuart 'Nev' Bonner, says, 'As I watched I wondered if the Aussie SAS would have a role to play. Not long afterwards I started to hear rumours of a deployment to Afghanistan; and of course the boys were itching to go . . . I bailed up the CO at a regimental meeting and asked – not very politely – if those of us on the [patrol commanders'] promotion course could leave it to rejoin training with our squadron. He said he'd "have a word" with the course senior instructors, and it worked.'[4]

By then, Special Forces command, led by a former SASR CO, Colonel Duncan Lewis, was in close contact with the American HQ in Florida, where they were planning a *coup de grâce* to take out Osama bin Laden in his mountain redoubt, the caves of Tora Bora. Unfortunately – and not for the last time – they misjudged the Afghan ethos and gave the lead to Northern Alliance fighters backed by US air strikes. The militia advanced on the terrorists' hideout. Anticipation ran high. But then the al-Qaeda leadership negotiated a 'truce' with the Afghan commander 'to give them time to surrender their weapons'. Bin Laden and his entourage escaped. The Americans were mortified.

The SAS commander, Lieutenant Colonel Peter 'Gus' Gilmore, had by now flown to the US command to ensure that his would be one of the units of choice within the ISAF forces. He and his operations officer, Major Pete Tinley, spent weeks liaising with the American Middle East HQ; and they succeeded in establishing the Australians as a 'stand-alone' operation, but with the capacity to call in US and other national air strikes as necessary. They would also share base facilities and intelligence product with the Allies.

The first element deployed would be 1 Squadron SAS, and they were working up to combat readiness with intensive live-fire training in their Lancelin and Bindoon facilities. A small group was detached and sent to the Kimberleys to complete a forward air controller's course to direct bombs and missiles from their American air cover onto enemy targets. Their training complete, they flew by C-130 to Kuwait and its huge Camp Doha airbase. From there the squadron – designated Redback One – was ferried in huge American C-17 aircraft that could carry their specially fitted LRPVs and all their battle kit into the war zone.

They landed at Firebase Rhino at the southern end of the Helmand Valley, where, after bombing raids, the US Special Forces had inserted by parachute and routed the Taliban defenders. Helmand Province was a major source of heroin, so was heavily impregnated with hostile elements. As soon as they dumped their gear in a massive hangar with US marines, the Australians were called to 'stand to' at the perimeter fence with weapons primed as enemy forces were spotted nearby. Apache and Black Hawk helicopters continually took off and landed just outside, creating a thick, choking dust cloud; while C-130 gunships fired mini-gun and 40-mm weapons at enemy positions.

'It seemed surreal,' Bonner says, 'like watching a movie.'[5]

The Australians combined with the marines on joint patrols over the next several weeks and then headed for the traditional Taliban stronghold, Kandahar. Arriving on the outskirts at night they sent scouts ahead and donned their NVGs for the dash to the airport base. When they reached the front gate of the massive

Russian-built facility, the American guards waved them down. 'They were really gunned up with missile systems mounted on the back of Humvees,' Bonner says. And they had placed heavy concrete blocks across the entryway to prevent an explosive-laden vehicle from reaching the base.

Once inside, they were guided to a compound that would become their patrol base for the next four months. 'In the coming weeks, we would spend only a few days at a time on the base,' he says, 'and when we were there we were always in frenzied preparation for the next job.'

On 16 February, the sense of ever-present danger was magnified by news of the first SAS fatality of the war when an improvised explosive device (IED) exploded under the vehicle carrying 33-year-old Sergeant Andrew Russell and his patrol on an operation in Helmand. American search and rescue helicopters were on the scene within minutes and rushed him to Kandahar but he died during the journey. The tragedy shocked the tight-knit unit. 'The boys were numbed,' Bonner says. 'Andy was so full of life it was hard to imagine that he could have been killed.'[6]

Meantime, the American command in Florida, stung by the Tora Bora fiasco, was planning another operation to decapitate the al-Qaeda leadership and wreak final retribution for the unpardonable attack of 9/11. Their Special Forces and intelligence agencies had identified a major training base and control centre in the folds of the massive borderland peaks.

The narrow Shahi-Kot Valley, at 8,000 feet (2,450 metres), was an ideal location for the al-Qaeda base, its vertiginous slopes pitted with caves providing shelter to its defenders from air attack and with well-used supply trails and escaping 'ratlines' to the Pakistan tribal areas. But the Americans believed it was vulnerable to a classic 'hammer and anvil' battle plan. They codenamed it Operation Anaconda and once again they gave the lead to a force of Afghan militia, under 'General' Zia Lodin in his first combat venture. He would swing the hammer supported by Special Forces closing in from the north-west; the anvil would be a unit of US Rangers at the southern end of the valley to take out the fleeing terrorists as the hammer descended.

A small SAS contingent would join the hammer force. Another SAS pair, Warrant Officer Clint Palmer and Signalman Jock Wallace, would be embedded as liaison with the anvil. And a troop from 1 Squadron – including Nev Bonner's patrol – would take up an overwatch position in the south prior to the battle to provide surveillance and to pick off those fleeing insurgents who escaped the Americans waiting for them in the 'turkey shoot' of the anvil.

23

IRAQ OPERATIONS

Anaconda was another debacle, but on this occasion the Afghans were not wholly to blame. At the last minute, American intelligence revised the estimated strength of the al-Qaeda forces in the mountainous training area from between 150 and 200 to almost ten times that figure. The US commander, General Franklin L. Hagenbeck, told his inner circle, 'This is bigger than we thought. There's going to be up to 1,500 bad guys out there.'[1] However, he decided to proceed with the original plan, believing their control of the air would allow them to destroy the enemy's fighting ability even before the ground battle was joined.

The US Air Force was scheduled to unleash a pre-emptive carpet-bombing assault on all the Shahi-Kot defensive positions – caves, mountain redoubts and training facilities – for a full 55 minutes. Unfortunately, according to the Australian liaison officer Clint Palmer, only one B-1 bomber arrived and dropped six bombs along a humpback ridgeline in the valley. The raid lasted a mere five minutes.[2]

More importantly, perhaps, the Afghan-led 'hammer' force was spotted by al-Qaeda lookouts before they reached the battle space in their convoy of trucks. They were assailed by a fusillade of mortars. Then, without warning, an American AC-130 gunship, wildly off course and 10,000 feet (3,000 metres) above the convoy, fired a deadly broadside of Howitzer shells into Zia's forces, killing several of his men and mortally wounding an American Special Forces soldier. Zia turned tail and fled. The SAS men escaped unscathed, but the hammer was no more.

When the American 'anvil' inserted by helicopter at 6 am, they were unaware that the hammer had been shattered. The 82 members of the Ranger Company were now exposed to a powerful counterattack from the enemy, and for the next 18 hours they were under constant mortar, rocket-propelled grenade (RPG) and sniper fire from the high ground. The American troops fought back valiantly and casualties were kept to a minimum. But, once again, the al-Qaeda leadership had escaped the Allies' clutches. The battered rangers were finally withdrawn at midnight, with the two embedded Australians among the last to leave. The SAS radio operator, Jock Wallace, would later receive the Medal for Gallantry.

The US Air Force then pounded the area with 2,000-pound (roughly 900-kilograms) bombs and mini-gun shells. Nev Bonner's patrol remained on watch from their mountain fastness. 'Some of the biggest shells hit just over the edge of our mountain top hideout and we felt the shockwave, saw the massive flash and heard the hot metal rip the air overhead,' he says. 'As dawn approached we could see the remains of at least two [American] helicopters that had been destroyed. We occasionally caught sight of scurrying Taliban fighters moving between small mud buildings.'

The Americans regrouped and pounded the target area mercilessly. 'The sky overhead was alive with aircraft all hours of the day and night,' Bonner says. 'One minute it was a predator droning slowly around 3,000 feet above; next we'd see a stream of B-52s fly in from thousands of kilometres away. Then it was Warthogs farting their deadly hail of 30-mm cannon fire down on to the rocks and ridges below. F-15s circled higher still and occasionally screamed down below the safe threshold to deliver a JDAM [joint direct attack munition] and then screamed upward again, sometimes followed by the snake trail of a surface-to-air anti-aircraft missile.' When the pilots detected the incoming missiles, they deployed magnesium decoy flares to divert their heat-seeking instruments. 'It was a fantastic, terrifying and awe-inspiring display,' he says.

Over the next two weeks the US forces mounted a further series of well-planned assaults on the training facilities and the caves that had sheltered the insurgents. While none of the leaders was captured, the area was effectively nullified as an enemy encampment. The Americans called it a 'victory' and the Australians then resumed their patrols.

'Over the next weeks and months,' Bonner says, 'we conducted many tasks searching for Taliban strongholds and training facilities. We had limited success, and some of the boys felt that the targets we were given were less than priority jobs. Whether or not this was the case, the lads were doing their best to perform well in difficult circumstances.'

Towards the end of his tour, Bonner's patrol was sent to establish an OP close to the tripartite borders of Afghanistan, Pakistan and Iran. It was a classic SAS long-range-surveillance operation. 'From there we could watch the activities of the Pakistanis on the high mountain range to our south and simultaneously the Iranian border stretching along a series of fences to our west,' he says. They could see Taliban supply trucks travelling back and across the borders. 'The intel gathered showed just how porous the borders really were, and how anything could be moved in and out of Afghanistan from any neighbour.'

Even in these isolated areas, American technology made its presence felt. 'When I tried to sleep I could hear the ever-present threat of the drones overhead watching us and searching the surrounds,' he says. 'It was supposed to be reassuring to have their extra eyes providing overwatch, but it put our nerves on edge.'[3]

When the squadron returned home in April 2002, they were given a month's leave before resuming training at their Swanbourne HQ. They were replaced by 2 Squadron, who stayed until August. Then 3 Squadron took over until the Afghan deployment was terminated in November 2002.

By then events in Washington and at the United Nations had conspired to open a new front in the Middle East, this time centred on Iraq and the catastrophic quest for a chimera: Saddam Hussein's weapons of mass destruction (WMDs). And while the opprobrium of history has fallen squarely on the political shoulders of President George W. Bush and his hawkish vice-president Dick Cheney, Britain's Tony Blair and Australia's John Howard were equally enthusiastic members of the so-called 'Coalition of the Willing'.

Australia's political parties were divided on invading Iraq, but then on 12 October 2002 the country experienced its own tragic attack at the hands of Islamist terrorists. In the Balinese tourist district of Kuta, inside Paddy's Bar that evening, a member of the Jemaah Islamiyah (JI) group detonated a bomb in his backpack. Some nightclubbers were fatally wounded; others fled into the street, where, 20 seconds later, they became the victims of a second and much more powerful bomb hidden inside a parked van. The explosions killed 202 people, 88 of them Australians. The second bomb left a crater a metre deep in the roadside. An audio cassette was quickly discovered with a message from Osama bin Laden that the bombings were a direct retaliation for Australia's support of the US 'war on terror' and Australia's role in Timor.

The incident was a serious blow to Australia's intelligence agencies, particularly ASIS. A 2004 inquiry conducted by the former head of the Department of Foreign Affairs and Trade

(DFAT) Philip Flood found that intelligence on JI was inadequate. '[I]n fact,' he wrote, 'little was known of Jemaah Islamiyah under that name . . . Australia and regional countries should have known, by the end of 2001, much more about Jemaah Islamiyah, its development of terrorist capabilities and its intentions towards Western targets.' Moreover, while ONA assessments 'reflected an increasingly deep understanding of the JI threat, [the] Defence Intelligence Organisation continued to assess that regional extremist groups were domestically focused and had little intent or capability to target foreigners or launch mass-scale terrorist attacks'.

Flood barely touched upon one of the continuing weaknesses of the intelligence and defence agencies: the inherent racism that has meant only a tiny proportion of operatives either come from a non-English speaking background or are fluent in a relevant language. And at the top executive level they are practically non-existent. The situation would improve slightly from initiatives in the relatively brief Rudd administration, but it remains a serious shortcoming.

Paradoxically, the Bali tragedy had the remarkably beneficial effect of transforming – at least for a time – the truculent relationship between Australia and Indonesia, particularly within the intelligence and security community. The AFP, ASIO and ASIS provided an unprecedented measure of cooperation with the Indonesian police and security forces in seeking out the culprits. At one stage the highly respected Australian ambassador to Indonesia, Ric Smith, was host to more than 100 federal and state police, DFAT and ASIS operatives.

Smith's presence was itself a happy chance. Born in Western Australia in 1944, he had risen through the ranks at DFAT and was acting secretary of the department in 1993. Prior to his Jakarta posting he had been ambassador to China from 1996 and would later become secretary of the Defence Department. His close links with key Indonesian Government figures would be a great asset in the early stages of the investigation.

The Indonesians responded, and Bali's police chief, I Made Pastika, developed a very close working relationship with AFP chief Mick Keelty. 'Pastika was a very good man,' Ric Smith says. 'He had been Chief of Police of West Papua where he did a very good job; and of course now he's the Governor of Bali.' Indeed, the sense of partnership against a common foe was reflected at all intergovernmental levels.

It was an extraordinarily successful operation. On 30 April 2003, the first charges were laid against one of the bombers, and by September three of the perpetrators had been found guilty and sentenced to death. A fourth was given life imprisonment. The executions would be carried out on 9 November 2008. Philip Flood called it 'outstanding work' between the two countries' police forces. In fact, it owed much to the work of DSD in tracking the bombers electronically and passing their information secretly to AFP officer Michael Kelsey. 'JI's rise,' Flood said, 'demonstrates the crucial importance of Australian agencies being alert to shifts in the regional security environment and the emergence of new threats.'

The plight of the victims' families in the aftermath of the bombings had resonated within the Australian community, so when the first publicly acknowledged military contingent departed for Iraq to fight in 'the war on terror' in 2003, both the prime minister and the opposition leader, Simon Crean, were on hand to wish them godspeed.

In fact, planning at Special Operations HQ in Canberra had been underway since May 2002. Whether this was an initiative of the special operations leadership or on orders from the prime minister is open to question. Howard consistently claimed that no decision to join the invasion was taken until the last moment. But in Canberra's labyrinthine corridors of power, signals come in many forms, most of them politically deniable. The likelihood is that Howard's security adviser quietly passed the word to trigger the military response. But signals were also, no doubt, semaphored from US intelligence sources to their Australian counterparts.

The SAS aspect of the operation was top secret, since it involved the clandestine cooperation of a supposedly neutral country – the Kingdom of Jordan – which was desperate not to be seen publicly as a cooperative American ally. Once again, 1 Squadron was chosen as the spearhead of the Australian force. Just before Christmas 2002, the OC, 'Paul', assembled his men at Swanbourne's Campbell Barracks and gave them a 'heads up' on the deployment. Soon afterwards a command group headed out to the Jordanian capital, Amman, to set up a base and begin battle planning.

On arrival, they were whisked by bus to Al Jaffa, a remote military facility in the north-east, where the Americans had already established a Special Forces encampment. British SAS soldiers were also embedded, and patrol commander Nev Bonner was among the Australian command group. 'No one told the others what we were doing,' he says, 'but it was generally friendly and the tucker was plentiful.'[4]

By the time the rest of the squadron arrived, the command group had developed a plan to insert a troop by helicopter into their AO deep in the Iraqi Western Desert prior to the invasion. They would observe and report on the main access routes when the 'shock and awe' bombardment of Baghdad began. The rest of the squadron would lead a combined Allied force in their LRPVs with the task of controlling the two principal roads east–west out of Iraq: Route 10 and Highway 1.

By now Australia's Special Forces had access to the most detailed satellite imagery in planning their route across the desert. 'Our biggest difficulty,' Bonner says, 'was avoiding all the military establishments and armoured units of the Iraqi Army. Once we agreed on the route, we decided that near our AO my patrol would split from the squadron and establish a food and water cache that could be a means of survival should any of our blokes become separated during the coming battles. After that, we would rejoin the squadron and be prepared for further tasks as they developed.'

With the squadron lined up in their LRPVs on the border early in the morning of 19 March 2003 the OC made a final check with HQ and then broke radio silence with a single order: 'Go!' The vehicles roared into life. 'Away we went to invade Iraq,' Bonner says. 'There were a few US soldiers around and some of them saluted. I was worried about the risk of landmines, but we got through without incident.'

For the next five weeks the SAS operators swept across the bare Iraqi landscape, patrolled their AO, monitored the escape routes, and took the Al Asad airbase with massive US air assaults and very little resistance. They captured more than 50 MIG fighters dismantled and buried in the sand, together with almost eight million kilograms of explosive.

Bonner says, 'On Anzac Day 2003, we were still in Al Asad where in typical Aussie fashion we commemorated the anniversary that means so much to Australian soldiers, especially the SASR. The lads all piled up on one of Saddam's command bunkers near the control tower in a formation reminiscent of that famous photo of the 11th Battalion on the pyramids in 1914 before they left for the Dardanelles.'[5] Soon afterwards they were told that US forces were on their way to take over. Al Asad would become the biggest American airbase in Iraq. The squadron then left for the return trip to Australia, where they received the Unit Citation for Gallantry – the first time it had been awarded.

For the moment, Australian forces withdrew from the Iraqi battlefield, while the Americans and British conducted their vain search for Saddam's fabled WMDs. Indeed, Philip Flood's review of the Australian intelligence agencies' performance in this area was unequivocal: 'Australia shared in the Allied intelligence failure on the key question of Iraq WMD stockpiles,' he said, 'with ONA more exposed and DIO more cautious on the subject.'

While noting that Saddam retained the 'ambition and intent' to have a WMD program, 'the lack of comprehensive assessment which might have been achieved by production of a National Assessment by ONA or an Intelligence Estimate by DIO to support ADF deployment considerations, was regrettable . . . Intelligence was thin, ambiguous and incomplete . . . the Inquiry recommends a number of changes to ONA and DIO processes to improve the robustness of assessments.'

Other conventional forces from the Big Army would later be deployed to provide security for a Japanese reconstruction unit in one of the less fractious provinces of Iraq. It was a clever political move by Prime Minister Howard, as it allowed him to win his spurs as a fighting ally of the United States (whose president would dub him – to his obvious delight – 'a man of steel'), while ensuring that Australia's troops were well out of the firing line. In the event, no Australian troops were killed or taken prisoner throughout the entire duration of the war.

Under the public radar, a new element of the Special Forces contingent had its first taste of war in the Middle East when a platoon of 4 RAR Commandos joined the SAS Squadron in Jordan. Their departure had been so hastily arranged that they arrived without adequate cold-weather or sleeping gear and they had to 'borrow' it from the SAS. They, together with the Incident Response Regiment support, joined them in the attack on Al Asad. They also returned to Australia when the SAS withdrew.

By now the commando unit had made good progress towards establishing itself as a viable commando force within Special

Operations Command (SOCOMD). But the pace of Special Forces activities in the Middle East and the region meant that responsibility for the military response to counterterrorism remained with the SAS. It also meant that the professional cadre of the reserve 1 Commando Regiment was pressed into service, providing support to Special Forces operations in Qatar and subsequently in Bougainville, the Solomon Islands and other regional trouble spots.

In September 2003, 1 Commando commemorated the 60th anniversary of the Jaywick raid on Singapore Harbour when it hosted the newly appointed CDF, General Peter Cosgrove, at a ceremony with the remaining members of the team – Moss Berryman and Horrie Young – at the National Maritime Museum. Also attending was the newly appointed Special Forces commander, Major General Duncan Lewis. Under General Lewis, the 126 Signals Squadron was transferred to provide communications for 4 RAR (Commando) and a new Signals Squadron 301 would eventually be raised to support the reserve unit.

The following year, the regiment's outgoing CO, Lieutenant Colonel Anthony John, said, 'As we reach the end of 2004, reserve members of the unit are in operations in Iraq, East Timor and preparing to deploy on Operation Relex in the Northern Australian waters as boarding parties. We are reinforcing a 4 RAR (Commando) rotation to Malaysia and on standby to provide support in responding to terrorist incidents in Australia. This displays a very high level of flexibility.'

The regiment's historian Peter Collins looked forward to an era of 'closer integration and co-dependence' of regular and reserve Special Forces. '1 Commando Regiment gives us a glimpse into the future,' he said. 'This is not simply a Special Forces structure but potentially the whole structure of the Australian Army.

'After the two world wars of the twentieth century, the prospect of global conflict has, mercifully, receded but in its place has been a never ending series of regional conflicts . . . if [this] trend continues then the demand for more highly trained and mobile forces will also continue. This translates to a probable demand for more Special Forces.'

In 2005 Duncan Lewis transferred from the command of Special Forces to a new position in the Department of PM&C to become the government's top civilian adviser on counterterrorism. He was replaced by a former SAS commander, Major General Mike Hindmarsh.

INTELLIGENCE PROBLEMS

Overwhelmingly, these overseas Special Forces actions were conducted well below the public radar. Secrecy is the essence of SAS operations on the battlefield. The same applies to the regiment's ongoing reconnaissance of potential hotspots in the region, the Middle East and as far distant as Africa. According to one defence planner, 'Wherever the threat – or the potential threat – that's where we need to be.'[1]

The official flow of information to the public is minimal and occasionally misleading, as befits a unit that operates in the shadowy world of international terrorism and where in combat zones it is routinely tasked to assassinate the enemy's high-value targets (HVTs). But, from time to time, the regiment does open its door a crack. In 1984, for example, the CO Lieutenant Colonel Chris Roberts commissioned a television documentary of the legendary selection course, entitled *Battle for the Golden Road*. It would enhance the regimental image and attract more candidates.

It was not the best news for the men on the course. Clint Palmer, who would later rise to become an SAS warrant officer, says, 'I'll never forget it. They were torturing us. They wanted to really portray the toughness of it. We had these guys running around saying, "Can we just do that again please? Run up the hill and jump over the log . . . now let's try a different angle so we can get the sun coming up".[2] Nevertheless it was an effective 'branding' operation and was repeated in 2010 with *The Search for Warriors*, which gained record viewing figures for the television network that screened it.

However, while it served its purpose from the regiment's viewpoint, it was also an exercise in public deception – an accusation that the SAS proudly accepts. There was no hint, for example, of the most gruelling element of the selection process – interrogation resistance – which uses physical and psychological devices deliberately designed to drive the candidates to breaking point and risks serious long-term mental damage. One candidate who actually topped his 1991 selection course and went on to a distinguished career in the SAS says, 'They were not allowed to injure us, but they went about as far as they could without doing physical injury. What mental trauma their actions might have caused I cannot say but I think there may be serious health ramifications from some of the techniques they used against us. Looking back now, I believe that experiences like these can shape the psyche of a person for the rest of his life.'[3] He is now retired and suffers from post-traumatic stress disorder (PTSD).

The interrogators on that occasion were from ASIS. 'They used the SASR selection to hone their interrogation skills and procedures,' he says. 'It must have been a great opportunity to do realistic interrogation techniques on Defence personnel, one that would normally arise only in times of war.'

It was indeed. And it is understood that the use of ASIS personnel in this way was later terminated. But if the SAS spearhead of our Special Forces operated in the twilight of public perception, their ASIS colleagues conducted their business behind a shield of almost total invisibility. At the time of the SAS interrogation, ASIS remained under the direction of its long-time head, Jim

Furner. The following year he retired and was succeeded by a career ASIS officer, Rex Stevenson. The new director-general had spent 20 years in the agency with postings to Bangkok, Kuala Lumpur and Washington. His appointment coincided with a period of internal turmoil, and a series of complaints against management boiled over into the media. They derived from the inherent tension between the Agency and its 'mother ship', the Department of Foreign Affairs, in the years prior to his appointment. And paradoxically they came at a time when its operational reputation was thriving. However, complaints from both sides had been left unattended by the office of the Inspector General of Security for 18 months. They had festered to the point where several ASIS officers enlisted the Liberal Opposition and then the press to vent their grievances.

'It was a little like a marriage break-up,' said one former close observer. 'It escalated to where people were taking sides.'[4]

It came to a head after a series of operational 'leaks' of classified information had caused severe disruption internally. And it culminated publicly when two ASIS officers and their wives appeared on *Four Corners* on 21 February 1994 alleging ASIS regularly flouted laws, kept dossiers on Australian citizens and hounded agents out of the service with little explanation.

The agency favoured a royal commission but the Labor Government's Foreign Minister, Gareth Evans, initiated a judicial inquiry by Judge Gordon Samuels and former Secretary of PM&C, Mike Codd. Coincidentally, it was signed off by former ASIS ministerial head, Bill Hayden, who now basked in the role of governor-general. The two commissioners were asked to examine the control and accountability of the service, the protection of its human intelligence sources and methods, and the resolution of grievances and complaints.

The result was much wider and more penetrating than expected. The commissioners found that the organisation needed a thorough overhaul. However, the initial complaints, they found, were not justified. 'It is not surprising that there should develop a culture which sets great store by faithfulness and stoicism and tends to elevate conformity to undue heights and to regard the exercise of authority rather than consultation as the managerial norm,' they reported. 'The nature of ASIS's operational activities inevitably means that members of staff are subject to pressures and restrictions, present in Australia but more onerous at postings overseas. They are bound to a level of secrecy rarely imposed on individuals in other organisations and cannot talk about their work even to family and friends . . .'

There were two fundamental reasons for secrecy – the effectiveness of the agency and the safety of both the ASIS spymasters and their agents in place. 'The Minister would rank these with the need to avoid damage to foreign relations,' they said, 'but arguably this is not as compelling a consideration; in any case, the secrecy required to protect operations and individuals should be sufficient to ensure that diplomatic embarrassment is avoided.'

They took evidence from some leading political journalists of the day including Michelle Grattan, Paul Kelly, Peter Harvey and Alan Kohler, and warned that prohibiting all information about ASIS to the media could be self-defeating. It meant that any information that reached the press became big news and there was no effective way to correct misconceptions. Indeed, ASIS officers present found Kohler's presentation 'spellbinding'.

The commissioners noted that ASIO had engaged more openly with the media and, 'while greater publicity can impose its own pressures on an intelligence agency, there is no indication that this has impeded the effectiveness of ASIO . . . We think it is clear that ASIS can no longer afford to maintain a wholly passive stance in public and media relations. It should engage with the media and adopt a positive approach to the management of its public profile.'

Management was far from perfect. 'There must be an acceptance within ASIS that staff will disagree with management decisions from time to time,' they said. 'Not only is that not disloyal, it can contribute to the diversity of ideas and the general health of the organisation . . . It is a case of managers not allowing the requirements of intelligence collection to dictate attitudes and actions in ordinary dealings with staff.'

It took the successive administrations until 2001 to act on some of its principal recommendations. That year, at ASIS's initiative – and with the support of DSD which also sought a legislative framework – legislation was passed to supersede the directive that until then had governed ASIS operations.

Even then, one of the original complainants – Warren Reed – told the ABC's PM radio program that the public was still unaware of the real problems within the service. 'Hardly anything has changed,' he said. 'Nobody was really disciplined. In fact some of the people involved have been given Orders of Australia, and very highly rewarded.' Nevertheless, the complainants themselves had received a multi-million-dollar settlement in a mediation with Mr Justice Street.

And publicly ASIS remained a closed shop.

By this time Rex Stevenson had retired and in 1998 was replaced by a career diplomat, Allan Taylor. Born in Wynyard, Tasmania, in 1941, he had served as ambassador to Indonesia and high commissioner to Papua New Guinea before heading the International Division of PM&C.

The commissioners' most detailed review focused on the manner in which other elements of government – through the National Intelligence Collection Requirements Committee

(NICRC) – set the priorities for ASIS operations, and indeed the other collecting agencies.

The committee, chaired by ONA, included the DIO, the Departments of Defence and Foreign Affairs, the ADF, ASIO, DSD and ASIS itself, with the AFP and Customs included for transnational issues. The requirements laid down were usually very broad and the commissioners noted that ASIS 'prefers its tasking to be in the form of a set of questions to which it can pursue answers'. Significantly, DFAT 'no longer has any control, over ASIS' yet 'the relationship between the two organisations remains of vital importance to ASIS'.

The commissioners found the tasking arrangements eminently satisfactory, particularly as they were being continually refined. They were unaware, however, that an agency of the federal government itself was even then preparing to perpetrate the biggest international scandal in Australia's history. And one of its most eager confidants – BHP – would be implicated.

Now known as the Oil for Food scandal, it had its genesis in the 1991 UN decision to impose a financial and trade embargo on Saddam Hussein's Iraq. However, as the effects were seen to be taking a terrible toll on Iraqi children – courtesy of Saddam's duplicitous propaganda campaign – the world relented in 1995 and allowed Iraq to sell its oil with the returns deposited in a UN bank account from which the regime, under UN oversight, could buy food and medicine.

For many years the Australian Wheat Board and its privatised entity, AWB Limited, had been a major supplier to Iraq, well ahead of its competition from Canada and the US. According to investigative journalists Marian Wilkinson and David Marr, 'Within hours of the resolution passing the UN Security Council, the AWB salesmen were back on the road to Baghdad. These were crazy, dangerous journeys that ended in brief meetings, long lunches and huge wheat deals.'[5]

The Australian Government was responsible for ensuring that all cargo left its shores in accordance with the sanctions. Over the next five years Foreign Minister Alexander Downer and officers of DFAT would approve 292 ships carrying 12 million tonnes of wheat worth more than $2 billion. Almost every cargo breached the UN sanctions. The contracts would include a phoney 'trucking fee' paid to the Iraqis, in reality a kickback worth millions to Saddam's regime.

By now Saddam had banned US wheat and Canada refused to pay 'trucking fees', which were clearly outside the UN regulations. This left the AWB master of the field. But in early 2000 a Canadian diplomat told the UN that the AWB was paying the fees in breach of the sanctions code. The information, this whistleblower said, had come direct from the Iraqi Grain Board.

A UN official, Felicity Johnston, immediately contacted Australia's UN mission seeking discreet, high-level inquiries to be made into the AWB. And here the record becomes fuzzy, with claims and counter-claims by DFAT and UN officials. There are also suggestions that intelligence generated overseas arrived at DFAT and PM&C in these terms: 'Alia [the supposed trucking company] received fees in Jordan for the discharge and inland transport within Iraq of goods purchased under the oil-for-food program ... the fees, less a small commission, were paid into accounts accessible by Iraq in violation of sanctions. The amounts involved were very substantial.'[6]

They became much more so after November 2000 when the new head of the Iraqi Grain Board raised the kickback to 10 per cent of all wheat contracts under the program. And DFAT continued to rubber stamp the AWB contracts en route to the UN for payment. According to Wilkinson and Marr, 'The last two contracts signed with Saddam's ministers were the dirtiest of them all. They were loaded with "trucking fees" of more than $US50 million; a further scam of more than $US2 million; and the repayment of a debt to Tigris Petroleum of a further $US8.4 million.'

This is where BHP came in. In 1995 and early 1996, BHP shipped 20,000 tons of Australian wheat valued at $5 million to Iraq 'to establish favour with the Government of Iraq in anticipation that sometime prior to 2000 the letter of credit may be exchanged with the Government of Iraq as a down payment for entry to the Halfaya [oil field] concession'.[7]

Now they were demanding payment of the 'debt', with $3.4 million in interest. And payment was made, but not to BHP, since almost all of it finished up in the pocket of a former senior executive-cum-internal consultant to BHP, one Norman Davidson Kelly and his company Tigris Petroleum. The AWB paid themselves a $US500,000 'collection fee' before transferring the funds to Tigris.

In his 2006 report on the scandal, Commissioner Terence Cole called the initial wheat shipment a 'soft bribe' by BHP and said Kelly was a 'thoroughly disreputable man with no commercial morality' who ought to be investigated 'for possible breaches of Victoria's Crimes Act.'

In the event, no charges were laid. Both Alexander Downer and Prime Minister John Howard were called to give evidence at the inquiry, and the commissioner found that neither 'were ever informed about or otherwise acquired knowledge of the relevant activities of AWB'.

In so doing, he exposed serious defects in the tasking system, amounting to tunnel vision among the intelligence agencies charged with the protection of Australia's national interests. Both ASIO and ASIS should have had a clear role to play in exposing the scam to the authorities within government – in this case the AFP.

While the AFP itself was not positioned to uncover the kickback scheme, it was carried out under the noses of the relevant agencies at home and abroad.

In the absence of a federal anti-corruption agency, it could well be argued that the intelligence services have a responsibility of maintaining Australia's reputation within the international body politic as well as its own ranks. In this case, they not only failed but also subsequently (so far as we know) chose not to review their procedures to prevent reoccurrences.

While the Cole Inquiry exonerated Prime Minister Howard and Foreign Minister Downer, it provided an opportunity for the opposition Foreign Affairs spokesman, Kevin Rudd, to show his forensic wares at question time in the parliament. His performance marked him out as a future leader, a perception that Rudd himself had nurtured from young adulthood.

At the same time, the government was increasing its armoury to deal with external threats. The Defence Imagery and Geospatial Organisation (DIGO) was established in November 2000. The new Special Forces pillar was a merger of the AIO, formerly attached to DIO, the Defence Topographic Agency in Bendigo, Victoria, and the Directorate of Strategic Military Geospatial Information. Its mission was 'to provide geospatial intelligence from imagery and other sources in support of Australia defence and national interests' – in short, to be Australia's spy in the sky. With facilities in both Bendigo and Canberra, DIGO worked to create the most detailed electronic mapping from space for military and peacekeeping operations. Their priorities too were set by the NICRC.

By 2004, they had more than 300 staff with an annual budget of $90 million, with capital expenditure of over $150 million expected in the next three years. Indeed, it was growing so fast that in his 2004 Inquiry into Australian Intelligence Agencies,

Philip Flood suggested the new boy on the block had become too pushy and had put some bureaucratic noses out of joint. 'Efforts by DIGO to promote the agency as having an all-source assessment responsibility were unhelpful to relations within the intelligence community,' he said. 'A balance needs to be struck. DIGO is not an all-source assessment agency. Neither, however, is it simply a provider of images and maps. DIGO undertakes single source analysis and dissemination of geospatial intelligence product. It needs the leeway to produce in this context.'

The settling-in issues were understandable. The Bendigo boys were of a new generation to whom electronic spyware from space was a panacea laying bare the enemy's command and control, weaponry and personnel as well as their disposition in the battlespace. They were impatient with old-style HUMINT, and this was guaranteed to provoke a reaction from the more mature agencies (who were not nearly as 'out of touch' as the newcomers imagined).

DIGO asserted its key role as 'support for the ADF', and Flood strongly suggested that the Defence Department needed to recognise its strengths. 'Too frequently,' he said, 'DIGO receives tasking to provide illustrative products to support briefings rather than being given specific intelligence requirements to produce against.' Moreover, the pace of ADF operational activity at the time – from East Timor to Afghanistan to Iraq – meant that DIGO staff were fully occupied on the highest priority targets. 'The tendency for current intelligence tasks to crowd out longer term intelligence work is an issue that affects all intelligence agencies,' he said.

It was partly to address this long-term issue that in 2000 the Howard Government created an organisation unique in Western democracies 'to provide alternative sources of input to government decision-making processes on major strategic and defence policy issues'. ASPI would be funded by the Defence Department as well as ASIS and ASIO up to $3 million annually for the next seven years. It would also be permitted to accept private funding, and in time the Commonwealth Bank of Australia would supply more than 10 per cent of its growing multimillion-dollar annual budget. Its board would include nominees of the prime minister and the leader of the opposition.

Its charter, signed by Defence Minister Peter Reith, said, 'The Government believes that contestability of advice is an important contributor to good public policy and is concerned that in the strategic and defence policy arena the range of alternative views on which the government can draw is not well developed. ASPI is intended to help remedy this.'

It was a remarkable step – the Defence Department was in effect funding an opposition to its own thoroughly considered advice to government on the key issues of its portfolio. 'It probably couldn't happen anywhere else,' one senior Defence official said. 'But Canberra's a small place and we have some very good people. A lot of that is luck.'[8]

As well as its advice to government, ASPI would have a public face through which it would 'increase understanding of strategic and defence policy issues among Australians . . . and promote international understanding of Australia's defence perspectives'. It would be a private company and its CEO (director) would be a figure of 'significant standing'.

The founding director ticked the appropriate boxes. Hugh White had been deputy secretary for strategy and intelligence in the Defence Department since 1995 and prior to that a senior adviser on the staffs of Defence Minister Kim Beazley and Prime Minister Bob Hawke. He had also spent time as a journalist on the *Sydney Morning Herald*, so (unlike many of his public service colleagues) he could actually string together a simple declarative sentence. He became a familiar figure on the nation's television screens, and in 2004 he handed the baton to retired major general Peter Abigail, the former land commander of the Australian Army.

Abigail was much less prominent publicly, but he brought practical military experience to the role having spent 37 years as a soldier. By then the institute was well established among the national and international lobby groups across the lake from the imposing domain of Defence's Russell Hill complex, where stood that most conspicuous architectural feature within its modest but orderly surrounds: the American eagle poised for flight on the phallic monument to the alliance that saved Australia in World War II . . . better known to the locals as 'Bugs Bunny'.

David Combe (*seated*) retires as national secretary of the Australian Labor Party and is given a farewell by (*left to right*) Bill Hayden, Bob Hawke and Bob McMullan. He would soon after come to the attention of the KGB and ASIO. (*Newspix*)

Soviet diplomat Valeriy Ivanov at Sydney Airport as he prepared to fly back to Moscow after being expelled from Australia following allegations that he was a Russian spy. (*Newspix/Simon Bullard*)

Justice Robert Hope led the Royal Commission on Intelligence and Security and the Royal Commission on Australia's Security and Intelligence Agencies.
(*NAA: A12386, EO/1/2*)

Harvey Barnett, director-general of ASIO from 1981 to 1985.

(*National Library of Australia/ Canberra Times*)

Brigadier Duncan Lewis and Prime Minister John Howard welcome back SAS troops from Afghanistan in 2002. (*Newspix/Megan Lewis*)

Then commanding officer of the SAS, Lieutenant Colonel 'Gus' Gilmore, at Swanbourne's Campbell Barracks in June 2002. (*Newspix/John Feder*)

The US–Australian Joint Defence Facility at Pine Gap, Northern Territory.
(*Newspix/Will Caddy*)

Head of the Regional Assistance Mission to the Solomon Islands (RAMSI), Nick Warner, talks to Malaita Eagle Force leader Jimmy Rasta in 2003.
(*Newspix/John Feder*)

Prime Minister Kevin Rudd talks to Dennis Richardson in Washington DC. Richardson was director-general of ASIO from 1996 to 2005, Australian Ambassador to the United States from 2005 to 2010, and appointed Secretary of the Department of Defence in 2012.
(*Newspix/Anthony Reginato*)

Rob Maylor (*centre*) of the SAS, outside Tarin Kot, Afghanistan. (*Courtesy of Rob Maylor*)

The SAS patrol a deserted Afghan village. (*Courtesy of Stuart Bonner*)

Victoria Cross recipients corporals Mark Donaldson (*left*) and Ben Roberts-Smith (*second right*) along with Lieutenant General Ken Gillespie (*second left*) and Major General 'Gus' Gilmore (*right*). (*Newspix/Colin Murty*)

(*Left to right*) Michael Thawley, secretary of the Department of Prime Minister and Cabinet; Duncan Lewis, director-general of ASIO; Nick Warner, director-general of ASIS; and Dennis Richardson, secretary of the Department of Defence, listen to Prime Minister Tony Abbott's National Security Statement at the Australian Federal Police headquarters in Canberra, 2015. (*Newspix/Kym Smith*)

25

INTELLIGENCE–MILITARY CONVERGENCE

By 2005, ASIO's operations had been transformed. The attack on the Twin Towers followed by the Bali bombing, the Afghan conflict and the war in Iraq meant that now well over 70 per cent of its resources were devoted to international counterterrorism.

These priorities were reflected in other elements of government. In mid-2003, Prime Minister Howard had created a National Security Division within his own department for independent advice on defence, intelligence and non-proliferation of WMDs. It also incorporated one of the natural consequences of the turmoil in the Middle East: so-called 'border protection' from displaced persons seeking asylum from persecution in their own riven communities.

The refugees were fleeing in their thousands and seeking protection and resettlement across Europe, America and other countries untouched by the warfare. And while there was some resentment among the settled communities of Europe, the reaction in Australia – particularly after the *Tampa* imbroglio – verged on the hysterical. It would continue to be a potent political issue for more than a decade.

But while ASIO was under pressure from refugee organisations to process claims for asylum more quickly, its overwhelming concern remained terrorism. In 2004 it created a National Threat Assessment Centre within its Canberra HQ to provide round-the-clock assessment by 40 analysts and support staff. Included in the team were ASIS and DSD operatives to ensure information was shared between agencies.

Director-General Dennis Richardson also developed a number of inter-agency bodies to improve communication and cooperation, such as the Joint Counter-Terrorism Intelligence Coordination Unit. And an ambassador for counterterrorism was established in the Foreign Affairs Department. Under his watch the government committed an additional $3.1 billion over seven years to fund these and other measures.

Though physically diminutive, Richardson is one of the towering figures of the recent Australian bureaucracy, with powerful supporters on both sides of the political spectrum. Born in rural Kempsey, New South Wales, in 1947, he took an arts degree at Sydney University in 1968 and was one of the 'famous 69' public service intake. He first made his mark in Foreign Affairs, then in 1986 he moved to PM&C. He was head of Immigration and Multicultural Affairs for three years before his appointment to ASIO.

Richardson increased the flow of intelligence from the US and other Allied countries; and while ASIS concentrated almost entirely on the collection of HUMINT from agents in the field, this product was now only a fraction of ASIO's operation. With input from the Australian network and its officers stationed overseas it had become a fully integrated collection, assessment and policy agency. According to Philip Flood at the time, 'ASIO's role is limited only by its function of security intelligence, not by geography.'

In his 2004 inquiry, Flood acknowledged Richardson's contribution. 'Effective communication is now one of the hallmarks of the Australian intelligence community,' he said. 'The cooperative nature of the community, the personal relationships between agency seniors and the relative lack of dispute between the agencies [are] highlights of the community.' The inspector-general of intelligence and security Ian Carnell, in his 2005 annual report, fully endorsed Flood's appraisal, calling Richardson 'a strong leader with a clearly evident commitment to transparency and accountability'. It was unsurprising then that the government selected him in 2005 for its most important and demanding overseas post, as ambassador to the United States.

By the time he took up his appointment in late 2005, the Allies' situation in Iraq and Afghanistan was on an accelerating downward slide. In Iraq, the Americans were losing up to 100 troops a month; they had suffered the international humiliation of graphic torture photographs from Abu Ghraib; US Secretary of State Colin Powell had publicly retracted and apologised for his support of the war based on doctored WMD intelligence; and the capture of Saddam Hussein only emboldened the Shiite majority, who dominated the 2005 election. Sunni and al-Qaeda militias were now sending car bombs and assassination squads into Shiite suburbs and towns.

When SAS 2 Squadron withdrew from Al Asad in late 2003, they had been replaced by elements of the Special Forces Task Group, including SAS and the Incident Response Regiment. In May 2005, Australian businessman Douglas Wood was kidnapped by insurgents from his Baghdad home and held for ransom. Prime Minister Howard publicly called for his release and refused to accede to demands that Australia pull out its troops. But he did nothing to discourage Wood's family from conducting a public-relations campaign on his behalf. Behind the scenes, he assigned his senior departmental security adviser Nick Warner to head an SAS operation to discover his whereabouts and rescue him.

Warner was well fitted for the task. He had been born in Singapore in 1950, the son of Denis Warner, a distinguished war and South-East Asian correspondent for the Melbourne Herald group, who maintained close connections with Australian and American intelligence services. Nick studied history at the ANU and in 1973 joined the JIO. He later worked in the ONA as liaison officer in Rhodesia (Zimbabwe) and its Canberra headquarters before transfer to the Department of Foreign Affairs, where his intelligence background was no impediment as he rose through the ranks.

In 2003, he was given charge of the Regional Assistance Mission to the Solomon Islands (RAMSI) when civil order collapsed in the face of systemic corruption and tribal conflict. An international security force of 2,200 police and troops successfully re-established the rule of law, but the operation would continue for a decade before Australian and New Zealand peacekeepers could be safely withdrawn.

Coincidentally, when Wood was taken, SAS 3 Squadron was in Adelaide training for overseas recovery operations. A member of the squadron, Rob Maylor, says, 'We reckoned the timing couldn't have been more perfect. We all returned to Perth and prepared to embark four patrols to Baghdad. Defence engaged a civilian charter plane and we flew direct to Kuwait where we put some gear together at an Allied base that had been maintained there since the first Gulf War. We landed at Baghdad international airport around midday and transferred to armoured vehicles for the drive to [the Green Zone] where the Australian Security Detachment (SECDET) were staying.'[1]

One patrol bunked with a team from the US Delta Force, while the other was attached to the British Special Boat Service, the Special Forces unit of the Royal Marines. They rehearsed each day doing building clearances, insertion and extraction operations and close-order combat. 'There was a lot of information coming forward to the Americans,' Maylor says, 'but nothing of substance. Our intelligence guys in Baghdad worked hard to get information also. It was the first overseas recovery job the Australians were involved in so the agencies wanted to do a top job.'

Warner worked with the ASIS operatives on the ground and liaised with the American intelligence community. The Americans were spreading lots of cash around, and the results were enthusiastic but largely unproductive. Warner and his team demanded a higher standard of proof than the Americans before the troops responded. 'However,' Maylor says, 'just as some really good information came forward a combined American–Iraqi operation swept through an area and found him. We were happy for Douglas Wood but disappointed we were not able to help with the recovery.' Before leaving, the SAS team completed a five-day security survey on the Australian Embassy and devised a contingency plan in case of attack.

When they returned to Australia, they resumed training but word soon passed around that reinforcements were needed for 2 Squadron in Afghanistan. In October, Maylor and five other members of his troop were chosen. 'We took the same chartered plane that had flown us to the Middle East earlier that year,' he says. From Kuwait they flew to Qatar and then to Tarin Kot, the Australian HQ in their area of responsibility: the hostile province of Oruzgan. 'Three days later we were heading out on patrol.'[2]

By now NATO had assumed command of Allied forces, though the Americans still dominated in the battlefield. The American-backed Hamid Karzai had been elected to the Afghan presidency with 55 per cent of the vote. But with major US resources diverted to Iraq, the Taliban, assisted by Chechen and other Islamist groups, were making a comeback. Maylor says, 'When speaking to the locals, the first standard response was, "Taliban? There hasn't been a Taliban here for 12 months." And the other was, "Yes, that village down the road is full of Taliban." So we treated every village with care.'

They patrolled in the field without a break for a full month, with contacts every few days. After a week's rest, they returned to the area around Saraw, a known Taliban hotspot, and soon were in combat against an elusive enemy. In an instructive example of Special Forces convergence, they worked with ASIS and DSD operatives at headquarters, while in the field they were joined by elements of 4 RAR (Commando), which by now had reached full strength and would take an increasing role in the Afghan conflict. The SAS would provide the reconnaissance and overwatch, with snipers tasked to take out high- and medium-value targets, while the commandos would deploy in greater numbers in the valleys with mortars and other weaponry.

In the early days, there was a sense of condescension bordering on resentment among some members of the SAS towards their 4 RAR compatriots. It would take up to a year of combined operations before each understood and appreciated the special skills of the other and operated as a mutually respectful unit. Afghanistan was a good proving ground, but such were the demands on Special Forces that there was little time for non-combat bonding exercises. Maylor and his 3 Squadron colleagues left Afghanistan in January 2006 and a month later they were training for a return to East Timor.

In February, about a quarter of the East Timorese military force of 1,500 soldiers deserted their barracks and, despite pleas from government leaders, refused to return. Then, in May, Major Alfredo Reinado and his unit defected to the rebels, taking with them two trucks full of weapons and ammunition. Violent gangs roamed the streets of Dili, burning down houses and torching cars. The civilians who fled Dili camped in tent towns or in churches on the outskirts. On 12 May, Prime Minister Howard announced that although there had been no formal request for assistance, two amphibious warfare transport ships, HMAS *Kanimbla* and HMAS *Manoora*, were being deployed offshore.

Soon afterwards the violence escalated, and Foreign Minister Ramos-Horta sent an official request to Australia, New Zealand, Malaysia and Portugal. By now Maylor and his team had reached Darwin, where they joined with a company of 4 RAR (Commando) as a cordon force. Maylor says, 'The majority weren't airborne-rappel or fast-rope trained so we spent a couple of days getting the boys up to speed.' Three days later they deployed to Dili and Maylor joined a group providing close protection for Xanana Gusmão and his Australian wife, Kirsty, as well as Ramos-Horta and Prime Minister Mari Alkatiri, who many believed was the guiding force behind the rebellion.

A month later, Xanana forced Alkatiri to resign and Reinado was captured. The violence quickly subsided. By August, the Australian troops had withdrawn from most points of the country, and later that month Reinado escaped from Becora prison in Dili. He fled to the mountains, and from his hideout he attempted to negotiate a pardon. In 2007, Australian Special Forces engaged his unit in a firefight at Same but he escaped. Finally in February 2008 he was killed during coordinated rebel attacks on Xanana Gusmão and Ramos-Horta.

The Special Forces intervention revived Indonesian memories of the earlier Australian-led invasion. And, by coincidence, in 2007 New South Wales Coroner Dorelle Pinch finally conducted an inquest into the death of Brian Peters, one of the Balibo Five. After taking evidence from both Indonesian and Australian witnesses, she found that he and his colleagues had died 'when shot and/or stabbed deliberately, and not in the heat of battle, by members of the Indonesian Special Forces'.

The killings, she said, were carried out 'on the orders of Captain Yunus Yosfiah to prevent [them] from revealing that Indonesian Special Forces had participated in the attack on Balibo. There is strong circumstantial evidence that those orders emanated from the Head of the Indonesian Special Forces, Major General Benny Murdani to Colonel Dading Kalbuadi, Special Forces Group Commander in Timor and then to Captain Yosfiah.'

She said the journalists had no risk-management training prior to undertaking the assignment. 'Nor was there a mix of experience and inexperience,' she said. 'The Balibo Five were all relatively inexperienced.' Training courses for such assignments were now available, but commercial television networks, it seemed, were the organisations least likely to have their staff trained.

'The other aspect that emerges from the facts of this inquest,' she noted, 'is that the journalists appeared to be unaware that their legal status could be jeopardised if they became involved in tasks that were linked to a combat role.'

In Jakarta an Indonesian Foreign Ministry spokesman, Kristiano Legowo, said the findings would not change its account of the killings. 'It will not change Indonesia's stance that for us it is a closed case,' he said, 'and we are still in the position that they were killed because of crossfire between conflicting sides at the time.'

The Australian Defence Department said the coroner had found that DSD 'had no intelligence which could have provided prior warning of the danger posed to the five journalists. None of the witnesses who gave evidence at the inquest about signals interception material they saw from 1975 onwards saw any material in terms of the alleged [intelligence] intercept.'

Either way, the resurfacing of the issue once again threw a wrench into the relationship, which since the Bali bombings had been running relatively smoothly. And it came at a time when Australia was particularly concerned to avoid the kind of Islamist terror bombings that had been visited on London as a result of Britain's involvement in Iraq and Afghanistan.

Ric Smith had transferred from his diplomatic role in Indonesia to become secretary of defence in 2002, until his retirement in 2006. Dennis Richardson had been replaced as director-general of ASIO by Paul O'Sullivan. And Nick Warner in turn was rewarded with the role of defence secretary in 2006 as Smith departed. A new figure had come to the fore in 2003 when career diplomat David Irvine was appointed director-general of ASIS, succeeding Allan Taylor.

At 55, Irvine was late to the spying game. But he quickly established himself as one of the agency's most astute leaders. A tall and imposing man with an engaging sense of humour, he was born in Perth and educated at the Hale School. He secured an Honours Degree in Elizabethan History from the University of Western Australia and played a sound game of cricket. His 33 years in the foreign service included postings to Port Moresby and Jakarta during the Indonesian invasion of East Timor. He not only learnt the Indonesian language but also absorbed sufficient of the national culture to author two well-regarded books on Javanese puppet theatre. Just prior to his ASIS appointment he had been ambassador to China at a time when the trading relationship with Australia was expanding exponentially. According to an Australian political leader, he provided 'a pair of very safe hands' during that period.

In his new ASIS role, he inherited an organisation about 200 strong, with one-third active in the field in most countries of the region. Its charter still forbade its operatives carrying weapons, except in special circumstances, and there were widespread suggestions that it had become overly dependent on American product.

However, Irvine's diplomatic skills would be essential in supporting his operatives and liaising with his Allied regional counterparts.

The appointments were another aspect of the emerging pattern of convergence within Australia's Special Forces establishment between the intelligence agencies, the military and the civilian departmental heads. The CDF in 2005, General Peter Cosgrove, was succeeded on his retirement late that year by Air Chief Marshal Angus Houston as commander of the Australian military within the unique arrangement of joint military/civilian control of the country's defence. The system is reflected in the office arrangements at Russell Hill HQ where the CDF and the defence secretary occupy adjoining suites on the top floor with a shared waiting room between. The offices themselves were then, and remain, modest by international standards and perfectly suited to easy personal communication. The occupants have developed a tradition of frequent informal chats as the need arises.

By 2007, their focus was directed principally on Afghanistan. Early that year the SAS was conducting a highly dangerous undercover operation in Kandahar, and once that was completed members of the unit drove to Tarin Kot. There they rejoined 3 Squadron and deployed in LRPVs for the journey to the American forward operating base (FOB), which, with a singular lack of imagination, they had also christened Anaconda. The Australians settled in for five days before heading out on the second phase of the operation.

By now they had been joined by a big detachment from 4 RAR (Commando) – about 120 troops in 40 vehicles, including support units of quartermaster staff and mechanics. In a classic Special Forces operation, the SAS patrols were inserted to a drop-off point in the dead of night about five kilometres into the countryside. From there they moved by foot to predetermined locations in the mountain range overlooking the village that would be cleared by 4 RAR.

They made two long-range 'kills' of enemy fighters and repeated the process several times over the next two weeks. They also combined with Canadian infantry mortar section, and were frequently accompanied by an American joint terminal attack controller (JTAC) to call in air support. The enemy was very active in the area, and IEDs were a constant hazard. Now they were involved in frontline hand-to-hand fighting.

From the Anaconda FOB they had to cross an open desert plain known as the 'dasht' until they reached the mountains and valleys – known as the 'green' – containing a sprinkling of village structures surrounded by crops and foliage. They were in deeply hostile territory. On one occasion, Maylor's patrol was travelling by LRPVs when the vehicle ahead struck a mine. 'It exploded right underneath the gearbox,' he says. 'I went to run forward but one of our guys shouted, "Stop!" He was concerned about the threat of a secondary device. Initially I thought, "Good call, mate" but then I thought, "No, bugger it, my mates are injured and they need help". So I ran forward with one other guy from my car.'

He found them bruised and battered but not seriously wounded. The troop sergeant organised a medical evacuation by two American Black Hawks flanked by Apache gunships and the patrol rigged a towline to the damaged vehicle. They headed back towards the dasht, but intelligence arrived by radio that another IED lay ahead. 'Everybody instantly became extra vigilant,' Maylor says. 'The dog handler and his dog Razz were out front with another engineer who was sweeping the ground with a mine detector. We were about 500 metres down the track when suddenly the dog got all excited.

'I must have been about 150 metres back at this stage. Razz ran back to the engineer wagging his tail, letting him know that he had done a good job, but then ran back to the device and started to dig for it. Boom! – Razz was vaporised. The explosion blew the engineer over and knocked him out. He was pretty upset about his dog but he was still alive. It was time to get out of there and head for Tarin Kot.'

26

RISE OF HOMELAND AND BORDER SECURITY

By late 2006, Kevin Rudd had parlayed his parliamentary performance on the Oil for Food scandal into a partnership with the highly respected shadow health minister Julia Gillard. Their political marriage of convenience had but a single ambition: to replace their leader, Kim Beazley, and his deputy, the popular Jenny Macklin.[1] And, by coincidence, the Cole Inquiry report, which Rudd had forced upon the government, was due to be released in the week before parliament rose on 4 December 2006. The cards were falling Rudd's way.

Beazley had been under siege by the contenders for weeks, and the pressure was beginning to show in a series of verbal gaffes; but he and his chief lieutenants, Wayne Swan and Stephen Smith, believed that if they could survive the final days of the session his leadership would be safe from challenge. However, as that last week loomed he publicly confused the popular television personality Rove McManus with the American political operative Karl Rove. The media pounced. Rudd and Gillard supporters, 'more in sorrow than in anger', plunged their verbal stilettos to the hilt. Beazley's backers panicked and in a shock move they declared all leadership posts vacant and called on the party factions to confirm his and Macklin's positions.

It was a serious misjudgement. When parliament resumed in February 2007, it was with Rudd as leader and Gillard as his loyal deputy, widely praised as 'the dream team'. And with an election due that year the opinion polls had Howard on the ropes. The mood of the country was for change.

While Rudd backed Australia's military commitment to Afghanistan, he gave notice that in victory he would withdraw the troops from Iraq. More importantly perhaps, the former diplomat was fluent in Mandarin and also a scholar of Chinese history and politics. As China was about to overtake Japan as Australia's biggest trading partner, relations with the giant regional neighbour were becoming ever more central to Australia's future prosperity and security. Rudd seemed to be the man of the moment.

In fact, Australia's relationship with China is more long-standing – and more consequential – than is commonly appreciated. In the 1850s and 1860s, for example, some 40,000 Chinese prospectors joined the worldwide gold rush to the diggings in Victoria and later New South Wales. Because of language and cultural disparities the Chinese tended to work together and thus became a focus for racist European resentment. The result was a series of increasingly violent outrages leading to the death of an unknown number of Chinese miners. In 1863 at Lambing Flat (now Young) in New South Wales, the civil authorities lost all control and marines from a British warship, replete with an artillery unit, had to be rushed from Sydney to restore order.

The racist resentment persisted, and when Federation created a national parliament the first legislation passed with the support of both sides of politics was a restrictive immigration act aimed squarely at the Chinese. This formed the foundation of the White Australia policy that disfigured the Australian polity – and relations with China – for the next 70 years. In the 1950s, following the civil war that brought Mao Zedong's Communist Party to power, Australian Government policy was at once antagonistic to the Chinese leadership but open to the prospect of wheat and mineral sales into the Chinese market.

When the Labor Party split in 1956, the Catholic-dominated Democratic Labor Party (DLP) was fiercely hostile to 'the international Communist monolith', despite the blazing antagonism between the USSR and Chinese leadership. Indeed, they and the other Australian conservative parties characterised the Vietnam War as a manifestation of 'the downward thrust of Chinese communism'. Defeat in Vietnam, they said, would lead inevitably to the fall 'like dominoes' of the other nations of South-East Asia.

The more perceptive noted the 2,000 years of Chinese–Vietnamese belligerence and refused to accept the received wisdom. Indeed, it was the sensational 1972 breakthrough visit to Beijing by Labor Leader Gough Whitlam that drew the teenage Kevin Rudd into the political process and set his sights on national leadership. This he achieved in a runaway election victory in November 2007 when even John Howard's own seat changed hands to the incoming government, the first such prime-ministerial humiliation since 1929.

One of Rudd's early initiatives in government was to commission the recently retired Ric Smith to conduct an inquiry into homeland and border security. In 2008, Smith recommended the creation of a national security adviser (NSA), with a deputy, in the prime minister's own department. 'The NSA's focus,' he said, 'would go beyond coordination to promoting a cohesive national security community culture.

'This better integrated and more strategic approach would be supported by broadening the mandate and membership of the Secretaries Committee on National Security to embrace the full range of national security issues.' These would include setting national priorities for intelligence 'across the foreign, defence, security and law enforcement domains'. On Smith's recommendation, a new body, the National Intelligence Coordination Committee, was established in 2009 to draw together no fewer than 14 federal departments and agencies under the chairmanship of the NSA.

In another striking step towards convergence, Rudd expanded the role of Duncan Lewis, the former commander of Special Forces, from counterterrorism to be the first NSA. His deputy was Dr Margot McCarthy, at the time a senior bureaucrat in the Defence Department. Rudd and his team were soon organising the phased withdrawal of Australian forces from Iraq, while reinforcing the military action in Afghanistan.

Though they protest to the contrary, prime ministers, and indeed national leaders of all stripe, like to preside over a small – preferably distant – war. 'They love to wrap themselves in the flag,' said a high-ranking Defence official, 'and of course the soldiers welcome them with open arms . . . they can't get enough of each other.'[2] This was certainly the case in Afghanistan, where Rudd and his defence minister Stephen Smith made frequent visits to Tarin Kot, invariably shrouded in secrecy until the accompanying television crews worked overtime to record their awkward, hail-fellow-well-met colloquy with the troops. One SAS soldier said, 'We quite enjoyed it but we were always pleased to see the back of them.'[3] However, despite their best efforts, the Labor leaders were unable to establish the sense of mutual admiration enjoyed by John Howard and the SASR.

In the second half of 2008, 3 Squadron SAS replaced 1 Squadron at Tarin Kot. It was the peak summer fighting season, and would encompass the biggest Australian battle against an enemy force since Vietnam. After a series of contacts beyond the base perimeter, in August an SAS detachment flew in Chinooks to the US Anaconda

FOB. The Australians were on the track of a Taliban leader the intelligence agencies believed to be operating in the area. And by now they were well practised at their 'kill or capture' operations. One former SAS trooper says, 'There's some of us that believe in putting them away permanently and there's others who would rather capture. There's pros and cons with both.' One of the 'cons' was that after the captives were questioned and then convicted by the Afghan judicial system, they would often be back in action within weeks. According to a former CO of the regiment who served in Afghanistan, 'That is why we as a task force had to operate on a number of levels – helping them develop a non-corrupt judicial system was just one of them.'[4]

When the detachment arrived at the Anaconda FOB, they discovered their quarry had retreated to Pakistan, but since the American force had been depleted by casualties, they joined with them in an operation that became known as the Battle of Khaz Oruzgan. In early September, they headed out from Anaconda with two SAS patrols embedded in a convoy of five armoured American Humvees. Three carried the Americans, while the Australians and members of the Afghan National Army (ANA) travelled in the other two, and interpreters were scattered through the convoy.

Corporal Rob Maylor was among them as they entered the danger zone. 'At the end of the valley the Americans dropped us off,' he says. 'We were to occupy a couple of overwatch locations. Basically we were the bait to stir things up. We didn't realise it at the time but by then all the [Taliban] fighters were probably concentrated in the valley behind us.'

While there had been no combat contact, there was ample evidence via radio that the enemy was all about, and at mid-afternoon the Australian troop leader met with the American commander. The best tactic, he suggested, was to lay up until midnight and deploy a Predator drone to reconnoitre the area before moving out under cover of darkness. 'But the Americans wouldn't agree,' Maylor says. 'They wanted to get back, so we started driving back into the valley. And that's where they were waiting for us – 100 to 200 fighters all armed to the teeth and determined to wipe us out.'[5]

They had been driving for about 20 minutes when suddenly machine-gun and mortar fire rained down on the convoy from about 300 metres. 'Our car was initially right in the centre of their fire, the killing ground,' Maylor says. 'That first volley was a bit off target but with such a weight of fire coming at us we knew we were in for a good fight.' The Americans stopped the vehicles and returned fire. That was when the Australians heard the Taliban leader on radio shouting, 'Kill them. Kill them all!'

They had been travelling along the slopes about 80 metres from the road to avoid IEDs and progress over the deep indentations was painfully slow. The valley was 3.5 kilometres long and they would have to travel most of it under fire before reaching the dasht. The Taliban were strategically placed on the high ground; the Allies had no choice but to run the gauntlet.

In Maylor's car, the American JTAC called in two F-18s. 'He was frantically working with a laptop and a radio in each ear on different frequencies, talking to the pilots and calculating targets with a GPS and a laser range finder,' Maylor says. As he walked beside his vehicle, all around him Allied soldiers were being hit. 'Then a volley of four RPGs from the high ground came in and straddled our car,' he says.

Maylor took a spray of shrapnel deep in the legs and back but he was still mobile and he began to run for cover. At the same time in another part of the action, an Afghan interpreter was blown out the back of a vehicle and SAS trooper Mark Donaldson ran back over 80 metres of open country to rescue him. 'Donno' loaded him onto his shoulders and under unrelenting fire carried him back to the convoy.

Finally the opening to the dasht yawned ahead. The Humvees roared towards it. Maylor says, 'We were in contact for about four hours. As we pulled in [to base] the medics were waiting for us.' He and the other injured were laid on the ground. Nine of the 13 Australian soldiers had been wounded in the ambush – seven SAS and two engineers. 'Donno came over and cut my uniform off,' he says. 'He had blood all over his face so I asked, "What happened to you, mate?"

'"Oh nothing, nothing."

'"Did you get hit?"

'"No, no, I'm good . . . One of the Americans was shot in the head so I took his helmet because I didn't have one, and when I put it on it was full of blood."' The American had been killed instantly.

For his actions in that battle, Corporal Mark Donaldson became the first recipient of the Victoria Cross for Australia on 16 January 2009, the honour having superseded the imperial system during the Hawke Government in 1991.

It was the beginning of an unusually prolific award of the supreme decoration for gallantry in the face of the enemy. By the end of the war, the SAS would have received a second for Ben Roberts-Smith; infantryman Daniel Kieghran would be decorated in 2010; and in 2014 the commando Cameron Baird would be awarded the Victoria Cross posthumously for his courage under fire in an attack on a Taliban compound in 2013.

Corporal Baird had already been recognised for bravery in action in Afghanistan and East Timor as a member of 4 RAR, which in 2009 completed its successful transition to 2 Commando Regiment. Along with the renaming, a new badge was developed that paid tribute to the independent companies of World War II by including the distinctive 'double diamond' colour patch and the traditional commando knife. The commandos also wore the revered Green Beret.

This was a major development in Australia's Special Forces cohort. It received very little public acknowledgement, since its ramifications included issues of high secrecy: 2 Commando Regiment, including 126 Signals Squadron, would relieve the SAS of some of its counterterrorism and hostage-recovery duties. It would form part of the Tactical Assault Group on the east of the continent, with a team of clearance divers from the RAN attached as necessary. (The SAS would retain prime counterterrorism responsibility in the west.)

Based at Holsworthy outside Sydney, 2 Commando Regiment conducted biannual recruitment in which candidates – restricted to qualified infantrymen – were required to complete a daunting six-hour physical test ending with a 15-kilometre walk in 2.5 hours followed by a six-week selection course at Singleton's Special Forces Training Centre. Once they passed selection they completed no fewer than 19 separate courses; failure in only one would mean instant disqualification.

As the courses developed they became almost identical to the SAS 'reinforcement' system, and included advanced parachuting, roping, helicopter insertion and extraction, signals, medic, amphibious, sniper, demolition, close-quarter combat, urban ops, heavy weapons, bodyguard, mountain and Arctic warfare.

In war, 2 Commando Regiment – whose motto is *Foras admonito* (Without warning) – was designated to take over some of the offensive operations previously carried out by the SAS. It quickly proved itself on the Afghan battlefield with the Special Operations Task Group, and in March and April 2009, during a four-week operation with the SAS, they killed 80 Taliban fighters in Helmand Province without suffering any casualties.

Freed of its continental counterterrorism responsibility, the SASR looked to break new ground in and out of uniform in cooperation with ASIS and some of the other intelligence-collection agencies. Most of its work was highly secret and incorporated new skills practised over a longer term in areas of potential insurgency and terrorist threat to Australian security.

It was at this time that David Irvine was promoted from ASIS to become director-general of ASIO, and his place was taken by Nick Warner, whose early undercover experience was in Africa. By now, Australia had become a wealthy middle power with ambitions to play a more significant international role beyond the region. Australian mining companies were increasingly expanding their investments to the African continent. Prime Minister Rudd had begun a campaign to secure a temporary seat in the UN Security Council, which would require votes from African nations to succeed. These factors combined to pave the way for the SAS to raise an ultra-secret 4 Squadron with long-term duties in Africa, particularly Kenya, Zambia and Malawi. However, their activities would go unnoticed publicly for another three years.

Meantime, the relationship with Indonesia was greatly enhanced by the 2009 re-election of President Susilo Bambang Yudhoyono (SBY) who, despite the difficulties emanating from both sides, developed a close bond with a succession of Australian leaders. 'He was the best friend Australia had in Indonesia,' one former ambassador said. 'Without his steadying hand several incidents would have blown up into quite serious issues.'[6]

Kevin Rudd responded with diplomatic finesse, and during SBY's official visit to Australia in March 2010 he became the first Indonesian head of state to address the federal parliament and was appointed an Honorary Companion of the Order of Australia (AC). At the same time the new ASIO chief's strong ties with

Indonesia paved the way for a greatly enhanced relationship with Indonesia's security establishment.

Rudd was less successful in improving relations with China.

While the Chinese leadership initially welcomed the Mandarin linguist, they were soon disenchanted by his Cold War attitudes. Indeed, the Chinese leadership was pivotal in his political downfall when, at the 2009 climate change conference in Copenhagen, they refused his entreaties to sign up for an enforceable reduction in greenhouse gases. Rudd had tied his political fortunes to action on climate change, calling it 'the great moral challenge of our generation'. But when Copenhagen broke up in disarray and the Liberal opposition elected a climate change sceptic in Tony Abbott to the party leadership, Rudd failed his own test and prevaricated. And when a leading journalist, Lenore Taylor, revealed that he had secretly postponed climate change action indefinitely, his popularity took a tumble from which it would never recover.

Rudd's disorganised style of government and his apparent indifference to the history, tradition and ethos of the Labor Party caused a backlash of resentment within the ranks. By mid-2010, members of his Cabinet and faction leaders allied to the better organised and more capable administrator Julia Gillard moved against him. On 23 June, the nation was rocked when without warning Rudd was deposed.

Gillard took the reins as the country's first female prime minister, and called an early election with strong community support reflected in the opinion polls. However, an angry and resentful Rudd orchestrated a series of embarrassing public allegations against Gillard that destabilised her campaign; while at the same time he privately pressed for inclusion in her Cabinet as foreign minister. In the event, the country split, and when three of the four independents sided with Labor, Australia found itself controlled by a minority government for the first time in 70 years.

Rudd gained his preferred ministry, secured his place as a member of the National Security Committee of Cabinet and remained responsible for ASIS within the Foreign Affairs portfolio. Nevertheless, his sense of raging injustice and bitterness was unassuaged.

The national defence and intelligence community in Canberra regarded the political turmoil and division with dismay. The essence of effective security, according to one leader in the field, is 'flexible continuity', and political disruption is anathema. 'There was a great deal of concern at the time,' he said, 'that we would be getting contradictory messages from above. It turned out that wasn't the case.'[7]

In fact, Julia Gillard made no change to the general thrust of defence policy. In 2010, Australia took a greater role in its Afghan AO, Oruzgan Province, when the Dutch contingent withdrew following a domestic political implosion. Under Gillard's watch US President Barack Obama announced his country's 'pivot' to Asia and during his visit to Canberra in 2011 negotiated an agreement for stationing a permanent contingent of US marines in Darwin. She elevated Margot McCarthy to become her NSA and posted Duncan Lewis – after a short stint as defence secretary – to Brussels as ambassador to Belgium.

There was, however, one major change of emphasis. According to a senior intelligence figure, 'Aside from anything else, both the PM and Mr Rudd were alive to the fact that a new element had entered the equation: cyber warfare.' Initially, the principal concern was what seemed to be a series of officially organised hacking operations from the Chinese mainland. Australia's response would test the growing sophistication within the country's political, security and intelligence establishment.

CHINA LOOMS

By 2011, China was making its presence felt in the region. Since the diminutive Deng Xiao Ping had released his country's entrepreneurial spirit from its collectivist chain, the economy had bounded up the international ladder past all but the United States. And forecasters confidently predicted that it was only a matter of time – perhaps three decades – before it reached the top.

Australia's defence planners had long reflected the nation's somewhat schizophrenic attitude to its massive northern neighbour. As a trading nation overwhelmingly dependent on the export of its products and services, Australia's prosperity was underpinned by China's astonishing rise. But that country's five-decade flirtation with communism, allied with an inherent racism among Australia's influential Anglophile population – not least among some of the planners themselves – meant that it was regarded as a potential adversary. This produced differing interpretations of the historical dynamics at play.

Not since the early days of the Qing Dynasty had the Middle Kingdom reasserted its place among the great powers of the world. Indeed, during the latter days of Qing it had suffered the humiliation of being carved up like a fat dumpling by the Western colonialists. And beginning in 1895 it had been tormented for half a century by its upstart oriental neighbour, Japan, culminating in the horrors of invasion, rape, pillage and degradation on a monstrous scale in World War II. So there was a special satisfaction in Beijing when it displaced Japan as the second-biggest economy in August 2010. But that did little to assuage the grievance held against the invader; and the communist leadership fanned the flames of resentment for its own political ends, while quietly welcoming Japanese investment and expertise.

The relationship with the United States was more complex. While the Americans had pressed for an open-door policy during the colonial era, it was their British cousins who led the European exploitation with their iniquitous Opium Wars. In the twentieth century, the Americans had betrayed China in Japan's favour at Versailles in 1919; but they had led the fight against Japanese imperial ambitions in World War II – and modestly assisted the Chinese struggle on the mainland.

When the US backed the Kuomintang forces of Chiang Kai-shek and isolated China throughout most of the Cold War, Mao Zedong responded in kind. President Richard Nixon's visit in 1972 began the thaw and when Deng and his successors threw their weight behind a market economy, America applauded. Indeed, successive presidents spoke warmly of bringing China into the community of nations. And as China invested massively in US bonds – and American consumers gorged themselves on less expensive Chinese imports – the two economies became ever more entangled and interdependent. However, after the Americans won the Cold War in 1989, the superpower jealously guarded its primacy and it was a small step from friendly competition with a resurgent China to international rivalry; and a smaller one to outright (if guarded) opposition.

By now Australia had not only followed America faithfully into all its imperial crusades but had also arranged its security and military systems to accord with those of its great and powerful friend. Australian political leaders from both sides brandished the American alliance as a symbol of their reliability – even their legitimacy – for the highest office. So as China loomed even larger than America in the economic health of the nation the policymakers devised a two-tiered formula for dealing with the Middle Kingdom – on the one hand asserting Australia's security alliance with the US (against the only possible sovereign threat, China itself), while on the other welcoming ever closer economic ties with the waking giant as she stretched her prodigious limbs.

Behind the scenes there was furious activity taking place in a heavily guarded building within the Russell Hill Defence complex. In 2010, Prime Minister Gillard and Defence Minister Stephen Smith jointly announced the name change of the DSD to the Australian Signals Directorate (ASD) to reflect the range of its activity in protecting government departments and industry from cyber attack as well as its defence functions. Inside that building, the organisation was now a combination of brilliant (and mostly young) men and women hackers, backed by the strongest computing power in the country.

The ASD's interceptors were using complex programs to decrypt foreign communications. Some of the technical devices were supplied by the Americans, but the agency employed its own research unit to develop advances in highly specialised areas. And according to insiders they made several significant breakthroughs. These were applied to the blizzard of electronic traffic to produce nuggets of valuable information within the mountains of dross. And while ASD has a broad remit, its principal mission is sharply focused on defence and security.

Its director in 2010, career intelligence operative Ian McKenzie, had begun his professional life as a schoolteacher, like Harvey Barnett and other prominent members of the Secret Service, before joining the agency in 1984. In 1996, he expanded his horizons with a stint as chief of staff to the defence secretary Tony Ayres. He was then blooded as a Defence bureaucrat cutting in half the staff numbers of a branch in less than three years. 'That was the hardest job I ever did,' he says. 'I have no doubt that it was my experience in these two areas that enabled me to win a [managerial] position back in DSD.'[1]

McKenzie witnessed the enormous expansion of DSD capability in the decade following 9/11. He was instrumental in the biggest DSD coup of the period, when they located and confirmed the identities of the Bali bombers and then quietly passed the information to the AFP, in Jakarta. He was also part of the development that would see DSD operatives support (from a discreet distance) the SAS and subsequently the commandos on operations in Afghanistan. Indeed, the foyer of the ASD building is proudly decorated with the plaques of fighting units that the Signals Directorate team has assisted. McKenzie had also spent three years in Washington early in the 1990s, and was a firm supporter of the American alliance. He was primed to respond to foreign cyber attacks from America's new rival, the Chinese.

The name change also signified the phenomenal expansion of the agency to keep pace as the internet spread its communication tentacles around the globe in its various guises and platforms. This, of course, was an impossible task. The whole world was in the process of becoming 'connected'. In this, the American experience is instructive. It took 70 years for the telephone to reach half the US population; seven years for TV to make the same inroads; but only seven months for the internet to achieve the same penetration. And in developing countries such as China and India the take-up rate was even more phenomenal.

ASD's sister agency, DIGO, was also expanding its reach under a former major general, Steve Meekin, who had resigned from the army to pursue a civilian career within the Defence Department. A Duntroon graduate with a Master's Degree in Science, he was even closer to the Americans, having joined the United States Defence Intelligence Agency as an analyst in 1986. He served as a UN observer of the ceasefire between Iran and Iraq and was later decorated by the Americans with the Legion of Merit for his 'command and leadership' in that troubled region.

After administrative posts in the Australian Army HQ, he became CO and chief instructor at the School of Military Intelligence at Canungra in 1994. He joined the Signals Directorate in 2005 in charge of the military element and two years later was promoted to deputy director, intelligence. His leadership of DIGO from 2009 would fit him well for a final promotion in 2012 to deputy secretary, intelligence and security in the Defence Department. In this he was responsible for ASD, DIGO, DIO and the Defence Security Authority (DSA). As head of DSA he would be at the very peak of the Australian security and defence establishment, since it sets defence protective security policy and undertakes defence security-clearance vetting for the whole of government.

Meanwhile, ASIO's new headquarters, a huge edifice down the slope from Russell Hill, was taking shape. With a floor area of 62,000 square metres the 'Ben Chifley' – named for ASIO's founding father – was easily Canberra's biggest building project since the new Parliament House in 1988. And it was entirely appropriate for an agency that now controlled an annual budget of $438 million, almost a third of the entire national security allocation of $1.4 billion.

The director-general of ONA, Allan Gyngell, said the expansion was inevitable. 'We're seeing all the consequences of the great changes associated with globalisation . . . the eroding of borders between domestic and foreign, the rise of transnational issues from terrorism, to cyber crime, to people smuggling. The world in which information was power has been replaced by a world in which the ability to sort and analyse information is power.'[2] Gyngell said the agencies now cooperated much more closely than 20 years previously when they behaved 'like powerful individual fiefdoms with limited contact with each other'. But inter-agency cooperation would always be 'a work in progress' as each sought to assert its primacy in the field.

The technology-based agencies had the advantage of spectacular advances and an aura of mystery for the lay observer, not least within the political community. One high-ranking Australian agency member said, 'The cloak and dagger boys are still useful in getting hold of codes or encryptions, but it's a different game these days.'[3] Indeed, the 'game' was then and remains dominated by America's National Security Agency, which has 120,000 operatives engaged in both aggressive and defensive cyber warfare with friend and foe alike. The 2013 revelations by former agency contractor Edward Snowden even surprised some other members of the Five Eyes grouping by the catch-all nature of its operations.

By 2011 the Chinese – principally through the PLA – were actively engaged in a wide range of cyber activities. According to Des Ball, writing at the time, 'Organisationally, the PLA has consolidated the computer and network attack missions together with Electronic Warfare into an Integrated Network Electronic Warfare [unit]. Computer network defence has apparently been included with cyber-espionage in the Signals Intelligence Department. Specialised militia units also share some aspects of these missions.'[4]

The Chinese corporate sector, from state-owned operations such as China Telecom to private corporations such as Huawei Technologies Company, cooperated with the PLA. 'Chinese manufacturers of electronic gadgets such as iPods, digital picture frames and navigation gear, have also been found to have installed viruses that send information back to Beijing,' he said. 'And the Chinese authorities have access to a large community of patriotic "Netizens" which is highly skilled in the design and implantation of Trojan Horse programs and other forms of malicious software [malware].' Indeed, there would soon be persistent reports that the Chinese had hacked into the floor plan of the new ASIO headquarters; and this was at least one of the reasons that it was 'opened' several times but would remain unoccupied until 2015. Other insider gossip, roundly denied by senior ASIO figures, suggested that they obtained the plans from a company asked to tender for the cleaning contract.

•

While both sides were engaging in a parry and thrust contest in cyberspace, the Special Forces spearhead on the ground in Afghanistan was confronted by real bullets and a very human crisis. The Australian soldiers reaped the technological benefit of DIGO and ASD input – and a growing force of American-made drones – but the Taliban was tightening its grip in the countryside.

In 2009, US President Barack Obama had authorised a 'surge' of a further 30,000 troops on the ground to counter a revitalised enemy. By June the following year, most had arrived in country, where they would be commanded by General David Petraeus, one of the Pentagon's high flyers with his own team of public relations flaks to burnish his personal and political profile. In time he would follow his predecessor General Stanley McChrystal in crashing to earth in a scandal of indiscretion. But for the moment the infusion of new blood appeared – to him at least – sufficient to turn the tide. 'We've got our teeth in the enemy's jugular now,' Petraeus exalted, 'and we're not going to let go.'[5]

In Oruzgan Province in the wake of the Dutch withdrawal, the Americans organised a gathering of the clans – known locally as a 'shura' – to encourage support for the central government. The Australian Government dispatched a number of DFAT officers to liaise with the locals in a 'hearts and minds' operation. And at Tarin Kot, Australia's Special Operations Task Force Oruzgan now comprised a provincial reconstruction team, the battle group of SAS and commandos, the Apache close air support group, a logistical team and a hospital. A Reserve force from 1 Commando Regiment deployed for four months over the 2010–11 winter when fighting subsided as both sides planned tactics for the next summer season.

The Task Force also operated with an expanding contingent of ANA units and the Provincial Response Company, an arm of the Afghan Police Force. Under the operational regulations, they were required to keep the Afghan authorities informed of all forthcoming actions in the field. In 2010, this liaison duty fell to SAS Sergeant Major Clint Palmer. 'It was a very, very sensitive juggling act,' he says. 'The security aspects and the sensitivity of certain missions were paramount and could be jeopardised with the more time they had to leak. So the idea was to seek approval just as the operation was launched.'[6]

His principal Afghan contact point was the Oruzgan governor, Ishmael Sherzad, a relative of President Karzai's. 'He'd lost his left arm in conflict with the Russians,' Palmer says. 'He was a big man and tough with it. And in [his] absence I would deal directly with the chief of police, [Matiullah Khan].' These contacts were kept to a minimum; the police chief had a particularly vicious reputation for thuggery.

'A couple of times they said "No",' Palmer said. 'They'd use any excuse. They might claim they were doing an operation in the same area and suggest we talk so we could deconflict. Or they'd come up with "local intelligence" so we couldn't go in that day. I'd ask, "Why is that?" and they'd make up some excuse, but it was to let the bad guys out before our team went in. They'd be talking to the Taliban quite often, but of course they'd deny it. "Oh no," they'd say. "No, no, no, Taliban no good."' These denials were themselves helpful to the Australians. 'It was double edged,' Palmer said. 'We'd tell our own intelligence agencies and systems. And they'd be right on it.'

In all relations with the Afghan authorities, the metaphorical elephant in the room was the heroin trade. Since the Allied intervention, Afghanistan had become the world's biggest illicit opium producer. By 2012 it would account for an estimated 75 per cent of traded heroin. 'The poppy industry is the lifeblood of the country,' Palmer says. 'And Oruzgan is quite a prolific producer because you've got the Kajakai Dam and the river system running into Helmand and down to the intersection of Pakistan and Iran. That's why there was so much fighting in Helmand. The SAS didn't ignore it. The bad guys we were after were also running the drugs. Sometimes the boys would come across laboratories when they went to do a clearance [and] they'd blow [them] up.'

There were times when the situation became almost comical. On one occasion, Palmer and his OC went to the governor's mansion for a meeting and were told he was 'dealing with a problem'. They were asked to wait upstairs in a tea room. 'They brought in chai,' Palmer says. 'It was Nesh, the time when they're harvesting the poppies and collecting the resin. But when we looked down from the balcony, in the governor's backyard [are] all the guys [who] are harvesting the poppies, right there! And at the same time he's signing the authorities to go out and get these guys, burning the poppies . . .'

In the larger context of the war, the Americans were impaled on the horns of a perfect dilemma. They were by far the biggest illicit importer and consumer of the drug, while its massive financial returns were corrupting Afghan civil authority and financing the Taliban. So they were in effect the authors of their own tribulation. And they made virtually no attempt to resolve the paradox.

More immediately distressing for the soldiers on the ground was the sharp increase in attacks by ANA soldiers on coalition troops. While in 2008 there had been only two green-on-blue incidents, there were five in each of the two succeeding years. And on 30 May 2011 at Chora, Australian Lance Corporal Andrew Jones was shot dead by an ANA soldier who then jumped the perimeter fence and fled. He was located and killed two weeks later. On 29 October, another Afghan opened fire shortly after morning parade, killing three Australian soldiers and one interpreter, and wounding ten others. The Australians opened fire and killed him on the spot. Then, on 8 November, three Australians and two Afghans were wounded in a further incident.

By 2012, green-on-blue attacks were accounting for 15 per cent of all coalition deaths. Military authorities responded by separating the two forces on FOBs by barbed wire and locked doors. As well, an Australian soldier dubbed 'the guardian angel' accompanied any Australian personnel entering the Afghan area. An ANA operations commander, Lieutenant Colonel Waleed Khan, said the 'wall' was 'not a division that can stop our cooperation. This was only a security measure and there is no other consideration.' He blamed the 'insider' threat on Pakistan. 'They train their personnel amongst our personnel,' he said.

In May 2011 came a pivotal moment in the struggle when a detachment of US Navy SEALs stormed a compound in Abbottabad, about 110 kilometres from the Pakistani capital, Islamabad. The CIA had spent several years tracking al-Qaeda couriers until they were almost certain they had pinpointed the hideout of the terrorist mastermind Osama bin Laden. As President

Obama and his top advisers watched the outside scene from the White House Situation Room, the SEALs advanced through three floors of the residence, and killed three men and a woman before they reached bin Laden's bedroom. As they burst in, bin Laden pushed one of his wives towards them but a SEAL fired two shots in quick succession into his head. After he fell, two other operatives shot him in the chest. Then the detachment radioed their commander: 'EKIA' (enemy killed in action).

While there was jubilation in America and quiet satisfaction among the other coalition forces, bin Laden's death added to the public sense of approaching finality. It solidified a growing opposition in the US and Australia to the sacrifice of Australian lives in a seemingly measureless war. President Obama signalled that America would 'transition' the security responsibility to the Afghans, and it soon became clear that most US forces would be withdrawn by 2014. Prime Minister Gillard also gave notice of a drawdown of Australian forces, though she indicated that the commitment to Afghanistan's reconstruction and governance could well continue until 2020.

Over the previous decade, Australia's Special Forces had been stretched to the limit by their operational demands. But along the way they had consolidated their reputation in the field as a formidable and highly professional fighting force. Despite the traditional tension between the Special Forces and the Big Army, there was growing public and political momentum for a greater concentration on the elite soldiery backed by the very latest in technological advance and intelligence expertise as Australia's force of the future.

However, there were indications that both SAS and the commandos were in danger of becoming victims of their own success. It was a simple equation of demand and supply. The demands for their expertise were increasing, but so too were the problems of replenishing their numbers. And that decade of unparalleled activity in the field had cut a gaping hole in their establishment as SAS operators were falling prey to the debilitating PTSD. Some left the regiment voluntarily, others were medically discharged, and still others remained but were deployed to non-combat roles. Even more troubling, some disguised their condition and self-medicated with drugs and alcohol.[7]

At the same time, the pool from which recruits were traditionally drawn – the Big Army – was itself shrinking; and the High Command resisted expanding eligibility to include women in the Special Forces front lines. The government clamped down on pay and conditions, offering less than consumer-price-index inflation rates at a time when there was a rising demand for former Special Forces troopers among private security contractors. The result was an expanding gap between the public perception of the 'super soldiers' and the reality within the forces.

28

RISE OF COUNTERTERRORISM

By the end of 2011, Australia's political and security communities were preoccupied with the arrival of seaborne refugees. Most were escaping from countries shattered by the coalition in which Australia was a willing participant. Now the continent that had nurtured a proudly bipartisan immigration policy since 1945 was rent asunder by it. Moreover, almost all the newcomers had used Indonesia as a transit stopover on their flight to an Australian sanctuary.

President Yudhoyono was willing to cooperate with the Gillard Government's attempts to disrupt the people smugglers; but it was more a gesture of *noblesse oblige* than partnership in a common cause. To the leader of a polyglot nation of 240 million souls, it was not just a third-order issue; it was difficult to understand, let alone sympathise with, Australia's hysterical fears of a relative handful of Muslim asylum seekers.

In the federal parliament, the opposition leader Tony Abbott and his immigration spokesman Scott Morrison taunted the prime minister daily as the dilapidated Indonesian fishing boats dislodged their unwelcome cargo on Christmas Island. They attacked in tandem, Abbott delivering a three-word mantra, 'Stop the boats', and Morrison striking at Gillard's credibility, bare of the protection of a viable policy. And when the boats' desperate passengers drowned as the flimsy craft overturned in high seas or broke to pieces on the island's rocky shore, even her own side of politics despaired.

Gillard and Immigration Minister Chris Bowen had tried many increasingly scrambling solutions – from the exponential expansion of detention centres in the Outback to the reintroduction of the offshore processing that Kevin Rudd had swept aside in the wake of his election. But when her first offshore choice – East Timor – rejected Australia's approaches Gillard's electoral stocks plummeted. Her next option was a 'people swap' with 800 asylum seekers being taken to Malaysia in exchange for 4,000 refugees already processed in that country. The former chief of staff of an adjacent Labor minister at the time says, 'We'd see these young characters from Bowen's office thinking they were in *The West Wing* and coming up with these crazy ideas. It was depressing to watch. We knew the Malaysian solution would never get off the ground.'

Malaysia was not a signatory to the UN refugee convention, and this allowed the opposition to bemoan the asylum seekers' fate among fellow Muslims in a judicial system that condoned corporal punishment. More pertinently, the Australian High Court stunned the prime minister when it ruled that the agreement with Malaysia was invalid on the grounds that it contravened human rights protections under existing laws. Frustration and despond haunted the government corridors.

The intelligence agencies and the ADF were working overtime on the issue. RAN ships were patrolling the enormous body of water between the Indonesian archipelago, Christmas Island and Darwin. It was tough work for the officers on the bridge, even tougher for the sailors, petty officers and young midshipmen who had to board the vessels and deal with the men, women and children. In

Canberra, it meant long, demanding shifts at the ASD listening posts aimed at detecting the plans and positions of the people smugglers scattered along the southern Indonesian coastlines; then, in cooperation with DIGO, spotting and tracking the progress of the boats when, except in emergencies, the passengers and crew were ordered to keep radio and mobile silence.

ASIO and ASIS resources were stretched in checking the identities and backgrounds of the rising tide of arrivals, many of whom had no documents or were carrying false papers. The only members of the country's Special Forces cohort to escape the issue's poisonous tentacles were the frontline troops of 2 Commando Regiment and the SAS. Coincidentally, the new CO of SOCMD Major General 'Gus' Gilmore, had been the CO of the SAS in 2001 when John Howard ordered the detachment onto the *Tampa*. That event is seared into his memory. The orders had reached him from the man in the seat he now occupied.

More recently he had commanded the ISAF Special Forces Operation in Afghanistan from 2009. Now he was accommodated in the new, ultra-secret headquarters of Joint Operation Command, the General John Baker complex, equidistant from Canberra and Bungendore on the King's Highway to the coast.[1] And while the posting provided some physical distance from the asylum-seeker imbroglio – and the battle in Afghanistan occupied most of his waking moments – he could not escape entirely from the political obsessions of the day.

He was well suited to the multidisciplinary demands of the twenty-first century Special Forces commander. Born in Sydney in 1962, he had attended Geelong College and then Duntroon, where he graduated in 1983 and took an arts degree from the University of New South Wales. He then earned his Master's in International Relations at Melbourne's Deakin University. He would subsequently collect further academic and military qualifications at Britain's Royal Military College of Science, the Australian Staff College and the Centre for Defence and Strategic Studies at the ANU.

Gilmore is also among the leading thinkers on the future of Special Forces within the array of the nation's defence capabilities. And his return to Canberra would bring him in touch with a new generation of equally thoughtful planners, among them Peter Jennings, the deputy secretary for strategy at the Defence Department. Jennings, who also has an MA in International Relations (his from the ANU) in a long list of academic qualifications, had been carving a steady path through the thickets of the defence and security establishment before settling in as the ASPI executive director in April 2012. He was no stranger to this unofficial arm of defence policy, having been director of programs there for several years earlier in the century while teaching postgraduate studies on terrorism at the Australian Defence Force Academy (ADFA). In time, he and Gilmore would collaborate in one of the more significant explorations of the future direction of Australia's Special Forces.

Meantime, the Rudd forces had used Julia Gillard's asylum-seeker problems in a continuing campaign to destabilise her leadership. And in February 2012, while Rudd was in the United States, a former Labor leader, Simon Crean, publicly attacked his 'undermining' of the prime minister. When Gillard declined to repudiate Crean, Rudd announced his resignation as foreign minister and returned to Australia to challenge for the leadership. Gillard called his bluff and won the party room ballot by 71 votes to Rudd's 31. The challenger retired hurt and covered his departure in a cloud of bathos. But behind the verbal smokescreen the ashes of resentment still glowed ruby red.

In the parliament, Abbott was ascendant. Already the election due the following year looked his for the taking; and in the defence and intelligence community preparations were underway for the necessary adjustments to a changing of the guard – not least the reassurance of an ever-increasing budget. In this they were particularly fortunate to have the leadership from October 2012 of Dennis Richardson, who on his return from America had spent the intervening years as secretary of DFAT. Now as secretary of defence he was bringing to the various components of his new bailiwick the same cooperative ethos he had engendered among the intelligence bodies as director-general of ASIO.

His military counterpart as CDF, Lieutenant General David Hurley, was a reliable, if uninspiring, figure with an enviable record in the Big Army. Hurley had taken over from Air Marshal Angus Houston on his retirement in 2011. Less than a year later, Julia Gillard recalled Houston to government service to devise a solution to her asylum-seeker dilemma. His expert panel's solution, it was hoped, would give the prime minister a political shield against the relentless savaging of the opposition.

Ever the gentleman, Houston grasped the tentacles, but with such consummate finesse that he alone would be able to release them without injury to his immaculate reputation. His panel proposed a 'firm but fair' response that attempted to select the best elements from the declared policies of both sides. However, this did nothing to relieve the pressure on a government that was now clearly terminal.

Gillard's defence minister, Stephen Smith, was besieged on several fronts and had pleaded with the prime minister to be given the Foreign Affairs portfolio in the wake of Rudd's challenge. She had instead appointed retired New South Wales premier and Macquarie Bank consultant Bob Carr, who had nurtured an ambition to be foreign minister since his teenage years. Carr was on the next plane to Canberra. A downcast Smith returned to his post amid shouts of 'failure' from the media commentators and the ginger groups that surround the portfolio. And when he suspended the commodore of ADFA in the wake of a student sex scandal, Smith was suddenly embattled from within.

It was during this most inconvenient time that the Fairfax press broke the news, 'A secret squadron of Australian SAS soldiers has been operating at large in Africa, performing work normally done by spies, in an unannounced and possibly dangerous expansion of Australia's military engagement . . . troopers from the squadron have mounted dozens of secret operations over the past year in African nations including Zimbabwe, Nigeria and Kenya.'[2]

It struck like a bombshell and, as is usual, neither the minister nor General Hurley would confirm or deny. In fact, as we have seen, 4 Squadron had been operating considerably longer than the 12 months alleged in the report. Based at Swan Island, they worked in very close cooperation with ASIS and their remit extended well beyond Africa. One SAS patrol leader says, 'I often worked with them on operations in Afghanistan and Iraq. If they couldn't find a role, they would try and insert with you so they might be some use; and they got their foot in the door. They'd be flying aircraft and getting us Intel. They're a little army within themselves. That was in the early days of their set-up.'[3]

The principal concern by military planners – then and now – was the legal standing of the 4 Squadron operators when they discarded their uniforms for civilian dress in pursuit of their surveillance, intelligence gathering, and the protection of ASIS secret agents who were prevented by law from carrying arms themselves. The former ASPI director, Professor Hugh White, said, 'Such an operation deprives the soldier of a whole lot of protections, including their legal status and, in a sense, their identity as a soldier.'[4]

While the SAS also refused to confirm or deny, the revelations did provoke a response from the intelligence community. The director-general of ASIS, Nick Warner, decided to give a unique public address concerning the role and nature of his agency to the National Press Club in Canberra. Despite the blustery winter chill, he had attracted a full house when he took the floor on 19 July 2012.

'In the 1960s,' he said, 'few people in Government knew of ASIS's existence.' Prime Minister Menzies had even withheld knowledge of it from his navy minister, John Gorton, even though the service was about to occupy a navy facility. Gorton only heard of it when he became prime minister. 'So why,' Warner asked, 'have I decided today, after 60 years, to shed some light on ASIS's functions and contribution to the national interest? What's changed?' In answer, he gave a broad response but referred specifically to the *Intelligence Services Act 2001* under which 'ASIS can use weapons in self-defence to protect its officers and agents but not to collect intelligence'.

The agency's first task, he said, was counterterrorism. 'We know that the intention to conduct mass casualty attacks against Western countries, including Australia, remains very real. We also know that many of these planned attacks are being conceived in places remote from Australia. As the reach of terrorism has spread, so has ASIS had to expand its collection capability to the Middle East, South Asia and Africa.

'We have for many years been involved in counterterrorism capacity-building with a range of intelligence partners to assist them to develop the professional and operations skills needed to tackle the extremist terrorist threat. Our counterterrorism work involves not only collecting intelligence on the plans and intentions of terrorist groups, but also working actively to disrupt their operations and to facilitate the work of law enforcement agencies.'

He acknowledged that ASIS provided 'support' for the ADF in combat operations in Iraq, Afghanistan and elsewhere. He claimed that his agents had been 'instrumental in saving the lives of Australian soldiers and civilians (including kidnap victims) and in enabling operations conducted by Australian Special Forces'. Moreover, it was 'difficult to see a situation in the future where the ADF would deploy without ASIS alongside.'

This was a remarkable statement. The agency – which now boasted a $250-million annual budget – had travelled a long way from its primitive beginnings under Alfred Brookes and Richard Casey. However, it too had been unable to avoid the lash of the asylum-seeker tentacles. 'ASIS has contributed intelligence and expertise leading to many significant and unheralded successes in recent years which have disrupted people smuggling syndicates and their operations,' he said. Perhaps so, but in the approaches to Christmas Island there was little evidence to support his claim.

Warner's speech was given wide and sympathetic coverage. But in parliament the pressure on Julia Gillard had become so great that it fanned the flames of Rudd's unquenchable desire to reclaim the prize he believed had been snatched illegitimately from his grasp. Across the aisle, the opposition fairly beamed in anticipation of their own imminent return to the Treasury benches.

By the middle of 2013, the prime minister, while retaining a brave public face, had become so dispirited that she offered to pass the prime-ministerial chalice to her minister for climate change and industry, Greg Combet. This, she believed, would at least put an end to Rudd's attempt at resurrection. A former president of the Australian Council of Trade Unions (ACTU), Combet had shown himself to be a competent administrator and an excellent performer at question time. But he was not well placed privately to take advantage of the offer. He had serious health issues and a disordered private life.

Rudd suffered no such impediments; his only concern was to be seen as the reluctant draftee to whom his party turned in its hour of greatest need. But that too was denied him. So intense and widespread was the hatred he had engendered among his fellow Cabinet ministers and backbenchers that in the end he would have to campaign publicly among selected enthusiasts and privately with promises and arm twisting among colleagues to regain the prize. Indeed, it was not until an erstwhile supporter of Julia Gillard's, Bill Shorten – who had helped to engineer Rudd's original downfall – publicly switched sides that Rudd was assured of the party room coronation.

Shorten had come reluctantly to his decision. He was well aware that Labor would be defeated and if Gillard led them to the election the party would be shattered; the younger brigade of ministers and talented backbenchers would be lost, probably forever. Rudd at least attracted a vestigial sympathy, particularly among Queenslanders where Gillard was electoral poison. He would 'save the furniture' around which a new leader – preferably himself – could reconstruct a viable political edifice.

And so it proved. There were even moments early in the campaign when the opinion polls actually gave Labor the whiff of an unlikely victory. But it quickly evaporated as Tony Abbott kept up the drumbeat of three-word sloganeering to 'axe the (carbon) tax', 'end the waste' and, of course, 'stop the boats', while Rudd reverted to type and careered out of control. In one of his less admirable policy initiatives he enjoined the prime ministers of Papua New Guinea and Nauru to take the asylum seekers and resettle them after processing in their decidedly less desirable communities. Abbott and Morrison could hardly have been more pleased.

When the parliament reassembled, it was with Abbott as the undisputed leader of a united coalition and Shorten as leader of a traumatised political movement that appeared set for a long, thankless trek through the wilderness of opposition. Abbott promised an 'adult' government with no surprises and a refocusing of the nation's energies. He would, of course, 'stop the boats' but his first priority in the parliament was to repeal the carbon tax, the one hard-won measure that Labor had notched up in the battle against climate change.

Abbott's alternative 'direct action' program was universally understood as no more than a sop to voters who might otherwise take fright at his firmly held scepticism about the reality of global warming. But nowhere did its consequences resonate more profoundly than among the thoughtful defence planners on Russell Hill, at the ANU and in the think tanks of the capital. And the role of Australia's Special Forces pillars would be front and centre in their strategic analysis.

HOMELAND AND BORDER SECURITY

Prime Minister Abbott's electoral victory was not quite complete. The vagaries of the upper house voting system and the prodigious spending of Queensland mining billionaire Clive Palmer resulted in the election of three senators from his Palmer United Party and a ragtag of independent and micro-party senators. They and the Greens would hold the balance of power whenever Labor voted against government legislation.

Initially, Abbot was sanguine. It was in Palmer's financial interest to repeal the carbon (and mining) taxes, and the government had won a mandate for change – so public opinion allied with traditional practice would compel an opposition still in disarray to wave his 'reforms' through. Moreover, by the time the new senators took their seats in July 2014, he hoped he would have established the authority of a well-regarded incumbency.

The Defence Department was pleased with the government's commitment to a 2 per cent real increase in its budget, and with the appointment of its new minister, Senator David Johnston, a long-serving Western Australian lawyer with virtually no public profile but a reputation in the party room as 'a safe pair of hands'. He could be relied upon to support his department at the Cabinet table and let them get on with the job on Russell Hill without political interference.

The several intelligence agencies within his bailiwick gave him – as well as the prime minister, Attorney-General Senator George Brandis and Foreign Minister Julie Bishop – a series of presentations to initiate them into their labyrinthine operations and the sources of real and potential threats to Australia's national security. Some of the politicians were distinctly more educable than others. 'It was really only a Cook's tour,' one departmental participant joked. 'There was neither the time nor the inclination to dig too deeply into the detail; and of course that's where the devil lives.'[1]

Brandis was unable to inspect his ASIO operatives at work in the new Ben Chifley building but was reassured that when finally opened it would house Australia's cyber warfare front line.

Indeed, ASIO along with ASIS, ASD, DIGO, DIO, the AFP and the Australian Crime Commission (ACC) would contribute to the 300 personnel in the building's Australian Cyber Security Centre (ACSC). The work is presently coordinated by Major General Stephen Day, the head of cyber and information security at ASD, and the operation is under the joint control of Defence and Attorney-General's. But according to one agency head its location is significant: 'This will inevitably mean that ASIO will take the reins.'[2]

Nevertheless, the principal responsibility for both defensive and offensive cyber operations remains with ASD and in December 2013 Dr Paul Taloni succeeded director Ian McKenzie on his retirement.

Taloni, who has a reputation for an incisive intelligence, had come from DIO, where he was deputy director. He had restructured that agency's systems to provide speedier intelligence to Australia's Special Forces and infantry in Afghanistan. The effect was not just improved 'situational awareness' for commanders in the field but better planning of operations. According to the department, 'Dr Taloni also initiated a number of improvements to the way in which DIO recruits key analysts and specialists; this has enabled DIO to maintain its analytical ability throughout periods of heightened operational tempo.' He would take these recruitment methods to ASD, where the best and brightest of Australia's computer geeks could exercise their idiosyncratic talents in defence of the nation.

Retention would be another challenge, since having ASD on your CV was a passport to highly paid positions in private industry. Indeed, it is said that one relatively low-paid operative was recently recruited by Google for more than $1 million. Nevertheless, it was, and remains, thoroughly absorbing work, and by the end of 2013 they were fielding up to 170 cyber threats a day; the numbers were growing and the rate of acceleration was increasing.

While their principal concern was defence and the integrity of government communications, they also assisted corporate Australia. This raised interesting questions about what constituted 'Australian' operations. Power, water and other community infrastructure would meet most criteria. And the banking system already boasted one of the strongest encryption systems in the world. But other cases were less clear cut. BHP Billiton, for example, was now 80 per cent foreign owned and its interests on issues such as climate change might well differ from established government policy. A company with minority Chinese investment in ten massive Aboriginal cattle stations in Western Australia might well seek ASD protection, but would it be eligible? Such questions, it is said, would be decided 'on a case-by-case basis'.

Most of the cyber threats came from China or – perhaps more correctly – were routed through China. According to an ASPI survey, while Beijing had 'an array of government organs involved in cyber issues', there was 'a seeming lack of overarching, comprehensible, national cyber policy goals or strategy. In February 2014, China established the Central Internet Security and Information Leading Group, a high-level committee charged with addressing increased cyber attacks, guiding public opinion and turning China into a global internet power,' ASPI reported. 'Headed by President Xi Jinping and including Premier Li Keqiang, the group has great clout, but it's unclear what impact, if any, it will have on Chinese cyber policymaking.'[3]

While Australia would be increasing its own cyber capabilities – including a $9.6 million expansion of its ASD facility at Geraldton – it would continue to rely on America's mammoth National Security Agency for much of its input. The extent of that reliance is illustrated by a 21 February 2011 extract from a signal sent by the acting deputy director of ASD to the National Security Agency seeking additional surveillance on Australians. 'While we have invested significant analytic and collection effort of our own,' it said, 'we would very much welcome the opportunity to extend that partnership with NSA to cover the increasing number of Australians involved in international extremist activities – in particular Australians involved with AQAP [al-Qaeda in the Arabian Peninsula].'[4]

The message was revealed by Edward Snowden and made special reference to the National Security Agency and ASD's Indonesian operations, which had been 'critical to [Australia's] efforts to disrupt and contain the operational capabilities of terrorists in our region'. The story passed through the media cycle with minimal public reaction. The lay community was largely sated by the flood of Snowden revelations. But then on 18 November 2013 came the disclosure that would reverberate through Australian–Indonesian relations for the next 12 months and would present Abbott with his first test in international diplomacy.

On that day, the ABC's defence correspondent Michael Brissenden reported that the Signals Directorate had sought 'a long-term strategy' from the National Security Agency to continue the monitoring of President Yudhoyono's mobile phone. And worse, they were also monitoring the mobile of his wife, Ani Yudhoyono. It could hardly have come at a less opportune time. The much trumpeted Abbott–Morrison election-campaign threat to 'tow the boats back to Indonesia' had already raised hackles in Jakarta. And reports from Indonesia indicated that on at least two occasions they had subsequently carried out their threat.

SBY was no doubt unhappy with this, and with his term of office coming to an end the following year, he was particularly sensitive about the relationship he had championed against opposition from within his own circle. However, that commitment paled before the offence to his public and private persona implicit in the Australians spying on his wife's private mobile phone. That went to the very heart of Javanese notions of impropriety.

The newly elected Australian prime minister was not well equipped to respond, either from experience or temperament. English born, he had shown very little interest in Foreign Affairs and even less in the Asian region. In his personal dealings, subtlety and empathy were not among his most obvious qualities. Indeed, his proudest achievement prior to his elevation to the Howard ministry had been the boxing blue he had won at Oxford University. His winning technique, he boasted to cricket commentators during an Ashes series, was to 'attack, attack, attack' until his opponent collapsed beneath his blows. And when the spying allegations were raised in question time he remained on the front foot. 'First of all,' he said, 'governments gather information and all governments know that every other government gathers information ... the Australian government never comments on specific intelligence matters. This has been the long tradition of governments of both political persuasions and I don't intend to change that today.'

SBY was outraged, and even took to Twitter to vent his fury. Former foreign minister Bill Hayden had often noted that in diplomacy, 'words are bullets'; if so, Abbott had just shot his front foot. And that was just the beginning of the imbroglio. Indonesia withdrew almost all cooperative links with Australia. Relations were thrown into disarray.

The situation was not assisted by Immigration Minister Morrison's uncompromising attitude to the asylum-seeker controversy. He not only obfuscated whenever questioned on the issue but also invented Operation Sovereign Borders, and sought to give it gravitas with a military figurehead. This was a rerun of Howard's *Tampa* tactic, but further up the chain of command.

The unfortunate soldier thrown into the front line was Angus Campbell, who was promoted to lieutenant general to accept the task. His embarrassed appearances at joint press conferences with Morrison in which he had nothing meaningful to say would have ended the career of a lesser man. Campbell had been deputy chief of the army with distinguished service as a squadron commander in the SAS and as chief of staff to both Peter Cosgrove and Angus Houston. He endured the appearances for several weeks before departing the public scene. From Morrison's viewpoint he had served his purpose in militarising the refugee 'threat'. Campbell would become chief of army in May 2015.

However, the fallout from Abbott's self-inflicted wounds eventually produced a very significant breakthrough. In the first half of 2014, the prime minister authorised the most remarkable gesture of rapprochement in the history of Australian–Indonesian relations. His top intelligence chieftain, the director-general of ASIO, David Irvine, led the director-general of ASIS, Nick

Warner, and ASD director Paul Taloni to Jakarta to meet in serious colloquy with their Indonesian equivalents.

Irvine had developed a professional relationship with his Indonesian counterpart even before the Abbott rapprochement. Many of their conversations centred on the return of radicalised fighters from the Middle East hotspots. With its 95 per cent Muslim population, Indonesia was particularly vulnerable. 'I might have 60 of these [radicalised] blokes returning,' Irvine says, 'but at the same time my counterpart in Indonesia would have 120. The threat from lone actors presents a significant challenge for security and law enforcement agencies – notably the difficulty in identifying such individuals in a timely enough manner to ward off an attack.' Most were activated by 'the motivating drive of violent extreme religious ideologies, the encouragement of a charismatic religious mentor and the acquisition of information from extremists in other countries, frequently over the internet'.[5]

During the Jakarta visit, as icing on the diplomatic cake, the Australians invited the Indonesian spymasters to Canberra for further sharing of 'issues of mutual interest' in their tightly guarded fiefdoms.[6] The Indonesians accepted and when they entered unannounced, agency personnel on Russell Hill were goggle-eyed at their presence in the inner sanctums. But genuine mutuality of interest overwhelmed all the leadership sensitivities and stumbles. According to the Institute for Policy Analysis, 'Indonesia is making some headway in countering violent extremism, but not through government programs. The National Anti-Terrorism Agency (BNPT) has not been as effective as hoped. There is still no consensus in the broader Muslim community about what constitutes extremism; radicalism in defence of the faith is considered laudable in many quarters. Many agencies and ministries that BNPT is supposed to be coordinating have little interest either in the subject of countering extremism or in being coordinated.'[7]

The ASD request for National Security Agency assistance had been the forerunner of a multinational operation to control the spread of the Islamist infection. But the growing religious and ideological chaos in the Middle East, triggered by the Bush–Cheney military adventurism and with deeper historical and colonial origins, made it almost impossible to check. The Israel–Palestine conflict, with America in thrall to the Zionists, was 'ground zero'. To the jihadists it was the *sine qua non* of Western oppression. But while it would continue indefinitely to fuel Muslim hostility, other centres of violent insurgency – from Iraq to Syria to Afghanistan, Pakistan, Yemen, the Caucasus and North Africa – would provide ample fuel to the jihadist fire. And the conflagration was already beginning to spread to areas within the region previously regarded as relatively stable.

Myanmar, with its substantial Muslim population imported by the colonial British and spurned by the Buddhist majority, was wracked by dissent just as it tried to re-enter the international community of nations. Bangladesh was also vulnerable. Less well appreciated was China itself with its 160 million Muslims, many of them alienated from the Han majority. Australia, widely viewed as a serial American camp follower, had its own well-merited concerns.

While the prime minister's Indonesian initiative was useful, it did not mark the end of Tony Abbott's clumsy diplomatic footwork. He led a relatively successful political and business mission to China in April 2014, but on his return he trumpeted Japan as 'our best friend in Asia' at a time of tension between the Japanese and China. He then invited the conservative prime minister Shinzō Abe to address the Australian parliament. Abe accepted, and Abbott, in his introduction, praised the 'skill and honour' of Japanese submariners who had attacked Sydney in 1942. While the official Chinese response was muted, behind the scenes they were appalled and ensured that his words were given wide coverage across the nation. The unofficial response – as reported by the Australian Embassy – was very different. 'If Abbott likes Japan so much, maybe he should move there' was one of many biting remarks to do the diplomatic rounds.

Part of the reason for Abbott's effusive welcome to Prime Minister Abe was an 'understanding' reached between Australia and Japan for a flow of Chinese intelligence product from Japanese listening posts into the Australian security network. There were also detailed discussions between the two leaders about Japan supplying Australia's new generation of submarines. The Australian prime minister had sent a clear signal to the defence planners in the departments, the think tanks and the universities that this security relationship with Japan – the only nation that had sought to overthrow Australia's sovereignty by force of arms – trumped the country's relations with its principal trading partner and third-biggest source of migrants.

The signal was quickly recognised by the ginger groups. In a lecture to the Kokoda Foundation soon afterwards, Paul Dibb, the Emeritus Professor at the ANU College of Asia and the Pacific and author of a seminal report for the Hawke Government, continually referred to 'our Japanese friends'.[8] Indeed, there was a movement within the foundation to change its name to the Institute for Regional Security, thus eliminating any implied anti-Japanese associations of combat on the Kokoda Track. The change was officially effected in February 2015.

Chinese cyber operations continued to expand. On 3 July 2014, for example, the official PLA newspaper announced the creation of a Cyberspace Strategic Intelligence Research Centre. It would be part of the army's general armaments department whose cyber spies 'will provide strong support in obtaining high-quality intelligence . . . and help China gain advantage in national information security'. But by then some 48 per cent of all cyber attacks on Australia were coming from 'unknown', 'friendly' or increasingly sophisticated jihadists. Moreover, technological advance was unquestionably on the side of the terrorists. A super-computer employed by the official agency a decade ago – at a cost of $50 million – provided abundant power at the time to overwhelm the encryption and coding precautions taken by the terrorists with their relatively primitive equipment. But by 2014 the same super-computing power could be acquired by the jihadists in portable form for only $120.

The Abbott Government responded with offers of additional funding to the relevant agencies, and in August 2014 allocated another $630 million to bolster their capacities. They also announced a suite of legislative changes to assist them to monitor suspected terrorist cells and individuals within Australia's Muslim community. The prime minister used the occasion to dispose of an unpopular proposal by Attorney-General Brandis to excise a provision in the Racial Discrimination Act that in his view infringed on freedom of speech. By associating his decision with anti-terrorist measures, Abbott balanced the political books, though the Act was not relevant since Muslims are not a 'race'.

The move was a reflection of his government's standing in a community that had reacted strongly to Abbott's international missteps and rebelled against the first budget brought down by his treasurer Joe Hockey in May 2014. Indeed, it was the most unpopular of its kind since the infamous Harold Holt 'credit squeeze' budget of 1961. In its wake, Clive Palmer felt sufficiently empowered to disrupt many of the government's most cherished measures. However, Palmer's bargaining power depended on his popularity in the ubiquitous opinion polls, and when he labelled the Chinese as 'mongrels' who 'shoot their own people' the cracks in his populist appeal quickly began to widen. He had backed the government to repeal the carbon tax to his own financial advantage but also to decidedly mixed reviews. At the time, the United States and China, the two largest emitters, had at last begun to take decisive action against global warming – the Chinese with emission trading schemes and the US through presidential decree. They would formalise their action at presidential level in 2015.

Abbott and Morrison had effectively stopped the people smuggling, but at a cost to Australia's international reputation. The prime minister had won praise for his forthright response to the death of 35 Australians in a Malaysian airliner shot down over the Ukraine. But behind the scenes, only firm resistance from the more level heads in Defence had advised him against sending 1,000 Special Forces soldiers to quarantine the crash site from the civil conflict between Ukrainian and pro-Russian forces. And when the ISIS terrorists threatened to take permanent control of northern Iraq, Abbott travelled to Amsterdam and London where he urged united action – with the Americans – by offering a reported 3,500 Australian troops to repel their advance with 'boots on the ground'. Again, wiser counsel prevailed.

Tony Abbott's brave expectations in the wake of his election victory had turned – for the moment at least – to ashes. Opposition Leader Bill Shorten had for some months outpolled Abbott as the nation's preferred prime minister. And as a New South Wales anti-corruption body, the Independent Commission Against Corruption (ICAC), continued its investigation of electoral funding malfeasance within his Liberal Party, the prospect of some phoenix-like revival seemed distant indeed.

However, like political leaders everywhere, he sought and found relief from domestic travail by identifying an immediate external threat. And the Sunni extremists calling themselves ISIS cooperated, with outrages to human decency. When two American journalists were publicly beheaded by ISIS in northern Iraq, Abbott dubbed them 'pure evil' and declared that Australia could not stand aside from the fight. When a British aid worker suffered the same barbaric fate, Abbott's rhetoric became even more bellicose. And when US Secretary of State John Kerry called for a 'global coalition' to stop the spread of the ISIS 'cancer', Abbott was first to raise an Australian hand.

The Australian prime minister ordered RAAF planes stationed at the US base in Dubai to drop supplies to Kurdish fighters with SAS soldiers in support. He followed this with a further Special Forces deployment, putting boots on the ground to train and advise the local forces opposing ISIS. Incrementally, it seemed, he was moving Australian assets into the front line.

On 18 September 2014, 800 police officers in Sydney and Brisbane, alerted by ASD intelligence, swooped on homes and business premises. They arrested 15 'terror suspects' in the wake of an intercepted phone call urging the random capture and beheading of an Australian citizen. Thirteen were released the next day; one was bailed after being charged with firearm possession; the other was held in custody on charges of committing a terrorist act.

In October, the government introduced a series of Bills designed to bolster the powers of the security agencies over the hard-won rights of the individual, but in the temper of the times they were allowed to pass into law with only a minimal protest from civil-liberties advocates. At the same time, parliament regularised the operations of the SAS and passed the Foreign Fighters Bill, which came into effect on 1 December.

Then on 15 December came the shocking siege in the heart of Sydney by a 50-year-old Iranian immigrant turned radical Sunni, Man Haron Monis. As the business district of Australia's biggest city ground to a halt he held customers and staff of a coffee shop hostage for 16 hours, demanding publicity for the Islamic State (IS) cause before New South Wales Police stormed in. Two hostages and the gunman were killed in the crossfire and three other hostages were wounded. Clearly it was a task for the Commando Regiment but emotional and political excesses at the time forestalled criticism of the SWAT squad.

One day later, Taliban extremists attacked an army school in Peshawar, Pakistan, and in a horrific bloodbath shot and killed more than 100 boys and girls before blowing themselves up and thereby massacring dozens more. Further civilian and military atrocities followed in Iraq, Afghanistan, northern Africa and Israel as ISIS sought to establish itself as the vicious cutting edge of jihadist terrorism.

Throughout the rising tide of international and domestic incidents, the pillars of Australia's Special Forces cohort responded as ordered. But their focus extended to issues that superseded the passing political fortunes of the day. Their troops were back in action in Iraq but out of Afghanistan, except for a few remaining instructors to the ANA and other arms of government and law enforcement. Once again they had distinguished themselves on the front lines of combat. But while their daily tasks were demanding, and tensions were rising, the decade of operational overload had tempered them for the challenges ahead. It was time to think and plan for a future that, by any measure, would require the very best of them.

NEW WARFARE
– AND OUR FUTURE

Apart from the Federal Cabinet itself, Australia's defence planners are a relatively small group – no more than two dozen decision makers – and after Tony Abbott abolished the office of NSA held by Dr Margot McCarthy, they are almost exclusively white, middle-aged, Anglo-European males. Many have a military background; all have been initiated into the operations of the intelligence agencies; all are respectful of the American alliance. While some have had diplomatic experience in the region – notably in Indonesia and China – almost all view the world through the reassuring prism of our 'Five Eyes' relationship.

They are not altogether homogenous. There are variations of age, background, education and personality. There are traditionalists to whom the communist menace lives on. There are rock-ribbed racists who conceal their atavism behind a clubby *politesse*. There are warriors to whom the resort to arms is the only credible response to international disagreements. Happily, they are balanced by a well-read, highly intelligent and perceptive brigade who abhor human combat except in the last degree. They revile the attitudes of their sexist predecessors and have escaped the ideological straitjackets of their seniors. And at the fulcrum between the two groups are a mix of the wise men of Canberra – five or six who have done it all and emerged with a steely realism.

The country, as a rule, is well served by them; and certainly better than by their political masters, no matter who sits on the Treasury benches. Indeed, the politicians are regarded as a necessary evil to be endured until replaced and then endured again. For, while high national policy will be decided finally in the Cabinet room, the broad streams of input that lead to those decisions are the province of the planners. And it is they who fashion the intellectual topography that divides and directs the flow to a bubbling centre or to the distant archival sands, never to be seen again.

As the twenty-first century gathered momentum through its second decade, they were confronted by a perilous landscape. Whether they are sufficiently flexible and quick-witted to chart a course through its rapidly changing environment is yet to be seen. In the distance, but coming unexpectedly nearer with each new report, is the defence planner's ultimate nightmare: international disorder caused by climate change. For despite the views of Prime Minister Abbott and a motley combination of right-wing extremists, greedy miners and professional controversialists, the ice is melting; the seas will rise; tornadoes are becoming more powerful; droughts longer and more intense; bushfires ever more destructive; and adequate food and water supply ever more problematic.

An ASPI report published in March 2013 warned that global warming 'has generated little interest in either the ADF or the Defence Department, [yet] climate change is transforming the conventional roles of security forces. As a threat multiplier, it has the potential to generate and exacerbate destabilising conditions that could reshape the regional security environment.'[1] The report confined itself to generalities. But it was plain to the planners and environmental scientists alike that no one could tell exactly how the Australian mainland will fare. As tropical conditions move south, for example, they might well bring higher rainfall to some marginal areas, while other more settled country crumbles to dust. But Australia is so big that in all likelihood it will be able to sustain itself almost indefinitely. The threat will come from those countries thrown into chaos around the globe with hundreds of millions of refugees in search of a place to live. Australian sovereignty will be under continuous hazard. Indeed, nationalism itself will be disputed in a world where the ravages of climate ignore all man-made borders.

In such a world, Australia's security as descendants of an invading force that dispossessed its original owners with barely a backward glance a mere two centuries ago is less manifest and incontestable than we might have hoped. Indeed, there is a hard core of Australians who use exactly this argument to deny Indonesia its right to claim sovereignty over the western half of Papua New Guinea.

This means that we must secure our coastline with a substantial and well-equipped navy and air force. But even more important, it seems, are international alliances with the great forces who would underwrite – with force if necessary – the right of nations such as Australia to decide (in John Howard's immortal phrase) 'who comes to this country and the circumstances in which they come'. The first of those great forces would, of course, be the United States of America, but unfortunately the words of President Obama in a frank interview with the *New York Times* in August 2014 were already looking prophetic. 'Our politics are dysfunctional,' he said. Gerrymandering, the Balkanisation (i.e. fragmentation) of the news media and uncontrolled money in politics – the guts of his country's political system – were sapping America's ability to take big decisions. 'We should heed the terrible divisions in the Middle East as a warning,' he said. 'Societies don't work if political factions take maximal positions.' A world order that dated back to World War I, he said, 'is starting to buckle'.

And that is well before the strains of climate change begin to be felt. Clearly, Australia must seek alternatives, and they must be as close to home as possible. The big three in the planners' focus are China, Indonesia and India. But there are obvious impediments to Australia seeking the firm alliances required. Most are historical rather than practical. China is decidedly at the wrong end of the Five Eyes telescopes. But as the two economies become ever more complementary, the momentum for change might well become difficult to resist.

During his first journey there as prime minister, Tony Abbott promised a new urgency in negotiations for a free trade agreement. It is a complex document but among the most serious sticking points was China's call for an investment regime comparable to that applied by Australia to the US. Americans could invest up to $1 billion without referral to the Foreign Investment Review Board (FIRB), whereas most Chinese investments were subject to FIRB disapproval. While the effect is more symbolic than real – since the board waved through almost all investment proposals – it was an important issue of face to the Chinese and an equally significant issue of perception for Australians, with their longstanding fears of the 'yellow hordes'. And of course China is America's 'rival'. Nevertheless the agreement was finally signed in Canberra in June 2015 and helped to consolidate the increasing co-dependence between Australia and the region's biggest power.

Similar problems needed to be overcome in the developing relationship with Indonesia. Though good progress had been made behind the intelligence curtains, and a new 'understanding' negotiated, SBY had departed. No doubt he warned his successor, Joko 'Jokowi' Widodo, a foreign policy tyro, that their southern neighbour was at best politically unreliable. This was reflected in

Jokowi's refusal to bow to Australia's plea for the commutation of the death sentences on reformed drug smugglers Andrew Chan and Myuran Sukumaran carried out in April. And the subsequent revelation of Australian payments to people smugglers to return their human cargo to Indonesia only confirmed it. But at least the Americans would favour a closer relationship with a newly democratised country that to date had kept its Muslim extremists in check.

India was an unknown quantity; work had begun to remedy the situation but, in any major climate change disruption, the populous subcontinent might well provide a source of Australia's unwanted immigrants rather than an official bulwark against their unregulated intrusions. The ASPI report highlighted the 250 million people living in the river deltas of Asia, a large proportion in the Ganges–Brahmaputra deltas where they were at 'extreme risk' from rising sea levels.

Dr David Brewster, a visiting fellow at the ANU's College of Asia and the Pacific, says, 'Australia recognises India as an important new security partner in the Indo-Pacific, but India is only beginning to see Australia as a useful partner. For India, in some ways, Australia represents a difficult case. India has no direct security interests in our immediate area and Australia's close relationship with the United States sometimes creates political unease in New Delhi.' Both countries, he says, have 'concerns' about China. But these 'should not be elevated as the moving cause of the relationship . . . in short, if Australia wishes to enhance its security and defence relationship with India it must be prepared to act outside its comfort zone.'[2]

Should we face an existential crisis, the experience of World War II has taught us that the old Anglophone ties are tenuous at best, and at worst a serious impediment to our territorial integrity.

It would be foolish indeed to rely solely on America to guarantee our national security at a time of unbridled global turbulence.

But that requires an intense reassessment of our national priorities. It involves a profound reordering of our self-perception, from an Anglophile colonial regime to a more realistic and enduring Asia-Pacific nationality blessed with a firm institutional foundation and an adventurous cosmopolitan population.

At the same time, the convergence between the Special Forces pillars has continued. Duncan Lewis's appointment as director-general of ASIO marks the first time since the legendary Colonel Spry that a military careerist steeped in the Special Forces ethos has headed Australia's top intelligence agency.

Within the ADF the movement towards a greater role for Special Forces is gaining traction. General Angus Campbell's elevation to the command of Operation Sovereign Borders had opened the way for the Special Operations commander Gus Gilmore to be appointed deputy chief of army. He immediately took the opportunity to engage with Peter Jennings at ASPI. The result was one of the more significant documents in the evolution of Australia's armed forces. Published in April 2014, it recognised that the traditional Big Army was not well suited to a security environment where the great set battles of the twentieth century had been replaced by smaller and more concentrated global operations in disparate terrain.

'Over the past decade,' it said, 'the Australian special operations capability has proven to be a major asset for the Australian Government. Its specific skill set, developed over the years, is likely to become more, not less, important to the new strategic environment. Looking to the future, special operations capability could be further upgraded relative to the regular Army, which might be cut as part of a "peace dividend".'

It recommended that SOCOMD be given control of much of its own budget. 'In the same way that other specialist organisations, such as the Australian Signals Directorate, have a capability development budget that's managed in house, an ongoing funding line for SOCOMD would be likely to give a better (and more efficient) return than requiring it go to through more elaborate processes within the Army or beyond.'

It also recommended the creation of a joint capability manager within the ADF – preferably the vice-chief of the Defence Force – to ensure that major ADF projects, such as the future submarines and amphibious equipment purchases, be coordinated with the needs of Special Operations.

The regular army should retain control of conventional combat operations, it said, but 'Special Forces offer the best value in unconventional operations and in so-called Phase Zero missions which focus on building and shaping defence relationships with key partners in a pre-crisis environment. SOCOMD has a lot to offer in Defence's regional engagement strategy . . . Augmentation of its capacity to contribute to regional and (limited) global defence engagement would be a valuable investment. It needs to have knowledge of allied and friendly country practices.' This would require a SOCOMD presence in selected headquarters in Australia's near region. 'That's where our security interests are most closely engaged,' it said, 'and proximity would make it easier for other ADF elements to provide support for operations as required.'

It recommended establishing Special Forces liaison officers in selected Australian embassies in Indonesia, Malaysia, Singapore and the Philippines, 'of which Indonesia is the most important'. In the South Pacific, fostering Special Forces cooperation with Papua New Guinea and Fiji should be a priority.

Increased Special Forces engagement with South-East Asian nations could lead to the establishment of a Special Forces Regional

Training Centre in Australia. 'The centre could also link to existing training centres beyond the Asia-Pacific region, such as NATO's Special Operations Headquarters.'

And in a groundbreaking recommendation it advocated 'an intensification' of cooperation with Chinese Special Forces. 'Defence should promote cooperation between SOCOMD and its Chinese counterpart,' it said. 'This would be a confidence-building measure in Australia–China military-to-military relations as well as a burden-sharing contribution to the US alliance. Exercises related to counterterrorism and humanitarian assistance and disaster relief would be well suited for this purpose.'

Nevertheless, it said, 'maintaining and strengthening Special Forces cooperation with our US ally is vital . . . while an agreement was recently signed for a SOCOMD liaison post at US Pacific Command, similar arrangements could be considered with US Central Command and US Africa Command to facilitate Australian special operations in the Middle East and Africa.'

It was a powerful contribution, generally well received within the establishment, except by the usual Big Army traditionalists with their obvious self-interest. However, mention of Africa raised the vexed issue of the SAS 4 Squadron with its longstanding African focus. The paper neatly avoided confirming their existence by implying that such missions 'might be needed in the future'. 'Clandestine operations which involve military personnel in ways other than uniformed and declared military operations could become important for Australia's Special Forces,' it said. 'If the government decides to use SOCOMD in this way, we need an unambiguous legislative framework and robust oversight mechanisms.'

It was a necessary charade perhaps, but it might well be time to inform the Australian people of actions being taken in their name. In any case, the United States has at least 700 Special Forces operatives on the African continent within a total military force that ranges from 5,000 to 8,000 personnel. Britain, France and Canada also support active Special Forces units in operations against terrorist groups. None are subject to the same degree of secrecy as that applied to the Australians.

The terrorist insurgents come in many shapes and sizes, from al-Qaeda in the Islamic Maghreb; Al Shahab in Somalia; Boko Haram in Nigeria; Ansar al-Sharia in Tunisia, Benghazi and Derna; Joseph Kony, the maniacal leader of the Lord's Resistance Army, and other Islamist and tribal groupings. However, while the Western Special Forces operators might occasionally become involved in armed contacts, their principal task is support, training and 'enabling' operations for government authorities. The US Special Forces leader General Linder says, 'The future of this war is about winning people, not territory.'[3]

Ironically, it is America's global rival, China, with no declared Special Forces operatives on the African continent, whose economic initiatives might well become a more effective weapon against the prophets of disorder. Chinese investment in some parts of the continent is transforming the lives of Africans and engendering signs of previously elusive social stability. In Uganda, for example, its operations had been so beneficial that when the government sought tenders for an $8 billion expansion of its rail network, only Chinese firms were invited to apply. Across sub-Saharan Africa, consumer demand is now fuelling substantial economic growth. Total Chinese trade with Africa has increased twentyfold since 2001. The African Development Bank projected in its May 2014 annual report that foreign investment would reach $80 billion that year with a larger share now going to manufacturing than to the former strip-mining of resources.

However, growth among the various economies is uneven. Inequality is rising in many areas and violence continues to simmer in the Central African Republic, South Sudan and elsewhere. In Kenya, where Australian Special Forces have long enjoyed a close association, economic advances have been patchy and violence is increasing. The scourge of AIDS has taken a terrible toll across the continent; outbreaks of Ebola and other killer diseases have ravaged communities and set back tentative economic advances. And nowhere is climate change more obvious, as the Sahara advances south at frightening speed.

Clearly, Africa will become a battlespace in the war against a loosely allied grouping of terrorists fired by the zeal of Islamist fundamentalism and simmering resentment against Western colonial exploitation. While it will be hard fought – and Australia's contribution will be strictly limited – it is by no means a lost cause. But it is only one of the fronts on which the battle will be joined. And already the zealous followers of a long line of terrorist autocrats from Ayatollah Khomeini to Osama bin Laden, Abu al-Zarqawi, Abu Bakr al-Baghdadi and beyond are spreading their poison through the most powerful weapon ever created: the internet. Indeed, it might have been tailor-made for just this purpose. As its tendrils snake around the globe they carry the toxic infection of hatred with its infinite capacity to adapt to local conditions.

Already, America has been drawn back into Iraq to confront the vicious ISIS advances, with Australia once again in full-throated support from the government if not the people. In China, the Uighurs have begun armed attacks in their native Xinjiang Province, while terrorist teams have conducted knife-wielding outrages as far south as Yunnan. Yang Shu, the director of the Institute for Central Asian Studies at Lanzhou University, says more attacks can be expected. 'For Islamist extremists in China,' he says, 'there's also this issue of ethnic identity and that adds to extremist hatred.'[4] In Indonesia, returning fighters from Syria and Iraq are already organising terrorist cells in West Java and Northern Sumatra.

Australia's defenders will themselves have to become as nimble and adaptable as their enemy. The stakes can hardly be overstated. It is a fight for civilisation itself, for the right to seek the full potential of the human individual in a world where knowledge is precious and freedom constrained only by consideration for the welfare of others. The alternative, where humanity surrenders its will and its quest for understanding to the vicious, primitive peddler of a supernatural formula, is not new. Nor is it confined to the mad mullahs of Islam or the other religious fundamentalists.

It is a task that will demand nothing less than the best of us. And the most perceptive of the planners have already reached the view that the most effective response lies within the pillars of our Special Forces. They are a powerful cohort – the ASIS, ASIO and DIO intelligence gatherers in the field risking sudden death or worse from a barbaric enemy; the ASD cyber warriors, code crackers and encryption specialists at their work stations across the continent; the DIGO observers at their space stations; the ONA analysts in their modest public service bunkers working round the clock. And at the sharp end where the combat is personal and deadly, are the men and women of the SAS and the commandos with their support teams by sea and air.

They draw their inspiration from the critical nature of the battle itself. But they are sustained by the knowledge of all those who went before, from the independent companies such as Sparrow Force who struggled against the Japanese tide when all contact with the home base was lost; to the jungle fighters of Borneo and Vietnam and East Timor; and to the troopers in the hellfire of ambush in the dusty mountain passes of Oruzgan. All served Australia well. They did what was asked of them and more. Now they, the Warrior Elite, stand on those broad shoulders as they face the longest, toughest fight of all.

ACKNOWLEDGEMENTS

It will be apparent to readers that I could not have written this book without the cooperation and guidance of a range of well-placed individuals within Australia's intelligence and military communities. I had worked on the personal staff of an Australian prime minister and deputy prime minister, enjoyed the confidence of another occupant of The Lodge, and written three biographies of former SAS operators. Yet I was unprepared for my induction into the world of military security and civilian intelligence that took place during the two years of this book's research and writing. It was both a surprising and reassuring journey for one who maintains an untrammelled allegiance to the journalistic precepts on which his writing career has been founded – not least a suspicion of the powers that be and a passion for the truth of the matter.

So, while I benefited greatly from the official access afforded, *Warrior Elite* is in no way 'authorised' by government; and those who provided me with insights and corrected some factual errors do not necessarily share the opinions and attitudes expressed within. They are entirely my own. Accordingly and unfortunately, I cannot name many of those who assisted. But they are aware of my enormous gratitude.

Among those I can name are Professor Desmond Ball and his colleagues at the Defence and Strategic Studies Departments at the ANU, Dr John Blaxland and Professor David Horner. The director of ASPI, Peter Jennings, was very generous with his time and permissions to quote from a range of ASPI's research papers. I would also like to thank Peter Collins whose excellent *Strike Swiftly: The Australian Commando Story* is a unique contribution to the field, and former SAS major Jim Truscott for permission to quote extensively from his several previously unpublished biographical works.

The former director-general of ASIO, David Irvine, the secretary of defence, Dennis Richardson, and former secretary of defence and DFAT, Ric Smith – three of Canberra's wise men – were kind enough to open some doors for me. I am very grateful. However, they did not contribute personally to the thesis I have advanced within these pages.

I would also like to thank my friend and frequent co-author Peter Thompson who read the manuscript and made his usual incisive marks; my agent Margaret Kennedy; my undaunted publisher Matthew Kelly; and of course my wife and fellow author, Wendy Macklin, without whom it would not be.

Robert Macklin
Canberra/Tuross Head, 2015
www.robertmacklin.com

ABBREVIATIONS

ABDA	American, British, Dutch and Australian
ACC	Australian Crime Commission
ACSC	Australian Cyber Security Centre
ACTU	Australian Council of Trade Unions
ADF	Australian Defence Force
ADFA	Australian Defence Force Academy
ADSCS	Australian Defence Satellite Communications Station
AFP	Australian Federal Police
AIF	Australian Imperial Force
AIO	Australian Imagery Organisation
ALP	Australian Labor Party
ANA	Afghan National Army
ANZUS	Australia, New Zealand, United States
AO	Area of operations
APEC	Asia-Pacific Economic Cooperation
AQAP	al-Qaeda in the Arabian Peninsula
ARDF	Airborne radio direction finding
ASC	Australian Services Contingent
ASD	Australian Signals Directorate
ASEAN	Association of Southeast Asian Nations
ASIO	Australian Security Intelligence Organisation
ASIS	Australian Secret Intelligence Service
ASPI	Australian Strategic Policy Institute
AWB	Australian Wheat Board

BAKIN	Badan Koordinasi Intelijen Negara
BNPT	Badan Nasional Penanggulangan Terorisme
CDF	Chief of the Defence Force
CHOGM	Commonwealth Heads of Government Meeting
CIA	Central Intelligence Agency
CIS	Commonwealth Investigation Service
CMF	Citizen Military Forces
CO	Commanding officer
COMU	Communication unit
CPA	Communist Part of Australia
CSS	Commonwealth Security Service
CT	Counterterrorism
DF	Direction finding
DFAT	Department of Foreign Affairs and Trade
DIGO	Defence Imagery and Geospatial Organisation
DIO	Defence Intelligence Organisation
DLP	Democratic Labor Party
DMI	Director of military intelligence
DSA	Defence Security Authority
DSCS	Defense Satellite Communications System
DSD	Defence Signals Division/Defence Signals Directorate
DSO	Distinguished Service Order
EOS	Electro Optic Systems
EW	Electronic warfare
FALO	Foreign Affairs liaison officer
FELO	Far Eastern Liaison Office
FIRB	Foreign Investment Review Board
FOB	Forward operating base
GCHQ	Government Communications Headquarters
HF	High frequency
HUMINT	Human intelligence
HVT	High-value target
ICAC	Independent Commission Against Corruption
ICBM	Intercontinental ballistic missile
IED	Improvised explosive device

ABBREVIATIONS

IS	Islamic State
ISAF	International Security Assistance Force
ISD	Inter-Allied Services Department
ISI	Inter-Service Intelligence
ISIS	Islamic State of Iraq and Syria
JDAM	Joint direct attack munition
JI	Jemaah Islamiyah
JIO	Joint Intelligence Organisation
JTAC	Joint terminal attack controller
KC	Kill confirmed
LRPV	Long-range patrol vehicle
LUP	Lay-up position
LZ	Landing zone
NAOU	North Australian Observer Unit
NATO	North Atlantic Treaty Organization
NCO	Non-commissioned officer
NICRC	National Intelligence Collection Requirements Committee
NRO	National Reconnaissance Office
NSA	National security adviser
NVA	North Vietnamese Army
NVGs	Night vision goggles
NZSAS	New Zealand Special Air Service
OC	Officer commanding
ONA	Office of National Assessments
OP	Observation post
PIR	Pacific Island Regiment
PKI	Partai Komunis Indonesia (Indonesian Communist Party)
PLA	People's Liberation Army
PM&C	Prime Minister and Cabinet
PTSD	Post-traumatic stress disorder
RAAF	Royal Australian Air Force
RAMSI	Regional Assistance Mission to the Solomon Islands
RAN	Royal Australian Navy
RAR	Royal Australian Regiment

RNZAF	Royal New Zealand Air Force
RPG	Rocket-propelled grenade
SAS	Special Air Service
SASR	Special Air Service Regiment
SB	Sleeping Beauty
SBY	Susilo Bambang Yudhoyono
SEATO	Southeast Asia Treaty Organization
SECDET	Security detachment
SHF	Super high frequency
SIA	Secret Intelligence Australia
SIS	Secret Intelligence Service (MI6)
SLR	Self-loading rifle
SO	Special operations
SOA	Special Operations Australia
SOCOMD	Special Operations Command
SOE	Special Operations Executive
SRD	Services Reconnaissance Department
STTW	Sense through the wall
TNI	Tentara Nasional Indonesia (Indonesian Armed Forces)
UDT	União Democrática Timorense (Timorese Democratic Union)
WMD	Weapon of mass destruction
WPLTN	Western Pacific Laser Tracking Network

ENDNOTES

Introduction

1 *Sydney Morning Herald*, 16 December 2014.

Chapter One

1 David Kilcullen, *Counterinsurgency*, Oxford University Press, New York, 2010, p. ix.
2 Christopher Wray, *Timor 1942: Australian Commandos at War with the Japanese*, Hutchinson, Melbourne, 1987, p. 14.
3 ibid., p. 17.
4 ibid., p. 28.
5 ibid., p. 37.
6 ibid., p. 42.

Chapter Two

1 Peter Dunn, Australia@War, <ozatwar.com>.
2 Judy Thomson, *Winning with Intelligence: A Biography of Brigadier John David Rogers*, Australian Military History Publications, Sydney, 2000, p. 144.
3 Richard Walker and Helen Walker, *Curtin's Cowboys: Australia's Secret Bush Commandos*, Allen & Unwin, Sydney, 1989, p. 3.
4 ibid., p. 6.
5 ibid., p. 5.
6 ibid., p. 9.
7 Peter Thompson and Robert Macklin, *The Battle of Brisbane: Australians and the Yanks at War*, ABC Books, Sydney, 2001.
8 Richard Walker and Helen Walker, p. 27.
9 ibid., p. 30.

10 ibid., p. 35.

11 Christopher Wray, *Timor 1942: Australian Commandos at War with the Japanese*, Hutchinson, Melbourne, 1987, pp. 104–5.

Chapter Three

1 Richard Walker and Helen Walker, *Curtin's Cowboys: Australia's Secret Bush Commandos*, Allen & Unwin, Sydney, 1989, pp. 32–3.

2 ibid., p. 34.

3 ibid., p. 45.

4 ibid., p. 87.

5 ibid., p. 61.

6 Christopher Wray, *Timor 1942: Australian Commandos at War with the Japanese*, Hutchinson, Melbourne, 1987, p. 132.

7 ibid., p. 143.

8 Richard Walker and Helen Walker, p. 93.

9 ibid., pp. 178–9.

Chapter Four

1 Robert Macklin with Peter Thompson, *Kill the Tiger: The Truth about Operation Rimau*, Hodder, Sydney, 2002, pp. 97–8.

2 ibid., p. 97.

Chapter Five

1 Robert Macklin with Peter Thompson, *Kill the Tiger: The Truth about Operation Rimau*, Hodder, Sydney, 2002, p. 183.

2 ibid., p. 195.

3 Judy Thomson, *Winning with Intelligence: A Biography of Brigadier John David Rogers*, Australian Military History Publications, Sydney, 2000, p. 190.

Chapter Six

1 Robert Macklin with Peter Thompson, *Kill the Tiger: The Truth about Operation Rimau*, Hodder, Sydney, 2002, p. 202.

2 Frank Cain, *The Australian Security Intelligence Organization: An Unofficial History*, Frank Cass Publishers, London, 1994, pp. 29–30.

3 ibid., pp. 67–8.

4 Rob Foot, 'The Curious Case of Dr John Burton', *Quadrant*, November 2013, p. 5.

5 ibid.

6 Desmond Ball with David Horner, *Breaking the Codes: Australia's KGB Network 1944–1950*, Allen & Unwin, Sydney, 1998, p. 173.

7 ibid., p. 286.
8 William Pinwill and Brian Toohey, *Oyster: The Story of the Australian Secret Intelligence Service*, Heinemann, Melbourne, 1989, p. 7.
9 ibid., p. 25.

Chapter Seven

1 William Pinwill and Brian Toohey, *Oyster: The Story of the Australian Secret Intelligence Service*, Heinemann, Melbourne, 1989, p. 26.
2 ibid., p. 27.
3 ibid., p. 28.
4 ibid.
5 Peter Collins, *Strike Swiftly: The Australian Commando Story*, Watermark Press, Sydney, 2005, pp. 34–5.
6 ibid., p. 42.
7 ibid., p. 50.
8 ibid., p. 54.
9 William Pinwill and Brian Toohey, p. 45.
10 ibid., p. 54.
11 ibid., p. 56.

Chapter Eight

1 David Horner with Neil Thomas, *In Action with the SAS*, Allen & Unwin, Sydney, 2009, p. 22.
2 ibid.
3 The author was on McEwen's personal staff at the time.
4 David Horner with Neil Thomas, p. 24.
5 *Australian Army Journal*, issue 2000, p. 89.
6 ibid., p. 28.
7 Peter Collins, *Strike Swiftly: The Australian Commando Story*, Watermark Press, Sydney, 2005, p. 71.
8 ibid., p. 73.
9 David Horner with Neil Thomas, p. 30.
10 ibid., p. 35.

Chapter Nine

1 Frank Cain, *The Australian Security Intelligence Organization: An Unofficial History*, Frank Cass Publishers, London, 1994, p 198.
2 Harvey Barnett, *Tale of the Scorpion*, Allen & Unwin, Sydney, 1988, p. 201.
3 ibid., p. 204.

4 Edward Woodward, *One Brief Interval: A Memoir by Sir Edward Woodward*, Miegunyah Press, Melbourne, 2005, p. 191.
5 The author had personal experience with this practice following a trip through Indonesia in 1965–66.
6 The author was on McEwen's personal staff from 1967 to 1971.
7 *CIA Status Report*, 1964.
8 Belief in the divinity of God; Just and civilised humanity; The unity of Indonesia; Democracy guided by the inner wisdom in the unanimity arising out of deliberations amongst representatives; and social justice for all the people of Indonesia.
9 The author was witness to some of the killings and their aftermath in Java and Bali.
10 Richard Hall, *The Secret State: Australia's Spy Industry*, Cassell, Melbourne, 1978, p. 145.
11 Author's interview with SAS personnel, 2014.
12 Richard Hall, p. 149.
13 The author attended the negotiation.

Chapter Ten

1 David Horner with Neil Thomas, *In Action with the SAS*, Allen & Unwin, Sydney, 2009, p. 44.
2 Gary McKay, *On Patrol with the SAS: Sleeping with Your Ears Open*, Allen & Unwin, Sydney, 1999, pp. 53–4.
3 David Horner with Neil Thomas, p. 51.
4 Gary McKay, p. 54.
5 David Horner with Neil Thomas, p. 56.
6 Gary McKay, p. 56.
7 ibid., pp. 66–7.
8 ibid., p. 69.

Chapter Eleven

1 David Horner with Neil Thomas, *In Action with the SAS*, Allen & Unwin, Sydney, 2009, p. 76.
2 ibid., p. 79.
3 ibid., p. 101.
4 Gary McKay, *On Patrol with the SAS: Sleeping with Your Ears Open*, Allen & Unwin, Sydney, 1999, pp. 62–3.
5 ibid., p. 64.
6 David Horner with Neil Thomas, p. 91.
7 ibid., p. 92.
8 Gary McKay, p. 72.

9 In 2008, the SAS began an investigation to try to find the remains. With the assistance of Kopassus, they located the graves very near to the place where they drowned. The bodies had been discovered on the riverbank and buried by the local pro-Indonesian Dayak tribesmen.

10 Gary McKay, p. 77.

11 ibid.

12 ibid.

Chapter Twelve

1 Gary McKay, *On Patrol with the SAS: Sleeping with Your Ears Open*, Allen & Unwin, Sydney, 1999, p. 89.

2 Author interview with retired SAS operator, Perth, December 2013.

3 David Horner, *SAS – Phantoms of War: A History of the Australian Special Air Service*, Allen & Unwin, Sydney, 1989, p. 108.

4 ibid., p. 110.

5 ibid., p. 111.

6 ibid., p. 119.

7 John Blaxland, *Signals Swift and Sure: A History of the Royal Australian Corps of 1947–1972*, Royal Australian Corps of Signals Committee, Victoria, 1998, p. 245.

8 David Horner, p. 125.

9 Gary McKay, p. 104.

10 David Horner, p. 229.

11 ibid., p. 230.

12 ibid., p. 255.

13 Letter to the author from Peter Young, 20 February 2014.

Chapter Thirteen

1 David Horner, *SAS – Phantoms of War: A History of the Australian Special Air Service*, Allen & Unwin, Sydney, 1989, p. 256.

2 ibid., p. 262.

3 ibid., p. 265.

4 John Blaxland, *Signals Swift and Sure: A History of the Royal Australian Corps of 1947–1972*, Royal Australian Corps of Signals Committee, Victoria, 1998, Ch. 5.

5 *Sig Tp* e-magazine, February 2014, pp. 1–4.

6 John Blaxland, *Signals Swift and Sure: A History of the Royal Australian Corps of 1947–1972*, Royal Australian Corps of Signals Committee, Victoria, 1998, p. 251.

7 David Horner, p. 292.

8 ibid., p. 349.

Chapter Fourteen

1 David Horner, *SAS – Phantoms of War: A History of the Australian Special Air Service*, Allen & Unwin, Sydney, 1989, p. 336.
2 ibid., p. 338.
3 John Blaxland, *Signals Swift and Sure: A History of the Royal Australian Corps of 1947–1972*, Royal Australian Corps of Signals Committee, Victoria, 1998, p. 251.
4 Interview with the author, January 2014.
5 Peter Collins, *Strike Swiftly: The Australian Commando Story*, Watermark Press, Sydney, 2005, p. 161.
6 ibid., p. 175.
7 ABC Interview with Mark Colvin, 27 May 2008.
8 Harvey Barnett, *Tale of the Scorpion*, Allen & Unwin, Sydney, 1988, p. 190.
9 John Miller, *National Observer*, No. 67, Summer 2006, pp. 26–39.
10 Harvey Barnett, p. 11.
11 John Miller, pp. 26–39.

Chapter Fifteen

1 Author's interview with Professor Desmond Ball, Defence and Strategic Studies, ANU, February 2014.
2 William Pinwill and Brian Toohey, *Oyster: The Story of the Australian Secret Intelligence Service*, Heinemann, Melbourne, 1989, pp. 139–42.
3 Richard Hall, *The Secret State: Australia's Spy Industry*, Cassell, Melbourne, 1978, pp. 153–4.
4 *The Australian*, 7 December 2009.
5 *The Australian*, 20 March 2010.
6 William Pinwill and Brian Toohey, p. 186.

Chapter Sixteen

1 Interview with the author, February 2014.
2 William Pinwill and Brian Toohey, *Oyster: The Story of the Australian Secret Intelligence Service*, Heinemann, Melbourne, 1989, pp. 225–7.
3 Harvey Barnett, *Tale of the Scorpion*, Allen & Unwin, Sydney, 1988, p. 22.
4 ibid., p. 119.
5 ibid., p. 124.
6 ibid., p. 142.
7 ibid., pp. 37–8.
8 ibid., p. 130.

Chapter Seventeen

1 William Pinwill and Brian Toohey, *Oyster: The Story of the Australian Secret Intelligence Service*, Heinemann, Melbourne, 1989, p. 247.

2 ibid., p. 251.

3 'Jim Wallace', Centre for Public Christianity, <publicchristianity.org/person/Jim-Wallace>.

4 Interview with the author, Perth, November 2012.

5 Interview with the author, Perth, November 2012.

6 David Horner, *SAS – Phantoms of War: A History of the Australian Special Air Service*, Allen & Unwin, Sydney, 1989, p. 447.

Chapter Eighteen

1 Peter Collins, *Strike Swiftly: The Australian Commando Story*, Watermark Press, Sydney, 2005, p. 159.

2 ibid., p. 160.

3 ibid., p. 163.

4 ibid., p. 171.

5 ibid., p. 174.

6 David Horner, *SAS – Phantoms of War: A History of the Australian Special Air Service*, Allen & Unwin, Sydney, 1989, pp. 470–1.

7 *Jane's Military Communications*, cited in Desmond Ball, *Defence Aspects of Australia's Space Activities*, Canberra Papers on Strategy and Defence, 1993, pp. 37–8.

8 The author was among the media contingent, representing *Canberra Times*.

Chapter Nineteen

1 Peter Collins, *Strike Swiftly: The Australian Commando Story*, Watermark Press, Sydney, 2005, p. 183.

2 ibid.

3 Interview with the author, March–June 2014.

4 ibid.

5 David Horner, *SAS – Phantoms of War: A History of the Australian Special Air Service*, Allen & Unwin, Sydney, 1989, p. 479.

6 *The Age*, 7 March 2003, excerpt from Richard Woolcott, *The Hot Seat: Autobiography*, HarperCollins, Sydney, 2003.

7 Interview with the author, April 2014.

8 Interview with the author, March–June 2014.

Chapter Twenty

1 Jim Truscott, *Australian Army Journal*, issue 2000, p. 88.

2 ibid.

3 Rob Maylor with Robert Macklin, *SAS Sniper*, Hachette Australia, Sydney, 2010.

4 Robert Macklin with Stuart Bonner, *Redback One*, Hachette Australia, Sydney, 2014, p. 156.

5 ibid., p. 160.
6 Jim Truscott, p. 94.

Chapter Twenty-One

1 Desmond Ball with David Horner, *Breaking the Codes: Australia's KGB Network, 1944–1950*, Allen & Unwin, Sydney, 1998, pp. 190–7.
2 Interview with the author, March 2014.
3 Robert Macklin with Stuart Bonner, *Redback One*, Hachette Australia, Sydney, 2014, p. 166.
4 Richard Tanter et al. (eds), *Masters of Terror: Indonesia's Military and Violence in East Timor*, Rowman & Littlefield, 2006, pp. 140–3.
5 John Blaxland, *Signals Swift and Sure: A History of the Royal Australian Corps of 1947–1972*, Royal Australian Corps of Signals Committee, Victoria, 1998, pp. 36–39.
6 Interview with the author, April 2014.
7 Interview with the author, March 2014.

Chapter Twenty-Two

1 Interview with the author, June 2014.
2 ibid.
3 Prime Minister Howard had permitted a group of Kosovo refugees from the war in former Yugoslavia to come to Australia temporarily. They were housed in a former immigration facility.
4 Interview with the author, May 2013.
5 ibid.
6 ibid.

Chapter Twenty-Three

1 Robert Macklin with Clint Palmer, *SAS Insider*, Hachette Australia, Sydney, 2014.
2 ibid.
3 Robert Macklin with Stuart Bonner, *Redback One*, Hachette Australia, Sydney, 2014, p. 214.
4 ibid., p. 245.
5 Interview with the author, June 2014.

Chapter Twenty-Four

1 Interview with the author, June 2014.
2 Robert Macklin with Clint Palmer, *SAS Insider*, Hachette Australia, Sydney, 2014, pp. 88–89.
3 Interview with the author, September 2013.

4 Interview with the author, July 2015.
5 *Sydney Morning Herald*, 15 April 2006.
6 ibid.
7 Report of the Commissioner of Inquiry, Terence Cole, into the oil for food scandal.
8 Interview with the author, July 2014.

Chapter Twenty-Five

1 Rob Maylor with Robert Macklin, *SAS Sniper*, Hachette Australia, Sydney, 2010, pp. 187–92.
2 ibid., p. 194.

Chapter Twenty-Six

1 No relation to the author.
2 Interview with the author, July 2014.
3 Interview with the author, August 2011.
4 ibid.
5 Rob Maylor with Robert Macklin, *SAS Sniper*, Hachette Australia, Sydney, 2010, pp. 284–300.
6 Interview with the author, May 2014.
7 Interview with the author, May 2014.

Chapter Twenty-Seven

1 *Defence Magazine*, series 114, 2014.
2 Sally Neighbour, *Monthly*, November 2010.
3 Interview with the author, July 2014.
4 'China's Cyber Warfare Capabilities', *Security Challenges*, Winter 2011.
5 *New York Times*, 24 February 2011.
6 Robert Macklin with Clint Palmer, *SAS Insider*, Hachette Australia, Sydney, 2014, pp. 266–76.
7 Interviews with the author, 2012–14.

Chapter Twenty-Eight

1 The site is about four kilometres from the unrelated Molonglo Observatory Synthesis Telescope operated by the University of Sydney to map the Southern sky. But since it was a radio telescope, special arrangements were developed to insulate each facility from interference from the other.
2 Rafael Epstein and Dylan Welch, *The Age*, 13 March 2012.
3 Interview with the author, March 2014.
4 Rafael Epstein and Dylan Welch.

Chapter Twenty-Nine

1 Interview with the author, July 2014.
2 Interview with the author, June 2014.
3 *Cyber Maturity in the Asia Pacific Region 2014*, International Cyber Policy Centre, ASPI, 2014, p. 21.
4 Glenn Greenwald, *No Place to Hide: Edward Snowden, the NSA, and the US Surveillance State*, Metropolitan Books, New York, 2014.
5 Security in Government Conference, 13 August 2013.
6 Interviews with the author, July 2014.
7 Institute for Policy Analysis of Conflict, 30 June 2014.
8 Paul Dibb, 'The Defence of Australia'. The author attended the lecture.

Chapter Thirty

1 Anthony Press, Anthony Bergin and Eliza Garnsey, *Heavy Weather: Climate and the Australian Defence Force*, Special Report – Issue 49, ASPI, March 2013.
2 *Security Challenges*, vol. 10, no. 1, pp. 84–5.
3 Eliza Griswold, 'Can General Linder's special operations forces stop the next terrorist threat?', *New York Times Magazine*, 13 June 2014.
4 Andrew Jacobs and Didi Tatlow, 'Attack kills more than 30 in Western China market', *New York Times*, 22 May 2014.

ABRIDGED BIBLIOGRAPHY

Aldrich, Richard J., *The Hidden Hand: Britain, America and Cold War Secret Intelligence*, John Murray, London, 2001.

Asher, Michael, *The Regiment: The Real Story of the SAS*, Penguin, London, 2007.

ASPI: *Cyber Maturity in the Asia-Pacific Region 2014*; *The Cost of Defence – Defence Budget Brief 2014–2015*; *Terms of Engagement – Australia's Regional Defence Diplomacy*, July 2013; *Moving Beyond Ambitions – Indonesia's Military Modernisation*; *A Versatile Force: The Future of Australia's Special Operations Capability*, April 2014.

Ball, Desmond, *China's Signals Intelligence (SIGINT): Satellite Programs*, ANU Strategic and Defence Studies Centre, Canberra, 2003.

——*Security Trends in the Asia-Pacific Region: An Emerging Complex Arms Race*, ANU Strategic and Defence Studies Centre, Canberra, 2003.

——*The US–Australian Alliance: History and Prospects*, ANU Strategic and Defence Studies Centre, Canberra, 1999.

Ball, Desmond with David Horner, *Breaking the Codes: Australia's KGB Network, 1944–1950*, Allen & Unwin, Sydney, 1998.

Ball, Desmond with Hamish McDonald, *Death in Balibo Lies in Canberra*, Allen & Unwin, Sydney, 2000.

Ball, Desmond, Gary Waters and Ian Dudgeon, *Australia and Cyber-Warfare*, ANU Press, 2008.

Barnett, Harvey, *Tale of the Scorpion*, Allen & Unwin, Sydney, 1988.

Bennett, Bruce, *The Spying Game: An Australian Angle*, Australian Scholarly Publishing, Melbourne, 2012.

Bennett, Richard M., *Elite Forces: The World's Most Formidable Secret Armies*, Virgin Books, London, 2003.

Cleary, Paul, *The Men Who Came Out of the Ground*, Hachette Australia, Sydney, 2010.

Collins, Lance and Warren Reed, *Plunging Point: Intelligence Cover-ups and Consequences*, Fourth Estate, Australia, 2005.

Cunningham, Michele, *Hell on Earth: Sandakan – Australia's Greatest War Tragedy*, Hachette Australia, Sydney, 2013.

Hall, Richard, *The Secret State: Australia's Spy Industry*, Cassell, Melbourne, 1978.

Hastings, Michael, *The Operators*, Plume (Penguin), New York, 2011.

Horner, David, *SAS – Phantoms of War: A History of the Australian Special Air Service*, Allen & Unwin, Sydney, 1989.

Horner, David with Neil Thomas, *In Action with the SAS*, Allen & Unwin, Sydney, 2009.

Jones, Seth G., *In the Graveyard of Empires: America's War in Afghanistan*, W. W. Norton, New York, 2010.

Kilcullen, David, *Counterinsurgency*, Oxford University Press, New York, 2010.

——*Out of the Mountains: The Coming Age of the Urban Guerrilla*, Scribe, Melbourne, 2013.

Lee, Sandra, *18 Hours: The True Story of an SAS War Hero*, HarperCollins, Australia, 2006.

Macklin, Robert, *The Battle of Brisbane*, with Peter Thompson, ABC Books, Sydney, 2001.

——*Kevin Rudd: The Biography*, Penguin, Melbourne, 2008.

——*Kill the Tiger: The Truth about Operation Rimau*, with Peter Thompson, Hodder, Sydney, 2002.

——*Redback One*, with Stuart Bonner, Hachette Australia, Sydney, 2014.

——*SAS Insider*, with Clint Palmer, Hachette Australia, Sydney, 2014.

——*SAS Sniper*, with Rob Maylor, Hachette Australia, Sydney, 2010.

McKay, Gary, *On Patrol with the SAS: Sleeping with Your Eyes Open*, Allen & Unwin, Sydney, 1999.

McKnight, David, *Australia's Spies and their Secrets*, Allen & Unwin, Sydney, 2004.

McPhedran, Ian, *The Amazing SAS*, HarperCollins, Sydney, 2005.

Mortimer, Gavin, *Stirling's Men: The Inside Story of the SAS in World War II*, Cassell, London, 2004.

Naylor, Sean, *Not a Good Day to Die: The Untold Story of Operation Anaconda*, Berkeley Books, New York, 2005.

Scahill, Jeremy, *Dirty Wars: The World is a Battlefield*, Nation Books, New York, 2013.

Spigelman, Jim, *Secrecy: Political Censorship in Australia*, Angus & Robertson, Sydney, 1972.

Stevens, Gordon, *The Originals: The Secret History of the Birth of the SAS*, Ebury Press, London, 2005.

Thomson, Judy, *Winning with Intelligence: A Biography of Brigadier John David Rogers*, Australian Military History Publications, Sydney, 2000.

Vogel, Ezra F., *Deng Xiao and the Transformation of China*, Belknap Press, Cambridge, Mass., 2011.

Wong Sue, Jack, *Blood on Borneo*, L. Smith (WA) t/a Jack Sue WA Skindivers Publication, Perth, 2001.

Wray, Christopher C. H., *Timor 1942: Australian Commandos at War with the Japanese*, Hutchinson, Melbourne, 1987.

INDEX

INDEX

INDEX

INDEX

INDEX

'This is the truth about Operation Rimau. It was written in anger, and justifiably so.'
Daily Telegraph

In the last months of 1944, a group of elite Australian and British commandos took part in the biggest Special Forces operations of the Pacific War. Their mission: devastate the Japanese shipping fleet in Singapore Harbour.

Operation Rimau takes us inside that fierce conflict and tells what really happened to these brave commandos – from the very beginnings of the operation through to their intense and courageous fighting in the South China Sea and its aftermath. It exposes the poor planning behind the raid, names those who betrayed and abandoned these heroes in their hour of need, and details the double-dealing which for so many years hid the real story behind the red tape and bureaucratic lies.

Previously published as *Kill the Tiger*, this revised edition includes extensive updates to a gripping account of this most ambitious and dangerous covert operation.

'The shocking betrayals provide so much of the impact of Operation Rimau.'
Canberra Times

In *SAS Sniper*, Rob Maylor takes us inside the closed world of the Australian Special Forces – it's tough to get in, but the fighting that follows is even tougher . . .

Royal Marine . . . SAS marksman . . . Elite soldier

Rob Maylor has seen action in the world's most dangerous combat zones. From East Timor and Iraq to Afghanistan he has been places where no-one else wants to go.

He was there when a Black Hawk helicopter crashed, drowning two of his mates. He was there at Australia's biggest battle in Afghanistan when a Taliban ambush left him shockingly wounded.

He has walked for hours, sometimes days, through hostile country until he has found the right position, sometimes more than a kilometre away from his target, then when the moment is right he aims, and with absolute precision, puts the bullet just where it is going to have the most effect . . .

This is a gritty, no-holds-barred behind-the-scenes look at life on the front line from an elite SAS sniper.

'A rare beast in this genre, this honest, insider's account of the dark arts of sniping and special forces.'
Herald Sun

'A chilling glimpse of the hazards encountered by SAS troops.'
Daily Telegraph

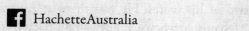
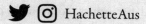